NEVER
NEVER
land

DAVID WILLIAMS

NEVER NEVER *Land*

A LIFETIME LOVE AFFAIR
WITH SOUTHEND UNITED

First published by Pitch Publishing, 2025
1

Pitch Publishing
9 Donnington Park,
85 Birdham Road,
Chichester, West Sussex,
PO20 7AJ
www.pitchpublishing.co.uk
info@pitchpublishing.co.uk

A CIP catalogue record is available for this book
from the British Library.

ISBN 978 1 83680 209 9

Typesetting and origination by Pitch Publishing

Printed and bound on FSC® certified paper in line with
our continuing commitment to ethical business practices,
sustainability and the environment.

Printed and bound in India by Replika Press Pvt. Ltd.

Contents

DEDICATION

For my darling wife, Kim, who's been
stuck with Southend United – and me -
for thirty-four years and is happy to be
stuck with both of us.

Prologue

The English Football League

SATURDAY, 17 April 1888 was a big day for English association football. On this day, a group of wealthy businessmen from England's north and Midlands created the Football League. These late-Victorian worthies decreed that there would be 12 nascent professional football teams in the competition: six from Lancashire and six from the Midlands.

The original 12 teams were:

Accrington
Aston Villa
Blackburn Rovers
Bolton Wanderers
Burnley
Derby County
Everton
Notts County
Preston North End
Stoke
West Bromwich Albion
Wolverhampton Wanderers

Professionalism was very much a regional affair in those early days and had not taken root in the south, so no club south of Birmingham got a look-in.

The founding fathers were already owners and directors of their respective football clubs, so the love of the game would have been a major motivation. But commercial interest was also, as always, in the mix: the Football League was a mechanism to deliver a consistent, predictable revenue stream for the first generation of professional clubs; a solution for a patchy, unreliable network of 'friendly' matches and getting knocked out of the FA Cup early. At first, the league had a one team per city restriction, so there must have been fierce competition for places: Notts County instead of Nottingham Forest. Blackburn Rovers instead of Blackburn Olympic. Derby County instead of Derby Junction. Everton instead of Bootle.

One of the principal exponents of the early professional game, Preston North End, won the first championship in 1888/89. And then won it again the following season. Everton seized the title from Preston's grasp in 1891. The temporary demise of Stoke brought forth new boys Sunderland, who added their name to the honours board one year later.

The Football League was a success. So successful, in fact, that the Second Division was established in 1892. Expansion of the First Division and the introduction of a Second Division meant that the original one team, one city rule was quickly consigned to history, so in came Nottingham Forest – and Bootle FC. Expansion also brought in clubs from Manchester, Sheffield and Newcastle, industrial powerhouses of the north.

The arrival of the Second Division also introduced promotion and relegation. At first, automatic ups and downs were subject to the intervention of the Test Match, which gave a First Division struggler one last chance at salvation if they could beat a second-tier aspirant in a winner-takes-all tie. In its very first season of operation, Second Division champions Small Heath (soon to become Birmingham City) missed out by losing their Test Match, after a replay, to Newton Heath (soon to become Manchester United), who stayed up as a result. Not the only time that the football gods have smiled on that part of Manchester, some cynics might suggest. Test Matches finally disappeared from the scene in 1899, and the promotion/relegation meritocracy intrinsic to the Football League has remained virtually unchanged since then. The model has also been adopted by most of those countries whose football infrastructure can viably support it, and provides its own echoes of glory and despair for those clubs not fortunate enough to take up long-term residence in the top tier of their league hierarchy.

The Second Division welcomed the arrival of London's first representatives, Woolwich Arsenal, in 1893. As London and the south of England gradually knocked harder on the door, the league expanded to accommodate the burgeoning ambitions of Chelsea, Tottenham Hotspur, Fulham and Clapton (to eventually become Leyton) Orient as the 19th century moved into the 20th. By the time the first world war forced its temporary close-down in 1915, the Football League comprised 40 teams in two divisions, including romantic anomalies like Derbyshire's own Glossop FC, who had been punching way above their weight for 17 years, but didn't survive the postwar league reboot in 1919.

But waiting in the wings were a new wave of clubs from the ranks of satellite southern, northern and Midlands competitions who were incorporated into a new third tier in 1920. First came the Third Division which became the Third Division (South) when joined by Third Division (North) in 1921. Some, like Southampton, Norwich City and Crystal Palace, were already quite substantial clubs in their own right (Southampton had already made it to two FA Cup finals, both of which they lost); others, like Merthyr Town, Nelson and Ashington, not so substantial. Most of the clubs making up the original Third Divisions are still in the league. Some have fallen away over time to the lower reaches of the English football hierarchy, whether because of a shortage of money, a shortage of support, a shortage of decent players or just plain bad luck, to be superseded by wealthier, better-supported, more talented and luckier replacements. However, allowing for a few tweaks and a few nips and tucks here and there, the 1921 model is the basic foundation for the 92-team structure we see today. All of the football league structures across the world are descended from the original English model; from Germany's Bundesliga to the Gabon Championnat National.

From moustaches to tattoos, from cloth caps to this season's replica home shirt, from mud-banked open terraces to air-conditioned executive boxes, the world's oldest football league competition has seen it all, gradually evolving all the while. The song remains pretty much the same, but the words change occasionally, which can make navigating the evolution quite complicated, especially over the last 60 years. This brief summary of the what, the where and the when of the Football League since its inception excludes the multitude of corporate sponsors since 1983 to keep things (relatively) simple.

TOP TIER
Football League:	1888–1892
Football League First Division:	1892–1992
Premier League:	1992–present

SECOND TIER
Football League Second Division:	1892–1992
Football League First Division:	1992–2004
Football League Championship:	2004–present

THIRD TIER
Football League Third Division:	1920–1921
Football League Third Division (South):	1921–1958
Football League Third Division (North):	1921–1958
Football League Third Division:	1958–1992
Football League Second Division:	1992–2004
Football League One:	2004–present

FOURTH TIER
Football League Fourth Division:	1958–1992
Football League Third Division:	1992–2004
Football League Two:	2004–present

Chapter 1

In the Blood

IF FOOTBALL is in the blood, it runs deep in the north-west of England. On the final weekend of March 1979, everything is as it should be. Here I am in Merseyside, the land of my birth. My lifetime Football League team has just won 2-1, which is good. The winning goal comes in the very last minute, which is even better.

Football is a part of my family too. Not the kind of family that would sell their souls for FA Cup Final tickets, but enthusiastic enough with a history nonetheless. Both my parents were Liverpool born and bred. Or Scousers if you like. The consensus of opinion is that the term 'Scouser' was inherited from 'lobscouse', a beef (or something resembling meat) and potato stew introduced to the port of Liverpool by Norwegian sailors in the 18th or 19th century. My gran used to cook Scouse sometimes; it was pretty awful to be honest, but so was most of her cooking, bless her.

I arrived on the scene at Oxford Street Maternity Hospital, deep in the city centre of Liverpool, in September 1955. My father was a secondary school teacher of English in the northern suburb of Bootle; my mother had worked in accounts at the massive Scott's Empire Bakery in the nearby suburb of Netherton, and was what used to be called a housewife. Our family home in Litherland was more or less between the school and the bakery. Litherland's main claim to fame was its town hall where, according to legend and my grandfather, The Beatles performed 20 times before they were famous. It was also less than four miles away from a major Liverpool landmark: Goodison Park, the home of Everton Football Club and less than five miles away from another major Liverpool landmark: Anfield, the home of Liverpool Football Club; as Liverpool as you could get.

Dad was a firm Liverpool supporter, as was his father before him – and his father before him. In the halcyon pre-second world war days, when getting into football was dirt cheap, Dad would go to Anfield one week to see Liverpool win and Goodison Park the next week to see Everton lose. Before I was born, Mum had already paid her footballing dues as a distinctly uncomfortable attendee in Liverpool's record home crowd: 61,905 for the FA Cup visit of Wolverhampton Wanderers to Anfield in February 1952. Dad's penance for this discomfort was tickets for Mum to see Frank Sinatra play the Liverpool Empire – twice – and Mum spent the years following as a mildly interested and unexpectedly insightful armchair critic.

That was the way it was. Liverpool or Everton. Red or blue. The year before I was born, Everton won promotion back to the First Division by beating Oldham Athletic on the last day of the season after a short but painful three years in the second tier. Liverpool suffered relegation by losing to Blackpool on the last day of their season after a 50-year residence in the top division, and took Everton's place in the Second Division. The Monday morning canteen banter would have been something to behold in late April 1954.

At the end of March 1979, it's more like business as usual for the red and blue sides of Liverpool. Everton are second in the First Division with an outside shot at the title. Liverpool are a few points clear in first place with a couple of games in hand, but not yet certainties for the crown. This weekend, Everton draw 2-2 with Norwich City at Goodison Park, which does their title hopes no good at all. Meanwhile, Liverpool battle to a 2-2 draw with Manchester United in the semi-final of the FA Cup at Maine Road, the 'neutral ground' of Manchester City.

Wait a minute. I am in Merseyside, the land of my birth and the birth of my Liverpool-supporting parents. My team has just won 2-1, which is more than Liverpool and Everton are able to do. What's going on? Well, there is another English league team in Merseyside, five miles and the width of the River Mersey away from Litherland, Goodison Park and Anfield.[1]

Which is where I am on the Friday evening of 30 March 1979. I'm at Prenton Park, the home of Tranmere Rovers. In a woefully semi-deserted football ground for a Third Division match, I hear a grand total of 1,220 Rovers supporters maintain a skirling barrage of relentless hostility and partisan abuse through the entire 90 minutes. Sitting in the confines of the sparsely populated Main Stand, I am comfortably detached from the barrage, apart from a reporter from the local newspaper who roundly berates me for having the audacity to sit in close proximity to the press box cheering for my team. Twenty-eight slightly intimidated, muted away fans form a forlorn mosaic in the otherwise empty 'away end'. I know because I'm quite high up and can count them. A terrier-like midfielder called Ron Pountney scores the last-minute winner for the away team. For Southend United. My team.

If you think this is all rather strange, you're not alone. Some people just don't understand it, so when the immigration official at Mexico City International Airport studies my passport a few years ago and politely enquires, 'Liverpool or Everton?' I reply 'Liverpool' because it's easier. A true Scouser

---

1 Prior to local government reorganisation in 1974, Tranmere was in the county of Cheshire and Liverpool was in Lancashire. By March 1979, both were in the Metropolitan County of Merseyside.

by birth, a genuine football enthusiast, but the football club I love is not Liverpool or Everton or even good old Tranmere Rovers. How could this possibly have happened?

Chapter 2

The Mersey Beat

ERIC CANTONA, a fondly remembered Manchester United icon of the 1990s, has a chequered history of memorable quotes. Some perceptive, some just plain daft. But this is one of my favourites, 'You can change your wife, your politics, your religion, but never, never can you change your favourite football team.'[2] Personally, I've never really put it to the test. My team has been my team for 60 years. It will be for tomorrow, and for an indeterminate period into the future.

My family moved down south at the end of 1957. I had been too young to acquire anything other than the very faintest vestige of a Liverpool accent, let alone any memory of Liverpool FC. Nevertheless, according to Hoyle, who set the established rules on things unrelated to football, it would have been entirely reasonable and logical for me to join the expatriate community of Liverpool supporters which even then, and still does, covers the four corners of England. And Wales, Northern Ireland and the Irish Republic. But not Scotland, because of Rangers and Celtic.

Dad did try – sort of – because he was a supporter, not a fanatic. Relocating deprived him of part of his fortnightly routine, which he seemed to handle with fortitude. Despite our move, I was no stranger to the city of my birth. Every

2 Cantona's words of wisdom are courtesy of www.quickmeme.com. But I'd already read it somewhere, or heard it on TV.

Easter school holiday for several years, our little family lugged bulky suitcases into a dusty crimson London Midland carriage at London's Euston station for the express train northwards to stay with my gran and visit other ageing relatives in north Liverpool.

Liverpool in the early 1960s was a dark, brooding, hulking metropolis. I don't remember being very cold in Liverpool – nor being very warm either. A city of the year-round raincoat. Rattling in on the train past the national identikit sprawl of interwar and postwar suburbia was reassuringly familiar.

Then, at Edge Hill, something else happened. As if consumed by the maw of an enormous, smoke-belching prehistoric monster, we disappeared into a seemingly endless black tunnel, accompanied by the whistling and groaning of wheels and brakes, the lurching of carriages as they crossed over points, the dimming and flickering of the carriage lamps a synchronised light show. After about five minutes, the train almost reluctantly disgorged itself into the skylit, cavernous expanse of Liverpool Lime Street station.

We left the station and there we were: St George's Square, the city centre of Liverpool. Declared a borough as long ago as 1207, a small sea port for centuries, transformed by the Industrial Revolution, one-time hub of Empire, proud owner of the soot-streaked Neoclassical pillared grandeur of St George's Hall, the Walker Art Gallery and the Central Library, the vertiginous Wellington Column, the bronze Queen Victoria and Prince Albert on their bronze horses. A different world from a seaside town in the south-east of England.

More lugging of cases for the mercifully short distance to the Skelhorne Street bus stop and then the red Ribble bus northwards. As we gazed out of the window, the bus carried us through the gap-toothed, still bomb-scarred, shopworn ugliness of the inner suburbs: Vauxhall, Kirkdale, Bootle, past the Richmond Sausage Factory (dubbed the 'Mystery Works' by satirical Liverpudlian bus conductors); rumbled across the old Lift Bridge and into Litherland, where I spent the early years of my life and where my gran and most of my ageing relatives lived. Liverpool was Victorian at its core – damp, grimy, smoky, slightly smelly, somewhat faded – but it was my second home and I adored it.

* * *

That's why the first football match I ever saw in the flesh was between Liverpool and Stoke City at Anfield on a damp Easter Monday, 23 April 1962. Surely, this would clinch my permanent attachment to the Reds and a lifetime of triumphant trophy collection.

Founded in 1892 as a result of a dispute between Everton FC and the owner of the Anfield football ground, Liverpool only had to wait a year before joining the recently formed Second Division, but it didn't bother them overmuch as they won promotion to the First Division at the first time of asking. It only took them another seven years to lift the league championship trophy and my great-grandfather would have been there to see them lift it. By 1962, the trophy count stood at five championships but no FA Cups, underpinning Liverpool's slightly ambivalent historical relationship with that competition. When Dad and I arrived at Anfield, the club had spent all of my young life languishing in the second tier.

Liverpool had finally won promotion from the Second Division only three days earlier – yes, I know, Liverpool in the second tier and I was there to see it! At that time, football was just starting to dawn on me as an entity other than a kickabout in the back garden or the school playground. The novelty of being at a real football match was an event to savour and remember.

We were standing close to the front and almost at eye level to the pitch in the lower tier of the old Main Stand, instead of the neutral elevated centre-circle position adopted by the television cameras. Dad had manoeuvred us towards the front, partly because it was safer for a six-year-old, partly because the immortal 47-year-old Stanley Matthews might be playing for Stoke and we would get a chance to see him up close. Even I knew who Stanley Matthews was. The fact that he did not actually play was a let-down for Dad, and for me in retrospect because it was my one and only chance to see, live, a footballer who had plied his trade for Dad and his generation at the highest level before the second world war.

I had enough sensations to work with anyway. I gazed wide-eyed and wide-eared at the ebb and flow of the game, the ball and players scurrying towards me and then away across the grass-denuded late season playing surface, the thunder of studs, the gasped 'oofs' and 'aahhs' as the tackles came crunching in before my eyes, the constant bellowing of instructions from captain Ron Yeats to his Liverpool team-mates. You just didn't hear that stuff on the telly. In fact, you didn't hear that much of anything football-related on the telly, because 1962 belonged to the days before regular televised football, before even *Match of the Day* fronted by the doyen of football commentators, Kenneth Wolstenholme. A few perfunctory minutes of highlights on Saturday evening's *Sports Special* was our limited exposure to league football. There were virtually no live matches on TV: the FA Cup Final on the BBC every year, England against Scotland and that was about it. The World Cup in Chile, with its time-delayed broadcasts in those pre-satellite days (and trying to make sure we didn't accidentally hear the result on the radio), was still a couple of months away.

I had never been in a large crowd before. There were 41,005 in Anfield that day, not a sell-out, but more than slightly intimidating for little me. Not that there was really anything to feel intimidated about. Liverpool were safely promoted, the crowd basked in the relaxed indulgence that characterises football crowds in post-promotion mode, relieved of the gut-wrenching stress of needing a goal and needing a result. Even I have experienced the feeling sometimes, though not as often as I would have liked.

It didn't seem to reduce the decibel level, though. The noise was gratifyingly boisterous and loud. One sight left me awestruck. The icing on the Anfield cake was 20 yards or so to the right of us: the towering mass of humanity in the Spion Kop named, with no apparent sense of irony, after a prominent hill in South Africa and the scene of an infamous British military reverse during the second Boer War. Humanity was there all right – and noisy it was too. But here's a thing. I don't recall a single chant or a single song booming out from the Kop that day.

Don't get me wrong. I know Liverpool didn't invent the chanting and singing which now reverberates around football stadia everywhere. The 1927 FA Cup Final between Arsenal and Cardiff City was the first to be broadcast live on the radio. And the only bit of sound surviving from the match is a recording of the band of the Grenadier Guards and 92,000 spectators tunefully belting out 'Abide With Me'. The 1929 final between Bolton Wanderers and Portsmouth was the first to be filmed with sound by British Pathé. And the first thing we see and hear is 92,000 spectators lustily singing 'Pack Up Your Troubles in Your Old Kit-Bag', an old soldier's song from the first world war – followed by 'Abide With Me'.

The conductor of this mass choir was a youngish, stocky, tousled-haired gentleman in an all-white outfit called T.P. Ratcliff, waving his arms around on a tall white podium in the middle of the Wembley pitch next to the big regimental brass band. Thirty years later, elderly, bespectacled T.P. was still doing his stuff on cup final day. But I also heard the (rather reedy) strains of 'Glory, Glory, Hallelujah' echoing around Wembley from the Tottenham Hotspur supporters in the 1961 final against Leicester City. My collection of old VHS videos offers the distorted rumbling of 'Blaydon Races' from Newcastle supporters in the final of 1932 and the more melodious 'Play up Pompey' from Portsmouth supporters in their final seven years later. And, I dare say, Norwich's 'On the Ball, City' has been sung from the early Middle Ages onwards, 'When the Saints go Marching In' has been a Southampton anthem since before there were saints and 'I'm Forever Blowing Bubbles' has been around West Ham since before people started blowing bubbles.

The ingredients for an enduring massed choir were certainly there back in 1962. Twenty thousand predominantly working-class males managed to create a din all their own, with rolling crescendos at corners and near misses. But it took local pop group Gerry and the Pacemakers' 1963 cover of 'You'll Never Walk Alone' to assist the morphing of the Kop into an all-singing, all-chanting tribe of merry Scouse scallywags. I once asked Dad if Liverpool had a club song *à la* 'Play up' or 'Bubbles' before Marsden's immortal contribution. He couldn't remember one. 'The Fields of Anfield Road' wasn't even a whistle in the wind that afternoon in 1962.

I don't remember the match itself being much to write home about either. Liverpool scored early through a Ronnie Moran penalty, amazingly the first penalty I can remember seeing. Dennis Viollet equalised before half-time and City proceeded to 'park the bus' as Liverpool laid siege to the Kop end. The impressively named Horace Yates of the *Liverpool Daily Post* summarised the match as 'struggling, stumbling Liverpool, who scraped home by the skin or their teeth'. [3]Because, of course, they did scrape home, as they always seemed to, while the rain came tumbling down, as it always seemed to. With 94 minutes gone and with the last kick of the match, Jimmy Melia, to quote Horace again, scored 'a goal which produced a roar that could hardly have been greater had promotion depended on it'.

I can still feel the roar in my mind's ear. A crush had built

3 Horace Yates' match report originated in the *Liverpool Daily Post*. The report is reproduced in www.lfchistory.net

around us as spectators edged their way downwards towards the front of the terrace anticipating the foray on to the pitch at the final whistle. After Melia's goal, a few spectators who had left us diehards and begun edging their way towards the exits came bounding back down the terrace steps to rejoin the throng. The Kop was in ferment and responded with one of those surges and sways that used to define the Kop in its pre-seated days.

The crush and the noise must have spooked me somewhat, because it resulted in floods of tears. Dad carefully guided me clear of the mayhem, out of the ground and down to Walton Lane for the bus home. A quiet admonition from Mum, who thought I was too young for a day out at Anfield, welcomed Dad's return. Maybe I was too young, but there was no long-term mental damage; unless you consider attending a football match to be a form of derangement, as some misguided folk do.

***

Another year, another Easter holiday in Liverpool, and Dad tried again. This time, however, he exhibited true democratic spirit in persuading Mum to allow me a visit to the enemy's lair: Goodison Park, the home of Everton.

In 1878, the St Domingo Church Sunday School set up a football club. A year later, St Domingo FC became Everton FC. Five years after that, the club took up temporary residence at Anfield which, given the history of Merseyside football, was quite remarkable in itself. Even more remarkable was that, just ten years after its foundation, the professional footballers of Everton represented one of the original 12 clubs making up the English Football League. Everton had shaded selection at the expense of Bootle FC, conceivably depriving the world of the joy of seeing a team called Bootle take long-term residence in the football hierarchy. Bootle United. Bootle Rovers. On reflection, probably not. I'm sure Liverpool FC would have found its way into the narrative somehow.

And Everton it was who prised the championship trophy from the grasp of Preston North End in 1890/91, a year before Liverpool's formation. Even Bootle beat Liverpool to the punch and landed themselves in the brand-new Second Division in 1892. Unfortunately, poor old financially bereft Bootle only lasted one season, to be replaced by Liverpool with a cruel irony which so often attaches itself to football's ups and downs. By April 1963, Everton had matched Liverpool with five championships, but they had eclipsed the Reds by also winning two FA Cups, so they were ahead on the trophy front.

A big crowd at Goodison was a certainty, so Dad had taken the precaution of securing two tickets for the top-tier seats in the Bullens Road Stand. I never knew where the tickets came from, but tickets for Anfield, Goodison and even Wembley used to turn up periodically, so I suspect an old acquaintance with some clout in the ticket-getting game.

***

This match was on a different scale from Liverpool versus Stoke. It was just as well I was a year older. And, at the risk of exciting mass incredulity from English football watchers less than 60 years old, Everton were the pre-eminent club in Merseyside and top of the First Division on Saturday, 20 April 1963. And, oh yes, playing the mighty Tottenham Hotspur, FA Cup and Football League 'double' winners from two years earlier, current FA Cup holders and nearest challengers for the top prize again. A win for Everton would effectively seal the title. So a different scale altogether. In an era when FA Cup Final day was still regarded as the apex of the footballing calendar (that year it belonged to Manchester United and Leicester City), this was, without a doubt, the Football League's match of the season.

Everton had more money, courtesy of multimillionaire chairman John Moores and his mega-company, Littlewoods Football Pools. Everton had a bigger and better stadium, with layers of tiered wooden seats atop the traditional terracing on all four sides. Everton had bigger crowds and better players: the formidable centre-half Brian Labone, resident hardman Jimmy Gabriel, classy up-and-coming England international midfielder Tony Kay, the very lean and very mean Welsh forward Roy Vernon, and the unarguable *pièce de resistance*, the flower of Scotland, the 'Golden Vision' himself, inside-forward Alex Young.

Even in 1963, if you had tickets for a match, arriving at the ground at 1.15pm for a three o'clock kick-off should have granted you a relatively comfortable excursion to your seat. Wrong. The queue outside the Bullens Road Stand seemed to stretch to Manchester, as did the queues for the other stands. The attendance was 67,650, huge even for Goodison Park at that time.[4] Everton had managed to squeeze in 72,488 for the visit of Liverpool six months earlier, the first derby in 11 years. God knows how. I have seen old video of that game and the stadium looked packed to the point of overflowing. What I saw for the Tottenham match was pretty much the same. When we finally got within hailing distance of our seats at half past two, we found them occupied. Eventually, a harassed steward made his way down, inspected our tickets and leaned over to coax the interlopers from our seats, which they vacated with barely a murmur. I have no idea where they went but we finally sat down in our rightful position as the teams came out.

I recall the football being better than at Anfield, but not dramatically so. There was a nervous edginess to the game and quite a slow pace at the beginning. As it happened, there were another couple of 'neutral' (that is to say Liverpool-supporting) spectators to our right, so Dad was able to expound some of

---

4   Horace Yates reported the Goodison Park crowd as 72,000, which would not surprise me. Originally in the *Liverpool Daily Post*, I sourced his report from www.bluecorrespondent.co.uk. I have chosen to revert to the official attendance.

his less than generous views about certain Everton players. In particular, he opined that Alex Young was a 'bit lightweight'. Our neighbour nodded in sage agreement. After 17 minutes, Young rose unfeasibly high above the Tottenham defence and flicked his golden head to power a bullet header into the goal at the Gwladys Street End. Cue pandemonium. As 'neutrals' we did the tactful thing and rose to applaud the goal with some enthusiasm – and Dad went a bit quiet after that.

Mass crowd singing was still a year or two away, but Everton supporters had discovered chanting, adopting the 'BRA-ZIL [clap-clap-clap]' chant from the World Cup one year earlier with regular outbreaks of 'EV-ER-TON [clap-clap-clap]'. The world of football – at least as far as crowd noise was concerned – was definitely changing.

Everton relaxed and played with some swagger for the rest of the game, Labone immense, Kay pinging the ball around majestically, Vernon lean and mean, Young relatively quiet as if in awe of his own finish. Tottenham, as befitting players with their pedigree, battled gamely but Everton held on quite comfortably for a 1-0 win. The final whistle was accompanied by the kind of roar that you would expect from at least 65,000 committed home fans in a tightly confined space with a trophy on the line. I don't remember a pitch invasion, but we couldn't have got near the pitch from our upper tier seats even if we'd wanted to. It took two hours, but it felt like an eternity, to exit Goodison, walk to the bus stop and get the buses home. Dad copped more quiet admonition from Mum, but no tears from me. Progress indeed.

Everton did lift the championship trophy that season. Liverpool won it the following year, then won the FA Cup in 1965, then Everton won the FA Cup the year after that and Liverpool won the league again. I was an avid supporter of Liverpool for the day when they beat Leeds United in the 1965 final. I was even an avid Everton supporter for the day when they beat Sheffield Wednesday in the final one year later.

The red rose of Lancashire versus the white rose of Yorkshire undoubtedly had something to do with it. While all this was going on, The Beatles were in the vanguard of a genuine western world cultural revolution, together with Gerry and the Pacemakers, The Searchers, Cilla Black, Billy J. Kramer and the Dakotas, and all the rest of the Merseyside trailblazers. The police soap opera *Z-Cars* was on prime-time TV; OK, set in Kirkby New Town, a few miles away, but catching the wave of all things Merseyside. The *Z-Cars* theme tune 'Liverpool Shore' still greets the Everton players as they take the field at Goodison – and also the Watford players at Vicarage Road, all of 200 miles away, for some obscure reason. In the two years following my first visit to Anfield, hailing from Liverpool had suddenly become cool and interesting, with the reflected cachet that music, football and *Z-Cars* delivered – even for a youngster with no discernible accent.

Revisiting the confluence of pop and football culture, it occurs to me that the 1960s was also a decade of the 'what-if?' What if Nixon had won the presidential election in 1960 instead of Kennedy? What if Khrushchev hadn't 'blinked' over Cuba? What if Kennedy hadn't been assassinated in 1963? What if the US had won the Vietnam War? What if Dubček's Prague Spring in 1968 had succeeded? What if Gerry Marsden had been an Everton supporter?

In his football memoir, *Anfield Iron*, the late, great hardman of Liverpool, Tommy Smith, reported that, in late 1963, Gerry presented the Liverpool manager Bill Shankly with an advance recording of his pop cover 'You'll Never Walk Alone' lifted out of Rodgers and Hammerstein's musical, *Carousel*. Shankly, Liverpool FC and the Kop adopted the song with gusto, right at the beginning of their rapid elevation into English football aristocracy.[5]

---

5   From *Anfield Iron*, written by Tommy Smith. Bantam Press, 2008.

Just suppose that Gerry had offered his advance recording to the Everton manager, Harry Catterick. Not that Everton have done too badly on the honours collection front over the succeeding years, but maybe we would have seen year after year of blue and white dominance, hoovering up league championships and European Cups for fun. Maybe Mick Lyons, Mark Higgins and Kevin Ratcliffe would have lifted all those trophies instead of Emlyn Hughes, Graeme Souness and Alan Hansen. Maybe Liverpool would have had to resign themselves to decades of underachievement in the shadows of the world-famous Everton. Maybe, to this day, it would be the Gwladys Street End belting out Gerry's anthem, blue scarves and banners aloft. Maybe the Kop would have been stuck with 'It's a Grand Old Team to Play For'.

But it still begs my biggest 'what if?' question. With my newly acquired Scouse cool and the footballing riches before me, why did I not then hitch my wagon to one of the Merseyside big hitters? It could have happened; probably should have happened; nearly did happen. But at seven years of age, I had not experienced the total immersion into a football club that young children enjoy today as excited youngsters bounce on their parents' knees, decked out in their junior replica gear. The terraces and wooden seats of the old-style football grounds didn't lend themselves to that and the old Boys Pen at Anfield was not a place for the faint-hearted of any age.

Whatever the reason, in the end I did not make Liverpool my team, to Dad's chagrin. Neither did I make Everton my team, to Dad's relief. It wasn't their fault. Something else, something irrevocable, got in the way.

Chapter 3

December-on-Sea

A COLD winter's night of steam and smoke.

Steam rises from the tea kiosk on the south-east corner of the open terrace called the South Bank. Halfway down the other side, more steam rises from those having a last-minute pee in the roofless male toilet block. Clouds of cigarette smoke spiral upwards from the well-populated terrace.

Steam and smoke, mingled together and captured in the glare of the floodlights perched on two skinny metal towers 60 feet above. An English FA Cup second round replay on Monday, 18 December 1978.

I have arrived nice and early and shiver in the icy wind gusting through the covered West Stand. At quarter-past seven in the evening, I can already see frost forming on the pitch. Despite my 23-year-old mop of hair and my three-quarter-length Parka, I huddle closer to the cold, steel crush barrier. For this ground is only 25 years old yet slightly old-fashioned, even by 1978 standards, and built for standing.

The reported capacity of Roots Hall is about 35,000 though this has never been tested.[6] Tonight, the crowd is 15,635 but feels larger. It is, after all, the biggest attendance for five years. The first game on Saturday had inconclusively ended 1-1. The third-round draw, announced after the final

6   The Roots Hall capacity was reported as 35,000 in the *Rothmans Football Yearbook 1978/79*. MacDonald and Jane's, 1978.

whistle, explains the size of the crowd and the building buzz of excitement.

The prize for the winner is a home tie against league leaders and reigning European Cup holders – the mighty Liverpool. But tonight Watford, long-term lower-division contemporaries, occasional bogey team, and now *nouveau riche*, thanks to Elton John's largesse, are in town.

***

The 1978/79 season holds potential for both clubs. Watford are already firm favourites for the climb to the Second Division, whereas Southend United sit on the fringe of the promotion places. The opportunity to lock horns against Liverpool is a big deal for both clubs.

Elton, we understand, is present and will be sitting in the directors' box of the East Stand. In the years before executive boxes and Roy Keane's 'prawn sandwich' brigade, Elton will emerge from the relatively warm, though rather spartan directors' lounge to a narrow wooden seat for a couple of hours. As his room for manoeuvre is limited, he will almost certainly feel the cold as much as I do.[7]

The yellow-shirted Watford players trot out from the East Stand to the cheers of their supporters housed in one half of the North Bank and a ragged chorus of boos from the home fans. Teams didn't take the pitch together in 1978; that was a 90s phenomenon. The Southend players in blue and white emerge at a more determined-looking canter to a louder crescendo of cheers. My team.

The match proceeds with the same staccato semi-rhythm we had seen at Watford's Vicarage Road. Under Graham Taylor, the future England coach immortalised as a popular root vegetable, Watford are what we used to call a 'kick and

---

7   'Prawn sandwiches' was coined by Manchester United icon Roy Keane in 2001 when lamenting the perceived lack of atmosphere at Old Trafford on matchday. From *Keane*, written by Roy Keane. Penguin Books, 2003.

rush' team – subsequently and more charitably renamed 'route one'.[8] Either the ball is spread wide to enable a regular stream of crosses into the middle or the full-backs are launching long, diagonal but fiendishly accurate punts at centre-forward Ross Jenkins's shaggy mane. To be fair, if you are in the Third Division, if you have the mountainous Jenkins and you're successful at it, why would you play any other way? The deceptively mercurial Luther Blissett is missing from the Watford line-up but the barrel-chested Keith Mercer provides additional muscle up front.

On the other hand, aerial football is not the style of Southend under Dave Smith's management; never really has been. Our oft-maligned centre-forward, Derrick Parker, is only five foot ten. As a result, the ball is worked more carefully through the midfield engine room of Laverick, Pountney and Dudley, frequently feeding the tricky feet of winger Colin Morris, who is most definitely not a practitioner of route one.

And it gets colder. The West Stand roof is quite low but there are no side panels to protect spectators from the elements. Therefore, it is ideally situated to maximise the discomfort of a cold, windy mid-December night in England. When the wind blows in from the north, the south or the east, you're, well, suffering, basically. On this night, the wind shrewdly insinuates itself into the West Stand as concentrated streams of freezing air. When this happens, and it frequently does, there is an audible, communal shiver from the occupants.

Approaching half-time, Andy Polycarpou heads United into the lead, close in, and the ground explodes in a guttural, tobacco-deepened roar. Poly's been at the club for a couple of years but has only recently broken through to the first team. His Mediterranean looks belie the fact that he hails from

---

8   Graham Taylor was a turnip, according to *The Sun*, complete with Taylor's superimposed head on the innocent vegetable after England's abysmal defeat by Sweden in the 1992 European Championship, with the headline 'Swedes 2 Turnips 1'.

Islington. His playing style is also more Mediterranean than north London, which makes him popular with the fans. Poly wheels away, arms outstretched in delight and is engulfed by team-mates. Not a ligament-crunching knee slide towards the corner flag, not a pious outreach to some heavenly power above, not a bellowed 'C'MONNN' in sight. It's 1978 and footballers don't do that stuff.

Half-time. Do I fancy a coffee? The queue stretches across the entire length of the stand. I don't drink tea as a rule, and the coffee is a scalding, grainy liquid of dubious consistency in a worryingly pliable white plastic cup; anaemic, discoloured milk self-served from open pint bottles; soggy, glutinous lumps of sugar artfully resisting best efforts to dissolve into the morass. That's a no, then. Instead, I take the opportunity to watch the glistening frost extending across the pitch, while I paw through the match programme because it's too cold to take my gloves off.

The teams return to the pitch, swathed by wispy clouds of exhaled breath. The tension has perceptibly increased since the break. Watford are executing 'the press', a tactic they adopted years before the football world coined a name for it, relentlessly challenging for possession of the ball, whereas our midfield engine room appears to be operating at half-throttle. An undercurrent of concerned muttering starts to build, with increasingly anguished cries breaking out around us. 'Parker! Hold the bloody ball! Hold it!!' 'Hadley, HADLEY!! Stop poncing about and get rid!' 'Ron! Man on, man on!! Oh, Jesus Christ...'

Roots Hall doesn't boast a massed choir of chanting, singing devotees. Southend's modest version of the Kop, incongruously named 'The Pak' and housed under the North Bank roof had disappeared into the mists of memory long since. Instead, a shrill cacophony of kids in the East Stand starts a rhythmic two-syllable chant of 'South-End [clap-clap-clap]'. This is then taken up by the grown-ups. The noise sounds like a rolling rumble echoing around the stadium. 'Come on you Blues, come on you Blues!' has now been picked up by supporters of all ages, even the ones who don't normally sing at football matches, and is periodically launched by the West Stand, then briefly taken up by the whole ground. The result is a transformed atmosphere, charged by impassioned desperation.

And the atmosphere seems to be recognised and absorbed by the players. United's surprisingly stylish centre-backs, Tony Hadley and Alan Moody, are holding the line – just. Parker is starting to make the ball stick. Pountney is everywhere in midfield, his 5ft 6in, nine stone frame covering the ground and nipping at the heels of the Watford midfield like a hyperventilating Jack Russell. Watford's long bombs towards the dangerous Jenkins and Mercer are increasing in urgency.

I nervously consult my watch on a minute-by-minute basis. In the days when 'added-on time' is called 'injury time', before electronic boards and the stadium public address system announces 'a minimum of x minutes', I have no clear idea how much longer the match will last. Neither does anyone else, so you start to speculate. How much injury time did the ref allow in the first half? Was half-time ten minutes, or longer? How much additional time will the ref allow at the end? Nobody knows except the ref. It's all in the lap of the gods for the rest of us. By my reckoning, encouraging whistles for full time from the home supporters start five minutes from the end and increase in shrillness as the seconds tick away slowly. So slowly. The referee obviously knows when to blow his whistle but there's no harm in giving him a bit of help. 'C'mon ref, your bloody watch stopped or what?' 'Oi! What's the matter, ref! Swallowed your whistle??'

The pressure from Watford is now incessant, long clearances from the Southend defence cheered to the rafters, misplaced passes from our midfield greeted with deep animal groans. The match has not been a classic by any means, but it seems to take on a frenetic momentum in the dying moments, as skill and technique are superseded by the imperative to either get or stop the goal. The result of this frantic to and fro is surprisingly few near misses and scares before the referee finally blows the full-time whistle.

***

Southend United 1 Watford 0. The roar is more relieved than triumphant. The players briefly offer congratulations and condolences, leaving the pitch with what fans today would probably regard as indecent haste. Kids run on to the pitch to celebrate, because they can. Manager Dave Smith performs a short pirouette of applause to the crowd, hands above his balding head gleaming under the lights, before being engulfed by youngsters. Many in the crowd, including me, stay in position a few more minutes to capture the moment before moving towards the exits. If mobile phones had been around, I might have filmed it for posterity. The Watford supporters have left very promptly. I wonder what Elton did. Maybe he's back in the directors' lounge having a consolation one for the road and waiting for the crowd to disperse and the traffic to clear. Maybe he's already on his way home, disappointed, right now.

As if to answer my unspoken question, the public address system starts to play Elton's latest hit, 'Song for Guy', which is shortly destined to make number four in the UK singles chart. Thanks to *Top of the Pops* and Radio 1, the song is already quite well known. In the clear, frigid air, virtually all of the pitch is blanketed in silvery-white under the brilliance of the lights, the dark shadows of people are snaking towards the exits, and the plangent chords of Elton's grand piano are played rather more loudly than usual, accompanied by his minimalist vocal. 'Life isn't everything ... isn't everything ... isn't everything', echoes funereally around the emptying ground. 'What a piss-take! Brilliant!' remarks someone close by, to a general ripple of laughter.

My exit routine involves a scramble over the front wall of the West Stand on to the running track. A 50-yard stroll and then a careful jump down into the South Bank and a walk up the 72 steps to the top exit, because it's a shortcut to the car. 'Song for Guy' comes to an end – but not for long. The final chorus promptly starts up again, and follows me as I finally leave the stadium; 'Life isn't everything … isn't everything … isn't everything'.

Let's face it, that's why we love English football. Atmospheric, passionate and a bit cheeky. You can find atmosphere and passion everywhere, not least on a December night in Roots Hall between two Third Division teams. I suspect that a long-standing fatalism underpins the self-deprecating cheeky humour frequently employed by supporters, stadium announcers, stewards, even police officers at lower division grounds. Some memories can still make me laugh out loud.

Well-placed in the Third Division. Watford defeated. Into the third round of the FA Cup. Liverpool at home next month. A day for Southend United Football Club to share the bright lights of the footballing elite – but that's a story for later.

Chapter 4

A Matter of Time

IF LIVERPOOL looked and felt like a brooding 19th-century throwback when I was a kid in 1964, my new hometown was brash and, for the most part, very 20th century.

Southend-on-Sea was, and is, a long skinny ribbon of habitation at the end of a 40-mile cul-de-sac reaching eastwards from London; 50 minutes away from the City by fast train and a couple of hours up the Southend Arterial Road or the London Road that every English town seems to have. The South End of what, you may ask.

The town began as a small fishing hamlet on the bank of the Thames Estuary at the southern extremity of an Anglo-Saxon district called Prittlewell, once a village in its own right, now an inner suburb of Southend. Apart from the shellfish boats operating out of Old Leigh, on the western extremity of town, the fishing ancestry of the south end of Prittlewell was long gone, unless you counted the shivering line of recreational fishing folk huddled over their rods and reels against the biting easterly winds on the pier. For the town has traditionally had a dual *raison d'être*: it was and is a seaside resort and it was and is a dormitory town for London office workers.

The Georgian Royal Terrace and adjoining Royal Hotel at the top of the cliffs, built for toffs in the 1790s, kicked off the seaside resort of New South End. The solid, stylish Victorian townhouses and wide, tree-lined streets of the adjacent Cliff

Town, built in the 1850s by the London, Tilbury and Southend Railway Company to accommodate well-to-do City gents and their families, kicked off the dormitory town. Thankfully, both areas wore the passage of time reasonably well as a moderately prosperous town of more dubious architectural merit gradually sprawled north, east and west, devouring settlements of more ancient vintage: Shoeburyness, Southchurch, Milton, Leigh, Eastwood and, of course, Prittlewell itself.

***

In the centre of Prittlewell is the site of the venerable Blue Boar public house. Rebuilt at the turn of the 20th century, the new Blue Boar was the venue for the foundation of a football club named Southend United on Saturday, 19 May 1906. The founding fathers comprised the following local worthies: Charles Albert Stein, a member of the stock exchange from what was then the posh end of town: Oliver Trigg, the landlord of the Blue Boar itself – a home fixture for him; Frederick England, landlord of the Nelson Hotel, another, less celebrated pub a couple of hundred yards from the Blue Boar; Thomas Stuart Tidy, a cigar merchant who lived a stone's throw from the house I lived in for 14 years; and last, but definitely not least, George Hatton Hogflesh, secretary of the Southend Harriers athletic club. Nobody seems to have a name like that now, more's the pity. Each gentleman Southend to the core: not an American franchisor, Arab oil sheikh or Russian oligarch in sight.

Across the road stood Roots Hall, an 18th-century timber-built manor house of debatable charm and style, judging from the old photographs. It was quite rightly pulled down around the time of the Blue Boar rebuild to make way for the new club's first stadium, which retained the name of its stately predecessor. 'Stadium' was a relative term, of course. As befitting a pre-first world war non-league football club, the ground consisted of two modest parallel wooden stands, a shallow bank of mud terracing behind each goal and a pronounced longitudinal slope. The official record attendance was 7,200 for a match against Northampton Town in 1909 and that must have been pushing it. In the absence of football and funding, the ground basically fell to pieces during the first world war and ended up as a set of allotments. Succeeding years would see United's first home progressively buried under layers of organic manure.

If Southend ever had a reputation as a desirable bathing spot for well-connected, well-heeled gentlefolk, it didn't last long. Its destiny was to develop as an authentic oasis for working-class day-tripping Londoners.

An oasis of giggling teenage girls sporting 'Kiss Me Quick' hats and teeth-shattering, sticky pink sticks of rock. The incomparable Rossi's ice creams and sickly sweet candy floss. Plates of boiled sea snails unpromisingly known as whelks. Small chunks of boiled eel in congealed juice, unsurprisingly known as jellied eels. Bags of cockles, compared to salted snot by the unconverted – but don't knock 'em 'til you've tried 'em. Boiled shrimps, bucketloads of the little pink critters, all delivered courtesy of the shellfish boats operating out of Old Leigh. Crowds of Londoners in shirt sleeves and sundresses strolling down High Street towards the beach from Southend Central and Victoria railway stations on summer weekends. Lines of buses and coaches parked up the hill just back from the seafront. In 1964, Southend still had a cluster of traditional bed and breakfast guesthouses immortalised in creaky old black and white British movies. Peggy Mount appeared as the buxom, bruising, battleaxe landlady in a few of these movies – she actually hailed from Southend, so she could probably recognise the type.

My first experience of the new youth culture in England came in 1964. I was too young to remember the Teddy Boys of the 1950s, with their bizarre, Brylcreemed pompadour hairstyles engineered to a reverse quiff known as a 'duck's arse', retro drape coats and chunky suede 'brothel-creeper' shoes bopping to rock'n'roll. Southend now entertained convoys of Mods as they cruised down the Arterial Road from London on their Lambretta and Vespa motor scooters. The guys sported Beatles-type mop hair and parka jackets over their oh-so-trendy mid-1960s gear. Classy-looking girlfriends perched petitely on the pillions with and their own trendy Mary Quant-copied outfits. Their transistor radios blasted out The Who 'Talking 'bout my Ge-Ge-Generation'. Bombing down the Arterial came the Rockers on their growling Matchless and BSA motorbikes, guys and girls all swept-up hair, Brylcreem and black leather. Their trannies ground out Johnny Kidd and the Pirates' 'Shakin' All Over', competing for attention with The Who up and down Southend seafront on summer weekends.

Mods and Rockers didn't like each other. They cemented their mutual dislike with pitched battles at seaside resorts such as Brighton, Hastings and Clacton, tut-tuttingly reported as 'riots' by the media. Trouble was harder to find in Southend, but Marine Parade wasn't always the best place to be on Whitsun and August bank holiday afternoons after the pubs closed.

A ten-minute eastward stroll from the pier along the Marine Parade took you past a line of garish seafront amusement arcades of almost preternatural tackiness: all jingling bells, whooping sirens and flashing lights encouraging gullible punters to gamble away their hard-earned on the one-armed bandits. In between, the abomination of old-fashioned self-service cafeterias. Dark, gloomy, grimy wooden tables and chairs, grimy plastic food trays, grimy tubular stainless-steel counters. Stewed tea slopping in grimy white saucers, boot-leather fried cod, soggy albino chips, anaemic peas – symbols of the culinary awfulness that characterised Britain from time immemorial until at least 1970, when our collective palates were saved by the liberating balm of restaurants from Italy, China and the Indian subcontinent. Until they arrived, I preferred the burgers at the Wimpy Bar, an English fast-food fixture in the days before the McDonald's, Burger King and KFC invasion.

Between the tackiness and the abominations of Marine Parade were a string of seafront pubs exhibiting highly varying standards of charm and style: the Borough, the Criterion, the Ivy House, the Hope, the Falcon, the Cornucopia, the Ship, the Foresters, the Minerva, the Britannia, the Army and Navy – each one a stepping stone on the 800-yard seafront pathway to oblivion.

Between the Foresters and the Minerva stood a late-Victorian domed construction paying its own homage to Southend's heritage as a traditional seaside resort. The dome crowned the entrance pavilion for the Kursaal, billed at the time as the biggest amusement park in the south of England. 'Kursaal' was derived from the German language and meant a 'Cure Hall' or spa, conjuring up a vision of healthy recreation not usually associated with an amusement park. For more than 70 years it was a major tourist attraction but by the time I started to patrol its precincts, the place had clearly seen better days. I never liked it much; my memories are of a cold, windy, labyrinth of dodgy roundabouts and rollercoasters, draughty arcades of one-armed bandits and a slightly faded ballroom. The Kursaal was in decline when I was a kid, but it was a slow decline.

The amusement park also hosted Southend United for the first 15 years of the club's Football League life. Courtesy of old photographs and my imagination, I can picture the tight, claustrophobic little ground near the coast. Cloth caps and mufflers of the faithful were buffeted by the onshore gusts of icy wind from the River Thames 200 yards away with the indignant barracking of seagulls circling overhead and the drop of a fairground waterchute perched precipitously behind the shallow terrace at the Woodgrange Drive end. For 15 years, United home matches were accompanied by shrieks of terror and gales of laughter – sometimes from the amusement park as well.

A crowd of 18,153 people managed to cram themselves into the Kursaal for an FA Cup tie against Nottingham Forest in 1926. Some of them must have been hanging off the waterchute. At the end of the 1934/35 season, the club found itself on the move once again as the old football ground gave way to the Cyclone rollercoaster.

Southend's home was now a brand-new greyhound racing stadium built about a mile from the Kursaal and the old Roots Hall, with a football pitch occupying the centre of the oval dog track. From dereliction to amusement park, now United had officially gone to the dogs. Officially, it was known as Southend Stadium but some old-timers I knew preferred to call it Grainger Road, after the road fronting the main West Stand.

Grainger Road had two quite impressive covered stands but, once again, skinny, shallow terraces situated behind each goal, where United fans used to squint past the greyhound track at a football match in the middle distance. The semi-detached atmosphere meant that it was never popular with supporters, but in Southend's second season at the new ground, a new record crowd of 23,634 squeezed in for the visit of Tottenham in a 1936 FA Cup third round replay – which the Spurs won 2-1. United's tenure at Grainger Road was not long-lasting and the Blues were on their way once again in 1955.

***

One and a half miles long, Southend Pier was (and still is) the longest in the world, despite several attempts to incinerate or demolish it into submission from land and sea. In 1964, green and white electric trains trundled up and down it to serve those who were too old, too infirm or too lazy to embark on the 30-minute walk from seashore to Pier Head. An elegant

Victorian pavilion on the pier entrance had quite recently burnt to the ground, to be replaced by the Pavilion Lanes – a ten-pin bowling alley of rectangular Modernist grottiness.

In spite of this, the pier looked a picture on summer nights, lit up along its considerable length into the River Thames as part of the famous Southend illuminations. In fact, the whole promenade from the Borough to the Army and Navy, otherwise known as the Golden Mile, was a dazzling array of twinkling, winking multi-coloured lights from April to October. The Kursaal Flyer, a motorised railway locomotive built in the style of an old-fashioned American steam engine, provided a mobile representation of the light show as it slowly made its way up and down Marine Parade. Peter Pan's Playground straddled both sides of the pier, complete with kiddie-sized rollercoasters, bumper car track, a large boating lake for the rotational passage of glacially slow motorboats and a life-size replica of the *Golden Hind*, the 16th-century warship in which Sir Francis Drake circumnavigated the globe and now implausibly home to a slightly gruesome Waxworks and Hall of Mirrors.

Added to all this was an attraction to light up my excited childhood eyes. If you know where to look on the Cliffs, you can still spot the remains of a fantasy model kingdom called Never Never Land. Imagine an illuminated fairytale in miniature, complete with cascading waterfall and the most spellbinding model railway I have ever seen snaking around steep-sided little castles perched on rocks, chugging over rivulets and lakes on Lilliputian bridges. Southend was loud, neon, brassy – and totally magical in its own way.

My hometown also had a diligently self-promoted reputation for endless sunshine. 'Sunny Southend-on-Sea' was emblazoned on coloured picture postcards featuring impossibly deep blue sea, improbably radiant blue sky and suspiciously golden sands. Not true, this was England after all, but my distant recollections are mostly sunny: you don't generally remember the dull, wet, cold days; unless you're watching football.

The reality was that Southend could occasionally be sunny and Mediterranean-hot; occasionally, it could be dull and Siberian-cold; sometimes both in one day. And it possessed a pebbly beach more than five miles long, fringing a tidal sea that crept up and down the beach for half a day and then retreated into the bowels of the Thames Estuary for the other half. I grew up in the modern suburb of Thorpe Bay, a couple of miles from the Golden Mile, the Mods and Rockers but comfortably close to the pebbly beach and the sea. For the archetypal English beach kid that I was, it was a jolly nice place to live.

***

1964 also saw my interest in the beautiful game take firmer root. Not through any particular sporting prowess on my part, I confess. No football prodigy I: in my own head an aspiring inside-right, on the pitch a too often perspiring left-back.

The arrival of *Match of the Day* on television helped to expand my Merseyside experiences into a wider perspective. *Match of the Day* was something else: we got a new aerial and rented a modern 17-inch TV with a push-button channel selection supplementing the tuning dial so we could indulge ourselves in the delights of BBC2, where the show resided in its early years. I was allowed to stay up on Saturday night to watch the 'big four' teams of the era: Liverpool and Everton of course, Manchester United, the Spurs, as everyone called Tottenham, and slightly lesser lights like Arsenal, Chelsea, and Leeds United (ha-ha-ha! But this was the mid-60s: Arsenal a dull shadow of what they had once been and would soon be again; Chelsea living down their traditional status as a music hall joke with glamour and glitz; Leeds giving a whole new meaning to the word pragmatic). Plus Burnley, for crying out loud! Those were the days.

Then there was BBC1's *Grandstand* on Saturday afternoons, fronted by David Coleman, and the football results sequence from about 4.40pm. Absorbing the 'clack-clack-clack' of the teleprinter and scanning the staccato left-to-right and two-spaces-down rhythm of the typeface for the final scores, it dawned on me that there was more to league football than the big four – 88 more teams in fact – and that one of them was Southend United. The consolidated and tabulated results were recited with the curiously flattened vowels of Australian Len Martin at five to five, followed by the league tables. I could have watched the results on the ITV commercial station, but the BBC elucidated the team names with more of a sense of occasion – 'Brighton & Hove Albion'; 'Tottenham Hotspur', rather than the terse 'Brighton' and 'Spurs' favoured by the other channel. I have always had a taste for statistics, so I took an inordinate amount of time poring over the scores and the machinations of the four divisional league tables.

It was also around this time that I started to make noises about paying a visit to my hometown team. Roots Hall stadium was difficult to miss, after all. It was situated just off the main thoroughfare leading north out from the commercial centre of town towards the London Arterial Road, in the heart of what was now the inner suburb of Prittlewell, more or less the geographical centre of modern Southend-on-Sea.

Gazing across a gentle grassy slope from the second-oldest building in town, the mediaeval Cluniac Priory, there is an uninterrupted view towards the towering floodlight pylons marking out each corner of the football ground in the distance, with the tower of the oldest building, St Mary's Parish Church to its left. Today, you can see the tower lurking behind the East Stand when you watch a United home match on TV.

But Roots Hall was easy enough to miss in the early 1950s. The site of the original ground had evolved from allotments to hollowed-out rubbish dump. With United's first ground falling to bits, the second ground situated where people went to get scared or have a laugh, the third ground gone to the dogs and now a fourth ground built on a tip, it did have a strange symmetry. This was certainly not in the mind of the Southend United Supporters' Club, which was putting up most of the money and the local council which was actively supporting the development (not always a given in United's history). To them, the new Roots Hall was a natural bowl so some of the groundwork was already done, it was on the major road into town, walking distance from the town centre and two railway lines and it was, in a real sense, like coming home.[9] There they built a new ground which opened its gates for the visit of Norwich City in August 1955, the month before I was born.

And the point of this unashamedly parochial potted history and travelogue is that the heritage and physical identity of the football club is intertwined with the heritage and physical identity of the town it lives in. The quartered club crest says it all. At the top left are the three horizontal notched cutlasses representing the county of Essex. A modern-looking football is positioned top right. Bottom right are three wavy blue lines, representing the River Thames. In the bottom left corner is a shrimp: a nod to Southend's origin as a fishing hamlet, a nod to the generations of shrimp scoffers on the seafront and representing what is generally regarded as the club nickname – the Shrimpers.

* * *

Some friends and acquaintances at my primary school were already living the dream: a few of them possessed blue and white scarves. It was always going to happen, the only question was when. I am sure Mum and Dad had conversations about it. I found out, after the event, that Dad had made a couple of clandestine expeditions himself to check out the scene. In

---

9 For trainspotters everywhere, the railway lines in question are Shoeburyness to London Fenchurch Street and Southend Victoria to London Liverpool Street.

any event, my increasingly insistent enquiries were finally answered.

And Southend United was waiting for me. For some reason, my club has a wealth of truly wonderful history books cataloguing United's ups and downs from their foundation and their elevation to the Football League Third Division (South) in 1920. I will take the liberty of referring to them freely throughout this book. But none of them have used the word I came up with to describe the club as it was when I discovered it in 1964; my chosen word is 'somnolent'.

Sorry, but there it is. Somnolent because, in all their 44 years of Football League history, Southend United had never left the Third Division. Had never won a meaningful trophy; the Essex Professional Cup does NOT count. Had never made an FA Cup Final or even a semi-final. Had never won promotion. Had never been relegated because there was nowhere to go below the Third Division (South) for many years. A couple of re-election scares along the way, the ultimate shock to the system for the four lowest-placed teams out of 92 at the end of a season. Officially being one of the worst teams in the entire Football League required your club to rely on a favourable vote from its peers for the right to retain its league status for the next season. Not enough votes and your club immediately became a non-league outfit.[10] As simple and as cruel as that but, happily, failing re-election was never seriously in doubt for United on either occasion. Maybe United's achievement in finishing above 12th place in 1957/58 and avoiding demotion to the newly created Fourth Division was worthy of note, but all that did was maintain the status quo.

---

10 Re-election lasted until 1987, when automatic relegation to non-league was introduced for the club finishing bottom of the Fourth Division. In 2003, the jeopardy was doubled with automatic relegation of the second-bottom team. The dreaded 'trapdoor'.

Truth to tell, Southend United was a small club, but not that small. Clubs of similar size and scale included Brentford, Brighton & Hove Albion and Bournemouth (or Bournemouth & Boscombe Athletic as nobody ever called them). In a perpetual triumph of hope over experience, Southend would regularly pull home gates of 10,000 to 15,000 or more during times of promise, like a long unbeaten start to the season or a late run to challenge for promotion or to put relegation fears to bed. Saturday, 7 November 1964 was not one of those times. It was business as usual. United camped out in lower mid-table: relegation unlikely, promotion already a forlorn hope.

Just a reminder. I had been to precisely two live football matches: one at Anfield, one at Goodison Park. I had watched a few FA Cup finals, a few England versus Scotland games, a few early club forays into European competitions and a decent segment of a World Cup on the television. I had three months of *MOTD* under my belt, watching the big teams play in front of packed stands and towering terraces. Lower-division football was not on my radar.

***

I will never forget stepping out with Dad from a not-very-full number seven Corporation bus, appropriately painted blue and white. On a damp but not cold day, weaving through knots – not crowds – of supporters, the men mostly decked out in raincoats with sensible trilby hats, many in collars and ties, the kids wearing gabardine macs and school caps, just like me. Women and girls noticeable by the fact that there aren't many of them. Joining a slow-moving queue maybe 15 people long. 'Click-clack' of the turnstile as the coins change hands and then leisurely taking our place in the South Paddock, a small standing area a few steps deep below the East Stand. Other supporters gradually ambling in around us. No rush, no crush. Plenty of time to take stock.

Roots Hall Mark Two has taken years to build and will take another four years to fully complete. The working estimate for the capacity of the ground is 35,000 to 40,000. Therefore, it is not a small football ground by any means, but three sides of it are compact in a way that Anfield and Goodison most emphatically are not. By contrast, 20 yards to my left is the slope of the unexpectedly vast open terrace known as the South Bank, where the remaining concrete steps have only recently been laid. Fewer than 1,000 people occupy the South Bank today, mostly draped over irregularly spaced crush barriers, resembling a succession of elongated reptiles. A few individualists spurn the barriers and stand freestyle behind the goal. Yawning spaces on the open terraces adjoining the West Stand and North Bank which are not thickly occupied under their barrel-shaped roofs. Quite a few empty seats in the stand above me. A crowd of 6,915. I have never seen anything like it.

The visitors are Colchester United: the 'Enemy' (at least since Colchester joined the Football League in 1950), the 'Scum', 'Sheep-shaggers', 'Wurzels', 'Yokels', 'Country Bumpkins' and all the other friendly epithets we have lobbed at our local rivals over the years. 'Local' is another relative term, by the way. Southend and Colchester are geographically further apart than, for example, Liverpool and Manchester, but nobody calls Liverpool against Manchester United a local derby. West Ham United and Leyton Orient, Millwall and Charlton Athletic are closer. But these are London clubs, and Southend is not part of London (as Southendians will tell you *ad nauseam*), so they don't count. In November 1964, there are only two Football League teams in Essex. Therefore, bragging rights for both clubs are wrapped around the Essex Derby and the kudos of being 'Number One in Essex'.

Apart from the shortage of fans, there is another difference. Southend United has its own supporters' club brass band which marches past us, backwards and forwards, then congregates around the narrow players' tunnel in the middle of the East Stand to serenade the crowd with stirring martial music of a bygone age. The ebbs and flows of cultural mores and the remarkable public address systems that all grounds possess today – even the rubbish grounds – means we don't see marching bands any more. In November 1964, there are no cute, cuddly club mascots bouncing around the touchline, pleasing and terrifying small children in equal number and winding up visiting fans.

The Colchester players emerge from the tunnel, followed shortly afterwards by their Southend counterparts in their blue-and-white-striped shirts. Both teams take the stage to a more muted reception than I am accustomed to. Roots Hall, not surprisingly, does not chant and does not sing. There are not enough Colchester fans in the ground to make a material difference. The standard of football is not what I'm accustomed to either. It is at least half a yard slower, the passing is not as crisp, the crosses and shots at goal more erratic, the goalkeeping less assured; the solution to a defender's dilemma is generally to hoof the ball as far up the field as possible. When Colchester score after five minutes, it looks as if the Southend defence has attempted a three-sided, slow-motion mugging of the visitors' winger. If that is the case, it doesn't work because the ball runs free and is smartly dispatched by Pat Connolly, Colchester's centre-forward.

Over time, but not today, I find out that Southend supporters have a well-deserved reputation for Olympian moaning. On this first visit, it just sounds like the barracking I have previously heard on Merseyside, but with a different accent and fewer expletives. It only lasts five minutes anyway, because Southend equalise with a low, firm drive from short range by wiry Scottish left-winger John McKinven, the scorer of the first United goal I have ever seen. Then Colchester are taken mercilessly to the cleaners; Southend are 5-1 up after an hour, including an emphatic rat-a-tat-a-tat hat-trick from another wiry Scot, Bobby Gilfillan.

And it could have been more. United are cruising, the crowd is purring, and I'm pretty chuffed as well. Even two goals from Colchester around the 70th minute fail to incite the renowned barrage of complaint, for Gilfillan whacks the ball, yet again, high into the Colchester net immediately afterwards. The final score is impressive Southend United 6, abject Colchester United 3 – which is as it should be.

Because it's November, Roots Hall is floodlit as we leave, the first time under the lights for me; the first of many, many times. Because it's Colchester, the home crowd leaves Roots Hall in a buzz of satisfaction; and I'm thinking, 'This is a bit of all right.'

That's the story of my first Southend match. Lots of goals, the massacre of United's closest rivals and the revelation of my first football hero. Not Roger Hunt, not Ian St John, not Alex Young, not Roy Vernon from matches I had previously attended. Not Jimmy Greaves, not Johnny Haynes, not Denis Law/George Best/Bobby Charlton, not Geoff Hurst from the matches I saw on TV, although I had a lot of time for all of them. The angular four-goal Bobby Gilfillan, all elbows and knees, earned my vote.

I went to Roots Hall three more times that season. United beat Bournemouth 2-1 (Gilfillan scoring once), Oldham 6-1 (Gilfillan with two) and Hull City 2-1 (Gilfillan not scoring – a day off). In the curiously perennial on-again, off-again love affair that the quintessential rugby league city of Kingston upon Hull has with association football (it was on again in 1965 and may be on again soon), City were pushing hard for promotion and United's win effectively killed their chances stone dead. In the biggest crowd of the season and the best atmosphere I have experienced at Roots Hall, I am vaguely aware for the first time of a significant away support in a crowd of 11,023. City's quite large following behaves quite well despite the result, for hooliganism was no more than a wispy dark cloud on the horizon in 1965.

By the end of the 1964/65 season, I was hooked – at the age of nine, and for ever, as it has turned out. My first football sliding doors moment. From then on, Southend United became 'We' and have remained so to this day. Although We ended up in mid-table mediocrity, I had seen 16 United goals in four games and my hero had scored seven of them. Poor old Colchester suffered the ignominy of relegation to the Fourth Division, so there were more reasons to be cheerful. Of course, hopes were high for the next season – as always. For those of you who have ever supported a football team, have you ever known a time when it wasn't?

I went to most of United's home games the next season. An ageing Eddie Firmani, one-time Sampdoria, Inter Milan and Genoa goalscoring wizard (and you had to be a wizard to score his tally of goals in the ultra-defensive war of attrition that was 1950s and 1960s Italian football) was an unlikely recruit to the club and immediately stole the place of the great Bobby. Heartbreakingly for me, my hero barely got a start and departed to Doncaster Rovers by season's end. Gone also were Southend from the Third Division, with an away win record you could count on the fingers – one finger, in fact – of one hand. The BBC teleprinter clacked 'Brighton & HA 9 (Nine) Southend Utd 1' in November 1965, the 'nine' cruelly spelt out in case people thought it was a typing error. It was at that moment that I, for the first time in my life, began to nourish a sense of foreboding. However, the problem with being a football fan, especially a newly baked football fan, is that hope, however unrealistic, remains alive until the arithmetic tells you there's no way back.

At the end of May 1966, Southend were officially and dismally relegated to the Fourth Division for the first time in their history. Typically, in the cyclorama of pain and grief which circulates so often around United, it was Hull City that delivered the *coup de grâce*, thereby ensuring their promotion and Southend's relegation in one fell swoop. I suppose if you're a Hull supporter, and I've known quite a few, you would say that was poetic justice.

If life is a bowl of cherries, some could say I picked a gooseberry with my chosen football team. Should have been a lesson to me, but it made no difference. Eric Cantona was right – I had the scarf, so it was already too late. But it does have its compensations. Supporting a lower-division football team may not always be rewarding, but it is rarely dull. It is a singularity of experience, and a story worth telling.

Chapter 5

A Week in September

'TO TRAVEL hopefully is a better thing than to arrive.'[11] So said Robert Louis Stevenson. It doesn't quite ring true to me. For starters, Stevenson died in Samoa in 1894 – so he couldn't possibly have been a Southend supporter. Travelling hopefully is something all United fans can readily associate with. What arriving feels like is less certain.

When I started supporting Southend, the gulf between lower-division clubs and the elite in top division felt almost insurmountable. That was not strictly true, however. Ipswich Town had quite recently broken through and won the First Division in 1961/1962. Even Leyton Orient (1962/63) and Northampton Town (1965/66) had joy, fun and a season in the First Division sun. Nevertheless, these were outliers of short duration and were generally regarded as such.

Ipswich continued to defy their outlier status with cup, league and European escapades to come. Although a smaller town than Southend, Ipswich had the advantage of being a modest East Anglian regional centre with its own support catchment area.

And what was the competition for the affection of its sporting public? London? Just a bit too far. Colchester? Not in a million years – in fact, legions of fans in Colchester used

11 R.L. Stevenson's quote is in *El Dorado*, an essay in his *Verginibus Puerisque* (1881).

to make the 20-mile trip up the A12 to Ipswich on any given Saturday. Norwich? You must be joking.

No such luck for Southend United with the Big Smoke of London just up the road. The thought of breaking into the charmed circle seemed as remote as landing on Mars. In the very first sentence of his classic official history of the club, Peter Mason writes, 'Other teams dreamed of Wembley, some hankered for the First Division championship or a place in Europe – but Southend only ever wanted Second Division status.'[12] This was as true in the 1960s as it was when he wrote it 30 years later and, to a degree, remains so today. Even the more limited ambition of long-term second-tier residence seemed a big ask.

Quite a few of my school contemporaries supported bigger and better teams, mostly from London, and regarded my affection for United with the amused condescension normally bestowed on those following a quaint but rather eccentric hobby, like collecting spoons. This was particularly true of West Ham supporters, some of whom seemed to think, quite erroneously, that the Hammers and Southend were footballing rivals. Chance would have been a fine thing; we shared the same division with the Hammers for all of one season. Cup clashes have been few and far between and even fewer have left me with the feel-good factor.

It was a dead giveaway on a Saturday morning. Southend Central, Southend Victoria and suburban railway stations, even my own local station of Thorpe Bay would reveal these Essex charlatans in their true colours: the London-bound platforms shamelessly dotted with scarves in the claret and blue of West Ham, the red and white of Arsenal, the navy blue and white of Tottenham Hotspur, the royal blue of Chelsea, even a few followers of London's footballing odds and sods: Fulham, Charlton, Crystal Palace, Millwall. All waiting for

12 *Southend United: The Official History of the Blues*, written by Peter Mason, with statistics by David Goody. Yore Publications, 1993.

their trains to London Fenchurch Street or Liverpool Street (unless they were off to see West Ham at Upton Park and changed at Barking). Supporting the teams their fathers supported, so they said.

Suppose your team was never on the television and excited rare comment on the radio. Suppose your team's performance merited a few lines (if you were lucky) in the popular daily newspapers: the *Sketch, Mail, Express, Mirror, People, News of the World*. Nothing at all in the 'qualities', *The Times, Telegraph, Observer* or *Guardian*. If people outside London had trouble even knowing where your town and team were located, what was to be done?

The answer was simple. Get yourself a second, bigger team to support; and it could be done, too. In the 60s, going to the football was still relatively cheap, a few shillings in old money, a couple if you were a kid. Therefore, it was eminently possible to get to two matches a week without breaking the bank. And the Southend board of directors weren't stupid. At almost exactly the same time as I started supporting my local team, United reached an agreement with the Football League to play most of their home matches on Friday evenings instead of Saturday afternoons to potentially resolve the dilemma of who to watch. You could do both! Tranmere Rovers and Stockport County did the same thing, faced with the competition from the big clubs in nearby Liverpool and Manchester. And, remember, this was in the days before wall-to-wall season tickets. There was a time when you could get into almost any match, even the big First Division matches, if you were prepared to get to the ground early enough and stand in a queue for long enough.

It paid dividends for United. Playing on a Friday night almost invariably put a couple of thousand on the Roots Hall gate compared to playing on Saturday afternoon. In addition, the darkened stands and terraces made a small crowd look half-decent and a half-decent crowd look like a full house. It also meant that I could go to watch my first team on Friday evening and then grab my West Ham claret and blue, Arsenal red and white, Tottenham navy blue and white, Chelsea royal blue or any other chosen scarf on a Saturday morning and brazenly join the throng on the Thorpe Bay station platform. Quite a lot of genuine Southend supporters, including school contemporaries of mine, did this. But not me; my second team was too far away.

***

Maybe some residual attachment to my increasingly tenuous northern roots persisted. Perhaps some basic antipathy towards the top-tier clubs in the big bad Smoke up the road for being too close to home – especially West Ham. Or perhaps because I thought West Ham were a bit pretentious, Arsenal a bit boring, Tottenham a bit soft-centred, Chelsea a bit flashy and Fulham a bit nondescript. So much for the London giants.

In the midst of all this was the 1966 World Cup which England won, helping to soothe the pain of United's relegation. I presume it was Dad's anonymous ticketing source who managed to conjure up another set for England's group games at Wembley: a deadly dull 0-0 opener against Uruguay; a nerve-rattling 2-0 win against Mexico, redeemed by Bobby Charlton right-footed screamer from 30 yards to open England's account and a tense but ultimately gratifying 2-0 win against France, where Liverpool's Roger Hunt knocked in both goals – one from about six inches.

We watched the rest of the tournament on TV in glorious black and white, culminating in the Wembley final when England beat West Germany 4-2. 'And here comes Hurst. He's got – some people are on the pitch, they think it's all over. It is now. It's four,' the incomparable Ken Wolstenholme intoned with barely restrained glee as West Ham's Geoff Hurst galloped along the cut-up pitch in the last minute of extra time and blasted the ball into the roof of the German net. Mum,

Dad and I danced with Marty the boxer dog. My baby sister Estelle slept through most of it.

England won the World Cup on 30 July 1966. The new Football League season started precisely three weeks later. No rest for the wicked in those days. On Saturday, 3 September, Dad and I joined the claret and blue Essex charlatans on the rail trip from Thorpe Bay to Upton Park District line underground station, change at Barking. We followed them down Green Street with the rest of the gathering throng, strolling past the platoons of local police maintaining a dutiful presence, grabbing the matchday programme from the deafening roadside seller, avoiding the muttered offerings from the circling ticket touts, checking out the wood and canvas merchandise stalls for scarves, hats, caps, badges and rosettes, lining up alongside the grease-laden fug of a hot food van amid the cloying stench of chip fat, the miasma of frying onions and the ambiguous pong emanating from the burgers. All the sights, sounds and smells of a typical London First Division match in the 1960s. After negotiating a sizeable queue, I joined 32,951 spectators in a steamy, humid Upton Park to see West Ham play Liverpool, complete with autograph book, a cardboard photograph of England's World Cup winning XI – and a Liverpool rosette, bought at Dad's urging from one of said merchandise stalls, but wisely kept hidden in the duffel bag.

It was the World Cup that had brought us to Upton Park and five England heroes were taking to the pitch. For West Ham, central defender Bobby Moore was already a living icon as the England captain who had lifted the little gold Jules Rimet Trophy at Wembley. Attacking midfielder Martin Peters had burnished his reputation as 'being ten years ahead of his time' (according to England's World Cup-winning manager Alf Ramsey) and striker Hurst had written his name into the history books with the first World Cup Final hat-trick. And a perfect hat-trick at that: header, right-footed shot, left-footed shot.

Liverpool's Roger Hunt had also played every match, weighing in with three goals, and Ian Callaghan had played against France. All in all, the scorers of eight goals out of England's 11 were on the pitch this Saturday afternoon.

We stood with the home supporters in what was known as the Chicken Run, a cramped little covered terrace with more than a passing resemblance to other cramped little terraces that became familiar in visits to clubs of much lower status than West Ham. I remember next to nothing about the match, mainly because it wasn't very good. West Ham had started the season slowly and were in the relegation zone. Reigning league champions Liverpool had also started slowly, hovering around mid-table, so that possibly explained it. 'I'm Forever Blowing Bubbles', the West Ham anthem, didn't sound any quieter for all that. And, almost inevitably, I remember Hurst putting West Ham ahead in the first half with a trademark, full-blooded, straight-as-an-arrow drive – he took his penalties like that as well. Liverpool eventually got their collective act together and equalised late on through another Geoff – Strong – and that was that.

What happened next was more memorable. Dad and I rapidly made our way to the players' exit and I took up station near the closed door, autograph book and pen in hand. After a few minutes, the door burst open to reveal Liverpool's Ian St John striding out, face like thunder, muttering 'I've got a train to catch.' Dad was just behind me and was rather put out, so he called out, 'Son, when you're sweeping the streets in five years' time, you'll be happy if someone asks you for your autograph.' Quick as a flash, St John responded over his shoulder in what in future years would be a well-known Scottish brogue, 'I'll be sweeping the streets Monday if I don't catch that fucking train.' That's something you don't forget in a hurry. Dad hooted with laughter and it didn't bother me. After two years of visits to Roots Hall, I was no stranger to the kind of language you wouldn't use in front of your gran.

A few minutes later, the West Ham players started to emerge to applause and clamours for autographs. Moore, Peters and Hurst lined us kids up in tidy rows and proceeded to sign EVERY autograph book, photograph, programme, rosette, what-have-you with their own pens, including my colour cardboard photo of England's World Cup winning team. Class, pure class. Mind you, to be totally fair, they would soon be driving off to their leafy young executive homes and wouldn't have to catch a fucking train.

But the Ian St John encounter didn't finally put an end to any prospect of me adopting Liverpool as my second team. The reason is that I already had more than a sneaking regard for another team.

In the mid-60s, memories of the Munich air disaster of February 1958 were still relatively fresh. When the chartered flight returning from a European Cup tie in Belgrade failed to take off after refuelling in the ice and snow of Bavaria, 23 souls perished. Included in the death toll were eight of Manchester United's first-team squad, and another two were too badly injured to ever play again. The abiding legend that is Duncan Edwards, mooted as a potential greatest of all time at 21, passed away in hospital two weeks after the crash – so we'll never know. Because of Munich, the Reds of Manchester were the nation's favourite second football team for a few years so my regard was not without foundation. I knew all about Munich, but it wasn't just that. I was at the age where I was glued to the television screen watching the gliding runs and bullet shots of Bobby Charlton, the audacity and sheer cheekiness of Denis Law and the magic that was George Best, the mop-headed Beatle clone who could do anything with a football.

In the final analysis, it was a combination of the Munich effect, Manchester United taking a slim first-leg lead to Lisbon's exotic Estádio da Luz in a March 1966 European Cup quarter-final and Dad's fault for letting me stay up to watch it on TV. 'What a player this boy is,' gushed the ubiquitous Kenneth Wolstenholme as Best waltzed through the Benfica defence to notch his second goal of the night with only 15 minutes gone, setting up a 5-1 evisceration of the European superstars. And then came an afternoon in exotic north London.

***

It was no coincidence at all that, just one week after Upton Park, I was at White Hart Lane for Tottenham Hotspur against Manchester United. Liverpool and Everton fans of more advanced age may disagree, but on Saturday, 10 September 1966 it was difficult to dispute that this match was between the biggest two of the big four. And it was another World Cup pilgrimage, for Manchester United's Bobby Charlton and Nobby Stiles had played all of England's matches and Jimmy Greaves had played in the first three before his injury sprung Geoff Hurst into the spotlight. England had used just 15 players in winning the World Cup and I saw eight of them doing their day jobs in one September week, six of whom had played in the final.[13] As Bobby Charlton had contributed three goals to England's triumphant campaign, I had also managed to see all the scorers of all England's World Cup goals in that week.

It was a first visit to White Hart Lane for us and Dad wasn't sure about how to get there, as there was no underground station within reach in those days. But we both knew we had a long queue waiting. We left home super early and eventually fetched up at Seven Sisters overground railway station on a day so hot it felt as if the breath was being sucked out of us.

---

13 The heroes playing a part in England's 1966 World Cup campaign that I didn't see that week in September: Goalkeeper Gordon Banks (Leicester City), right-back George Cohen (Fulham), left-back Ray Wilson (Everton), centre-half Jack Charlton (Leeds United), midfielder/winger Alan Ball (Blackpool) and winger Terry Paine (Southampton). Another winger, John Connelly of Manchester United, did not play against Tottenham for reasons unknown.

The walk up Seven Sisters Road and Tottenham High Road seemed endless as we wilted under the burning sun. Even just after noon, there were plenty of fellow pilgrims making their way to the ground for the three o'clock kick-off, passing the different yet familiar ranks of local constabulary, programme sellers, ticket touts, merchandise stalls and rancid hot food trucks. Finally, after guzzling a couple of tepid Coca-Colas, we joined the serpentine queue stretching down the High Road, which we occupied for well over an hour. Wow! It was hot, even when we finally made it to the welcoming shade of the terrace steps below the posh seats of the old West Stand.

White Hart Lane felt like the epicentre of the football world. There were 56,295 shirt-sleeved spectators squeezed into the stadium which would have taken the breath away even without the heat: so hot that a few dozen youngsters were passed down the sunburnt Paxton Road terrace to our left and allowed to sit on the running track behind the goal. The local constabulary kept a wary eye on them, and I could hear them managing expectations by occasionally wandering past, quietly promising all kinds of instant and painful retribution if the youngsters misbehaved.

Football was changing. For the first time, I was aware of a clearly segregated away end, with a large congregation of Manchester supporters congregated on the terrace below the Park Lane stand chanting and singing away. Most of the chanting and singing from the Tottenham fans came from the human lasagne that was the mountainous multi-layered Worcester Avenue Stand. A steep terrace was topped by a larger bank of terracing known as The Shelf, itself topped by a large wedge of seats and surmounted in turn by a roof protecting the seated punters from the elements. Crowning the whole structure was a press box with the Tottenham golden cockerel perched on top, gleaming in the sunlight. White Hart Lane was buzzing, it was noisy, it was brilliant. It was an occasion.

A huge roar and the teams launched themselves at each other from the first whistle. First Tottenham had a spell, then United had a spell. The rhythm could have been set to music, interspersed with moments of sheer havoc around the goalmouths. Not the hundred-miles-an-hour firecracker instinctive touches and flicks of the modern game, but more measured and no less technically proficient. There were chances and misses at both ends. The ritual booing of Nobby Stiles, renowned as a snarling hatchet-man in the heat of battle but also beloved for his toothless grin as he danced around Wembley with the Jules Rimet Trophy, was mostly good-natured.

Shortly before half-time came a goal at the Paxton Road end. Manchester United's David Herd took a corner from the right. A mistimed clearance saw the ball drop to George Best, with his back to goal, at the left-sided edge of the penalty area. Almost right in front of me, he teed the ball up and performed a bicycle kick of outrageous virtuosity, lobbing the ball back into the penalty area, whereupon Denis Law was able to rise, as he so often did, at a backwards, diagonal angle and still power a header into the roof of the net from ten yards out. It was gravity-defying, pure flamboyant brilliance. Even the Tottenham fans around me were stunned into grudging admiration.

Tottenham 0 Manchester United 1. With half-time imminent, Charlton hit a shot which deflected directly to the feet of Law in the penalty area. This time, he took the ball past Jennings, the Tottenham goalkeeper, and tapped in number two, or so I thought. He had scuffed his tap-in and the ball was cleared before it crept over the goal line, but I couldn't see because the crowd, all of them taller than me, had already craned their necks even higher, expecting to see the ball in the back of the net. I heard a cheer, but I thought it was for the goal, not for the goal-line clearance and it took me a little while to understand that Law had not scored. Half-time and 1-0 to United.

The second half started, with Tottenham now kicking towards the Paxton Road end where the touchline kids were sitting – or kneeling. If anything, the pace was even more frantic, the noise even louder, the atmosphere even more breathless – and it wasn't just the heat. Wave after wave of Tottenham attacks seemed destined to end up in a goal, but United managed to stem the tide and reassert a level of authority. The longer it went on, the more control United seemed to have. Best hit the inside of the post, then he glided past three defenders as if on rails and forced a last-ditch save. To keep things interesting, Tottenham's Alan Gilzean hit the post with a header. Time ticked on. Four minutes to go.

Just when it seemed that the Manchester United defenders had weathered all the storms, Tottenham scuttled down the left wing in front of me, and a driven cross into the middle met with Gilzean's head for an equaliser of sublime simplicity and deadly accuracy. Cascades of toilet rolls and a minor pitch invasion from a few of the touchline brigade ensued and, just to be on the safe side, I applauded the goal with more enthusiasm than I felt. Some semblance of order was restored, with more loudly expressed assurances from the local constabulary of the retribution that would fall upon the touchline dwellers if they didn't behave.

'Tottenham [clap-clap-clap]' from all sides of the ground now. It was deafening in a way you didn't always get from a White Hart Lane crowd, not in those days. With less than three minutes to go, Jimmy Greaves sprinted in pursuit of a through ball, got to it a nanosecond before United goalkeeper Gaskell and prodded the ball into the middle of the unguarded net. This time, the invasion was tumultuous; the Tottenham kids on the touchline were either trying to get a piece of Greaves or generally bouncing around the pitch. A few of those around me joined them and I thought about a brief foray myself: not to celebrate, you understand, but just to say that I had once walked on a sliver of the lush green turf of

White Hart Lane. 'No you don't,' was Dad's firm advice and I contented myself with observing the lines of toilet paper snaking across the pitch.

There was a short delay while the bottles and cans thoughtfully donated by the grumpy ranks of Manchester supporters were cleared from the pitch at the far end. 'Glory, glory, Hallelujah, and the Spurs go marching on' rained down from The Shelf, the terrace I was standing on and even the folk in the posh seats above me; not that they were sitting down now. With an effort, the touchline brigade was reassembled. The local constabulary, helmets just about intact, now directed some of their attention towards my section of the West Stand, smiling tightly and meaningfully as they passed by. Full time: 2-1 to Tottenham. Not so soft-centred, after all.

After a few minutes, we agreed that autograph-hunting with Charlton and Stiles would be too hard today. Dad and I made our snail-like way out of the ground in a daze of mass Tottenham jubilation and turned toward White Hart Lane station because the long trek back down Tottenham High Road to Seven Sisters seemed too formidable in the crush and the heat. Not a wise choice, as the queue for the train was almost as endless as the queue to the ground had been, but eventually we found our way home as day turned to night, more than ten hours after we had left. Mum was relieved to see us. It was three days before my 11th birthday.

***

Tottenham's win was daylight robbery. But the result didn't really matter. The Ship of State that was Bobby Charlton in his prime, the crackling genius of Denis Law, the sensual relationship between George Best and a football, even the barking attack dog called Nobby Stiles confirmed what I had suspected: Manchester United were now officially my second team. My second football sliding doors moment, with apologies to Liverpool and Everton. That season, the Red

United ended up winning the league championship, sealing the trophy with a 6-1 victory over West Ham at Upton Park. Tottenham consoled themselves with the FA Cup. All's well that ended well; at least for half of Manchester and half of north London.

Nor did I bear any grudge against Ian St John or Jimmy Greaves. St John later became a sharp and witty television anchor with a gift for a quickfire pithy one-liner – no surprise there. Greaves had the insight and good taste to become a high-profile Southend United supporter and was closely involved with the club for several years as a sort of cheerful Dutch uncle. Between them, they hosted the weekly ITV lunchtime show *Saint and Greavsie* through the late 1980s and early 90s which, in my humble opinion, is the best football show ever, and compulsory Saturday viewing when I was around – or on video when I wasn't.

By the age of 11, therefore, I had a first club and a second club and both have remained unchanged to this day. I couldn't do anything about Southend United, I was stuck with them, but history shows that the other United was a fortunate choice. I have vicariously celebrated decades of glory and cabinets full of trophies. It's not quite the same, but it's something.

***

Two of my oldest friends, fellow long-suffering Southend United supporters from the early days, were living in the East Midlands. Both of them also supported second, more successful clubs: one supported Birmingham City for family reasons, but the other's chosen team was Liverpool. On a mild, cloudy Saturday afternoon in October 1986, after a beer (or two) at the ancient Ye Olde Trip to Jerusalem public house in the city of Nottingham, we were sitting in what is now known as the Brian Clough Stand at Nottingham Forest's City Ground to watch the Forest play Manchester United. Typically for an outfit managed by the legendary Clough in the late 1980s,

Forest had started the season at a gallop and were sitting top of the First Division. Typically for a Manchester United outfit in the late 1980s, United had started the season at a stumble and were just one place off the bottom. Nevertheless, Manchester United were Manchester United so the City Ground was full to bursting with 34,828 raucous partisans, both sets of fans resplendent in red and white. The perennial pressure on all underachieving United managers since Matt Busby was building to a crescendo for Ron Atkinson as his tall, heavily built frame restlessly prowled the touchline.

The match started off as you would expect from an early season top-versus-bottom clash: Forest brimful of confidence, United a bag of nerves. No undue sympathy for their plight in my immediate vicinity, however. 'Olsen!! Olsen!! You're a big girl's blouse! What are you?' shouted my Liverpool-supporting friend at United's stick-skinny Swedish winger Jesper Olsen. 'Kevin Moran! Kevin Moran!! Kevin MORON!!! That's what you are!' waxed my friend at the unfortunate United centre-back, well known at the time for summarily upending Everton's Peter Reid and becoming the first player to ever be sent off in an FA Cup Final – which United still managed to win.

As if aware of the calumny, Olsen's performance was largely ineffective and Moran clattered around like a runaway goods wagon. In the second half, Forest took a thoroughly expected lead through ex-United striker Garry Birtles to the visible and audible annoyance of the United travelling multitude filling the Bridgford End terrace to our left. However, Forest proceeded to disappear into a shell as United belatedly decided to make a fight of it. Right at the death, United's long-time Captain Marvel, Bryan Robson, slid in at the far post to touch a deflected low cross into the net, sending the Bridgford End into raptures and delighting an unexpectedly large number of previously unnoticed United fans in the stand around us.

As I retook my seat, my Liverpool-supporting friend muttered 'jammy, so jammy', head slowly shaking in disbelief.

Then he turned to me, his face racked with frustrated rage and announced, 'But they're so jammy. Bloody Jamchester United!'

One-all it ended, but United's season did not immediately improve and Atkinson prowled for only one month more; he was replaced by Alex Ferguson and the rest, as they say, is history. Forest's title challenge dissipated by March, United crept to safety and both teams ended up in mid-table. But 'Jamchester United' has been an enduring, gleeful refrain in my household since that day and even I am prepared to concede that the label has been justified more than once.

Naturally, I have been endlessly advised that I fit the bill for a typical Manchester United supporter: I wasn't born in Manchester, I've never lived anywhere near Manchester, I don't have a Manchester accent, I know my way round the M25 much better than the M60, I'm prepared to pay outrageous sums for a ticket once in a Blue Moon (I don't mean for Manchester City). Oh, and of course, Manchester United aren't really my team anyway. Yeah, yeah, yeah; been there, heard that. Too bad. I got over it years ago.

But maybe the sceptics have a point. My most fundamental footballing memories have always been attached to Southend United. And there's nothing like the immediacy of a new season, a time for renewal, to quicken the pulse and tighten the gut muscles.

Chapter 6

Settling In

'Who's that team we call United?
Who's that team we all adore?
They're the boys in blue and white
And they fight with all their might;
And they're out to show the world
that they can score.'

Copyright: every football club's 'Popular End' choir in
England and Scotland, circa 1966. Substitute 'United' and
'blue and white' at will, according to allegiance.

BY SEPTEMBER 1966, both first and second teams were
locked in my affections and Southend United were locked in
the Fourth Division. I could handle the indignity because it
was a new season and new realms of hopes and possibilities
opened up, as they always do for even the most battle-hardened
football supporters when the sun is shining and the winter gear
stays in the wardrobe for another few weeks. And I had just
started secondary school, so I had put the ways of childhood
behind me. Yeah, right.

The terraces and floodlights of Roots Hall beckoned
once again. A big ground for a small club. According to
Peter Mason's *Official History of the Blues*, the *Daily Mail*
once christened Roots Hall 'the Seaside Wembley'. Being

the Wembley of whatever was helped in no small way by the phenomenon of the South Bank, the immense 72-step open terrace that towered over the other three sides of the ground and seemed to cow them into awed submission. It was almost as if the architects of Roots Hall Mark Two had taken note of the poky little terraces of United's previous homes and decided to overcompensate.

That's not where I started, though. My vantage point was still the South Paddock below the East Stand, as it had been since my debut against Colchester United in 1964. I was joined in the South Paddock by Dad, and occasionally the dads of a small but passionate group of fellow sufferers from school. There I was, in my blue-and-white-striped scarf and bobble hat.

Life in the South Paddock had its pluses and minuses. On the plus side, it was a comfortable place for pre-teens to stand, and it was close enough to catch another thunder of studs, the gasped 'oofs' and 'aahhs' as the tackles came crunching in, the constant bellowing of instructions from our captain Tony Bentley – on our side of the pitch, at least. On the minus side, you almost needed binoculars to catch some of the action at the far end. If it rained or snowed or both, as it so often did, the unfortunate spectator was assailed by the weather from all points of the compass; if the crowd wasn't too big, it was possible to ease our way into the shivering huddle under the part of the terrace covered by the barely adequate roof of the East Stand. If that wasn't possible, be prepared to drown and/ or freeze.

Another minus was the fellow supporters in the South Paddock. I have already mentioned the reputation for Olympian moaning attached to the Roots Hall crowd. To the mostly respectable middle-aged gentlemen around me, continuous and trenchant complaint about our team, the opposing team, our manager, their manager, the referee, the linesmen, the board of directors (of course) and the world in general was the *modus operandi* of the South Paddock. Reflecting the social norms, most of the juicier Anglo-Saxon swear words were muttered or groaned, rather than bellowed out at full throttle, but the overall sentiments were unambiguous. In 1968, the East Stand was finally extended to completely overlook the North Paddock and almost completely cover the South, meaning that most of the hardy souls on both terraces were only battered by the elements on three sides. But it didn't matter to me by then – I'd already moved on.

As my small band of brothers and I got a year older, and a bit more self-confident, we started to look for a different home in Roots Hall. The seats in the East Stand scored a zero from us; too expensive for one thing, but most of the occupants were distinguished, if that's the right word, by an air of brooding semi-silence. On cold nights, inmates occasionally started up a rhythmic stamping of numb feet on wooden floor. The foot-stamping sometimes signified support, sometimes just hypothermia, but would typically begin at one end, gradually gather momentum across the whole stand, to diminish in volume and eventually die out at its furthest point from origin, unless the stamping made its way back along the stand again, which it sometimes did. Outrage and despair were frequently expressed by the tossing of plastic cushions (designed to relieve the numb bums of stand-dwellers perched on the wooden bench seats and yours for the evening at the price of an old shilling) on to the pitch; usually but not always waiting until full time.

Directly opposite us was the barrel-roofed expanse of the West Stand, darkened because the floodlights only illuminated the first few steps, and the lights in the stand itself were rationed to pre-match, half-time and post-match. Unreasonably, considering our surroundings, we harshly dismissed the inhabitants as 'moaning old gits'. But those guys could moan for Great Britain. Even from our position, we could clearly hear the howls of protest. If one of our players was clattered by one of the opposing team in front of the West Stand, if the referee made a 'clear and obvious error', to use the modern parlance of the Video Assistant Referee, a communal outburst of indignant fury arose. What it meant was incomprehensible to our ears. From 50 yards away, it sounded like an incoherent 'GAAAARRRRRNNNNNNN'. It wasn't Cockney, it wasn't East Anglia. With the benefit of hindsight, it was probably an explosion of Estuary English moaning, a regional accent intrinsic to the folk who live on or near the tidal banks of the River Thames, but nobody had come up with a name for it back in those days.[14] We weren't ready to become 'moaning old gits' at the age of 12, so the West Stand was out as well.

Instead, we made our way to the turnstiles on top of the South Bank on matchday. 'Click-clack' and we were immediately at the highest spot in Roots Hall. I would take a moment to admire the panoramic view around the ground and beyond: on Saturday afternoons I could even get a distant view of my school up the hill behind the North Bank. It was even better in the evenings when I could gaze down at the silhouettes of the building crowd contained under the glare of the floodlights. To my eyes, it was beautiful and never failed to give me a buzz of anticipation. Sometimes I would turn left to spend a few minutes browsing the football programme shop, looking for additions to my collection. And then down the steps I went to join the others behind the goal.

Which brings me to another phenomenon unique to some lower-division football grounds in the 1960s. Assuming a half-decent crowd and assuming we won the toss, United would generally kick towards a reasonably busy South Bank in the first half. From about the 40-minute mark – earlier if the weather was bad – small but growing streams of spectators

14 'Estuary English' was originally coined by Peter Rosewarne, an English as a Foreign Language teacher as recently as 1984, according to www.phon. ucl.ac.uk.

would start towards the quadrant between the South Bank and the West Stand. At the stroke of half-time, the streams became a tide as most of the South Bank inhabitants disappeared, to reappear moments later, 90 yards away, and rapidly fill up the much smaller, indifferently covered North Bank. Not something you would have seen at Old Trafford, Anfield, Goodison or White Hart Lane. Bugger a panoramic view of play: you were there to see your team win, and the best way of helping was to get yourself behind the goal and raise a racket.

***

The days of good old T.P. Ratcliff were passing by the late 60s, as crowds had devised their own homespun alternatives. My friends and I joined the migration along the perpetually muddy path behind the West Stand from South Bank to North Bank to add some heft to another growing phenomenon: the chanting and singing in the 'Popular End', known to the more devout inhabitants as the 'The Pak'. I even talked Dad into joining the migration, although he stubbornly remained part of the non-singing constituency.

Every English ground, big and small, had a 'Popular End'. And by 1966/67, chanting and singing had arrived, even at clubs like Southend United, even at grounds like Roots Hall. At first, it was pure copycat Liverpool; 'You'll Never Walk Alone', of course. 'Ee-aye-addio, we're gonna win the cup/league/whatever', a Merseyside version of the old nursery rhyme, 'The farmer wants a wife' went the rounds for a few years. Nobody sings that one any more. 'United' [clap-clap-clap] or [clap, clap, clap-clap-clap, clap-clap-clap-clap] 'Southend' came in around the time of the 1966 World Cup when Wembley used to rumble with the incantation directed at England, adapting the rhythmic beat of 'Hold Tight' by Dave Dee, Dozy, Beaky, Mick and Tich. I know this because I bought the single. The Rolling Stones donated another early musical effort as we trumpeted 'Duh, Duh, duh-duh-

duh, UNITED' to the opening bars of '(I Can't Get No) Satisfaction'.

I also recall hearing the 'Iggy-Oggy, Iggy-Oggy, Oi, Oi, Oi' chant barked out by Cornwall supporters at a rugby union match somewhere. This morphed into a pastiche rip-off by round-ball crowds when chanting and singing were getting going. 'Zigger zagger, zigger zagger, U-NI-TED! Zigger, U! Zigger zigger, UNITED! U-N-I-T-E-D, UNITED!!' was the Roots Hall version, concluding with a hearty cheer.[15] Oh, the innocent enthusiasm; the transition from the old world of football crowd noise to the new.

English supporters acquired a nostalgic affection for American martial anthems: why is an abiding mystery to me, but English football supporters like silly, as we see to this day. Among the better-known at Roots Hall were:

'From the Halls of Montezuma,
To the Shores of Sicily;
We will fight, fight, fight for United,
'Til we're in Division Three.
To hell with Luton Town, to hell with Brad City;
We will fight, fight, fight for United,
'Til we're in Division Three.'

'Where was the goalie when the ball was in the net?
Where was the goalie when the ball was in the net?
Where was the goalie when the ball was in the net?
He was sitting on his arse, singing United [clap-clap-clap]', to the tune of 'The Battle Hymn of the Republic'.

It's gratifying to note that 'Halls of Montezuma' is still sung at Old Trafford, but the Halls of Montezuma are replaced by the 'Banks of the River Irwell' and the teams consigned to

---

15 *Zigger Zagger* was also the title of a play, the first work commissioned by the National Youth Theatre in 1967. I saw it on BBC TV.

Hell by Manchester United fans are Liverpool and Manchester City (with the helpful clarification 'They're shit!' for those ignorant of the City situation) and the aspiration is ''til we win the Football League'.

To even things up a bit, football song composers channelled social commentary with the appropriation of well-known protest songs of the era: the upbeat and defiant 'We shall not be moved' is still doing the rounds today, but the downbeat and miserable 'We shall overcome' disappeared about the same time as the morose hippies who invented it.

It wasn't only the opposing team that copped it. Referees and the Essex Police force were also in the firing line:

> *'My eyes are dim, I cannot see;*
> *I think I'll be a referee.*
> *I think I-I'll be a referee.'*

An edited version of 'The Quartermaster's Stores', another little number of quasi-military lineage. Or the more succinct and prosaic:

> *'The referee's a bastard.'*

As for the local constabulary, a cheerful little rendering to the tune of 'Camptown Races' – another American song – paid homage to the homely Saturday evening cops and robbers show on BBC TV, more *Call the Midwife* than *Line of Duty*, as I recall.

> *'Who's the copper in the big blue hat?*
> *Dixon, Dixon;*
> *Who's the copper in the big blue hat?*
> *Dixon of Dock Green.*
> *On the beat all day,*
> *On the wife all night;*

Who's the copper in the big blue hat?
Dixon of Dock Green.'
Evening, all.

* * *

We didn't need drums. All we needed for percussion were a couple of big lads thumping the corrugated iron wall at the back of the North Bank. And, as a long-term observer of lower-division clubs, I know about the vocal fans at compact 'Popular Ends' all over England. They might think they're the Stretford End in full voice; in reality, they sound more like an altercation in a bus shelter. Maybe we sounded like that as well although, with two to three thousand gathered behind the goal for the second half, there were probably enough of us to make a decent noise. The roar that greeted a United goal in the North Bank was a discordant combination of adult bellows, adolescent croaks and schoolboy shrieks as we took part in the North Bank version of surge and sway, a pallid attempt to copy the Kop at Liverpool, and tried to dodge the cascades of unfurling toilet rolls streaming down to the pitch around our heads.

It was just a shame that the football did not live up to the evolving off-pitch atmosphere. In 1966/67, we were on target for promotion until late March; then things gradually fell apart with a distressing rash of 1-0 away defeats and a depressing 0-0 home draw against Rochdale, by which time even I had thrown in the towel. Ageing maestro Eddie Firmani had also disappeared for a brief cameo at Charlton Athletic and subsequent retirement. The season concluded with a miserable 1-0 defeat at home to Stockport County, who ended up as champions, while United finished five points and two positions short of promotion in sixth place. As I watched the modest gathering of County supporters celebrating on the South Bank after the final whistle, I fervently wished that I would never experience another let-down like this one. How young and naive I was.

* * *

Events off the pitch were also starting to impinge on my consciousness. Alvan Williams (no relation), an exponent of tracksuit management in contrast to the pipe and trilby hat demeanour of his predecessors, had taken United down to the Fourth Division. He then unexpectedly sloped off to take over at Wrexham in April 1967, at a crucial and highly inconvenient time for us. Then, three months later, he compounded the felony by pinching our top scorer, the tall and bustling Ray 'Smudger' Smith. This caused me vague and undefined disquiet, but it set a pattern for years to come.

Ernie Shepherd was United's latest tracksuit (with a bit of pipe and trilby thrown in) and relieved my Ray Smith angst by signing Phil Chisnall, the former Liverpool AND Manchester United midfielder. Chisnall had not been a regular starter for Liverpool, still less a regular goalscorer, but I had seen him on *Match of the Day* once or twice so his arrival felt like a big deal. Out marched Southend into the 1967/68 season armed with renewed hope, despite the non-prolific inside-forward Chisnall and the non-prolific centre-forward Andy Smillie as our attacking spearheads.

And John McKinven, the sinewy scorer of the first United goal I had ever seen. An out-and-out left-winger, a rarity today. A goalscoring left-winger, double rarity. As a touchline-hugger, he was a soft target for the more trenchant critics in the East Stand, the West Stand and the Paddocks. And, truth be told, he sometimes looked a bit lazy, meandering around the halfway line. Give him the ball, however, and a space to run into and off he went, haring down the touchline before crossing into the middle for a succession of United forwards. His deceptively languid persona also came in handy when he lurked without obvious intent 15 yards out at set pieces, and then arrived with the ball on his trusty left foot to drill a searingly accurate drive into the net – some of the time. 'Give us a goal, give us a goal, Johnnie Mac, Johnny Mac,' sang the

North Bank and give us a goal he did, and so did Chisnall and Smillie as we started off the season with confidence and style. United even managed to sign another ex-Manchester United player, born-again midfielder-cum-defender Sammy McMillan. The points and the goals started to stack up, as did the crowds: 11,000 to 13,000 to 15,000, with the burgeoning North Bank atmosphere as the musical accompaniment. As autumn turned to winter, we were challenging Luton Town for top spot.

So well were we doing that Mum decided to pay her one and only visit to Roots Hall for a football match. No Friday night under the lights, no North Bank singsong for us today. On 25 November 1967 we are halfway up the South Bank with a corner of a crush barrier to hand, in a respectable Saturday attendance of 10,850. On a chilly, misty afternoon, the Blues are hosting the perennially troublesome Bradford City in their retro claret and amber shirts (which have always irritated me for some reason); they are also in the early promotion mix.

United start the match brightly enough but the combined efforts of Chisnall, Smillie and McKinven are not unduly troubling the opposition defence for most of the first half. Eventually something clicks. United break down the left, the City goalkeeper embarks on an excursion to nowhere and is marooned by a low cross which finds right-winger Jackie Ferguson at the far post who touches into an empty net from four feet out. 'Goal!!' I shriek, and Mum applauds politely. And that is pretty much that for the first half. As the half-time whistle blows, the exodus for the North Bank begins. 'Where's everybody going?' asks a bemused Mum, until I point out the human tide emerging from behind the West Stand 90 yards away. 'That's interesting; never seen that before,' she remarks.

The floodlights are on now. When the teams return for the second half, the North Bank looks quite full, while the South Bank demographic is 30 years older and the noise level 30 decibels lower. Now we have most of a crush barrier to ourselves. Unfortunately, United's stop-start first-half performance becomes more stop than start. We are starting to play like, well, a Fourth Division team. The North Bank noise is subdued and an air of uneasy gloom descends. Mum keeps her counsel while my exhortations become more and more urgent without, of course, opening up the rich vein of swear words I have acquired by now. It seems inevitable that City will score and finally they do, right in front of us. 'Aarrggh,' I groan and Mum applauds politely. The match peters out in a tepid 1-1 draw; not a disaster, but somewhat disappointing. 'To hell with Brad City,' as the song so rightly puts it.

As the South Bank quickly disperses, there is time for a short post-match interview with the insightful armchair critic from home. What was the day like? 'Well, it was nice to have plenty of room to move about.' What about United? 'Mmm, they're not very good, are they?' Gee, thanks Mum.

The Bradford match heralded a problem, the impact of which we soon became all too aware. United needed a real out-and-out goalscorer – badly. After a dodgy Christmas and new year (not the last time that's happened!), United were just about holding their own in the promotion stakes but Chisnall, Smillie and McKinven had left their shooting boots at home. In January 1968, manager Ernie Shepherd acted.

William James Blaikley Best, mercifully shortened to Billy Best, was not related to the legendary George. But his name was encouraging. Short and Scottish, he arrived from Northampton Town for the sum of £3,000. Personally, I'd never heard of him. Neither had most of the Roots Hall crowd; Northampton were embarking on one of the biggest collapses in football history, free-falling from First to Fourth Division in five years flat, so their limited mass media exposure was not generally positive.

Early indications were not positive either. No goals in his first four games, as our promotion challenge hit a brick wall and the forever sceptical Roots Hall faithful started to wonder,

'Blimey, what have we got here then?' In his fifth game, Best finally gets off the mark in a 2-2 home draw against Halifax Town in front of me and United's lowest crowd of the season, a match in which United are absolute rubbish. Then the goals start – and they never really stop. Two games and three goals later, Billy scores his first United hat-trick against Chester at Roots Hall and marks his third goal, a towering header for one so diminutive, by shinning up the goalpost in front of the celebrating North Bank.

Securely back in second place, with aspirations towards Luton Town's top spot, confidence was back, the crowds were back, the Chisnall-Smillie-McKinven strike force was back and we looked forward with hope and expectation as the English winter almost reluctantly gave way to spring with ten games to go and the arrival of the season's sharp end.

***

Whatever else has changed in football over 60 years, one thing hasn't. Referees: the characters that football fans everywhere love to hate. The amount of referees that have raised the ire of Southend United supporters is too many to mention, but one name from the 1960s sticks in my mind. It could be that football fans are not always fair or even rational when it comes to referees. It could be the name that drew a heartfelt mixture of groans, boos and jeers from the crowd every time the Roots Hall public address announcer declared, 'Tonight's referee is Rex Spittle from Great Yarmouth.'

It's virtually impossible to even speak the name 'Rex Spittle' without some emission of phlegm. And huge quantities were spluttered at Roots Hall when Rex was in town. He was tall, spare, balding and immaculately attired all in black (including the prewar-era long shorts sported by referees well into the 70s). I was apoplectic when what I saw as yet another nailed-on penalty was imperiously waved away with a dismissive sweep of his long arms, free kicks endlessly delayed while Rex fished out his slide rule to ascertain the precise geometric location of the alleged offence, stern lectures to nonplussed Southend players for non-existent infringements before producing the dreaded little black book (in the days before yellow cards) and the laborious scribbling of the alleged miscreant's name.

In researching United's infamous nemesis from Norfolk, I unearthed a slim curio from long ago, sometimes found in the local newsagent but more frequently as a free insert into the matchday programme: the *Football League Review* magazine.[16] Two adjacent articles in a March 1968 edition caught my attention – 'From the Chair – Friday night football by F.W. Skinner, Southend United Chairman' and 'Meet the Referee – Rex Spittle'. There you have it: Southend United, Friday nights at Roots Hall, Rex Spittle – all joined at the hip in print.

A few other crucial elements were needed to generate the ultimate Roots Hall atmosphere in 1968. A decent-sized crowd was a must – 10,000 or more and you were talking business. A significant turnout of away supporters to bait and ridicule wasn't necessary as visits from well-supported local clubs were rare in the late 60s, due to most of them being in a higher division. Kicking towards the North Bank in the second half was highly desirable to maximise the noise cascading from the mass huddle under (or at least close to) the indifferent shelter provided to some parts of the terrace by the low, barrelled roof. Playing on a Saturday afternoon just didn't look or feel the same, so a night game under the lights, preferably a Friday night, was a must.

The *Football League Review* was truly prescient on Friday, 29 March 1968: a league match against Workington, under the lights at Roots Hall, almost has it all. Unbeaten in seven matches, United sit comfortably in second place, with their eyes firmly fixed on overhauling Luton. What's missing is an

16 The *Football League Review* in question was volume two, number 32, 23 March 1968.

away support to ridicule. From what I can see, there appear to be no opposition fans whatsoever in a monster attendance of 13,970. Not surprising, given that Workington is nearly 350 miles away and the team is struggling in the re-election zone. Maybe a handful of Cumbrian suits settle into the directors' box, but I don't frequent that area. The weather has relented, delivering an unseasonably mild evening. And United have the excitement of a new recruit making his home debut, and quite a well-known recruit at that: Eddie Clayton, a cultured midfielder from Tottenham who I had briefly seen in a white number 12 shirt on the White Hart Lane pitch on that 1966 afternoon against Manchester United.

I am tingling with anticipation, with just a touch of nervous tension. The public address announcer calls out the teams: loud cheers for the Southend players, louder still for Best and Clayton; subdued boos for the Workington lads. Then, even more mournfully than usual, comes the declaration, 'Tonight's referee is Rex Spittle from Great Yarmouth.' The groans confirm that I'm not the only one feeling the Rex factor.

United start slowly but gradually take control and lay siege to the South Bank goal. Smillie nets on the quarter-hour. Fittingly, Clayton slaloms through the opposition defence to score the second. Billy Best latches on to a Clayton pass and his shot is helped into the net by an unlucky Workington defender. McKinven thumps in one of his trademark strikes and it's 4-0 at half-time. No surprise that the South Bank empties *en masse* to ensure that everyone can see the fireworks up close.

It doesn't take long. McKinven drives in his second, then our centre-half Eddie May, renowned for his inability to score goals, meets a free kick. Even today, my memory can capture his mistimed looping header as the ball rises to momentarily disappear into the glare of the floodlights, then reappear as it clears the defenders and dips over the flailing goalkeeper to flop into the back of the net to the delight of the North Bank;

6-0 and still more than 30 minutes to go. The ground is in full voice, all the current songs belted out with gusto, with the hammering feet of the East Stand as an accompaniment. 'We want seven' bays the North Bank, but we have to wait until the final few minutes when Clayton drills a square pass low into the net from the edge of the penalty area to cap one of the more unforgettable debuts.

'We want eight' insists the North Bank, selfishly. But seven is enough as the final whistle blows to a mighty roar, a standing ovation and a mini-pitch invasion as I leap over the North Bank wall and walk the length of the pitch, jumping into the South Bank and climbing the 72 steps out of Roots Hall to join the whooping and singing multitudes along Victoria Avenue. And good for Rex; on this night, it's all about the team. Thirty-seven games gone and 50 points on the board in the days of two points for a win. A point a game should be enough now.

And it would have been too, but the aftermath of the Workington match saw the wheels fall off our season, although Billy Best scored virtually all of the meagre collection of goals we managed during a demoralising tumble down the table. 'Miracle Cure needed for United's April Blues' lamented the *Southend Standard*. But miracles were in short supply at Southend United – I already knew that. A 4-3 defeat at Notts County sealed our fate. Our first win since the Workington massacre comes in the last match of the season against Rochdale, with all promotion hopes extinguished and a quiet half-crowd at Roots Hall. Best scores two goals, but declines to celebrate either of them, which earns him quite a few brownie points with our diminished band of disconsolate fans. In any event, 14 goals in 20 starts have helped to establish Billy Best as predator *par excellence* and on the road towards Southend United legend.

The day after that inglorious finale, Manchester United decided to hand the league championship to Manchester City by losing at home to Sunderland, to cap my week of woe. Recovery was soon to hand, however: less than three weeks later on Wednesday, 29 May, my second United defeated Benfica 4-1 before a jubilant horde of northerners in the European Cup Final at Wembley. More dancing with the boxer dog. It wasn't quite the same, but it was something.

But for my first United, the bottom line was stark. Another sixth-place finish. Four points short of promotion. Another summer pondering what might have been. Next season had to be different. But how?

Chapter 7

So Much Promise: The First Half

WHEN I started buying *The Guardian* in the late 1960s, it did not signify a precocious interest in politics, not even as a political counterweight to the *Daily Telegraph* that my parents used to buy. The clue is that I only bought *The Guardian* on a Monday. The reason was that, in the days when all the major English daily newspapers printed regional editions, it was the only source of a Manchester United match report (unless United were playing in London); otherwise, it was endless servings of Tottenham, Arsenal, Chelsea, West Ham, Fulham and the rest from the London editions. Even *The Observer*, the Sunday counterpart of *The Guardian*, was locked into the parochial bubble of London football. If not for *The Guardian*, where else would I have found the material for my Manchester United scrapbook?

Fodder for my larger and more lavishly illustrated Southend United scrapbook was more limited. If I was lucky, the Blues occasionally merited a passing mention in the London dailies – maybe two or three short paragraphs.

Until the *Southend Evening Echo* started up in 1969, my reference sources were restricted to the *Southend and District News Review* (published weekly on Wednesdays) and, more importantly, the *Southend Standard* (published weekly on Thursdays). United's anonymity stretched beyond the print media, however.

Blame it on television. Back in the 1960s, there weren't many league football matches on TV and none were shown live. Southend United on the BBC? Good luck with that. As for the commercial TV alternative, which was all we had for years and years, the good news was that highlights of Southend matches were very occasionally shown on ITV Sunday afternoon football shows. The bad news was that these games were shown on what used to be called Southern or Anglia Television and the TV aerial at our home was pointed towards London, initially to Associated Television then later to London Weekend Television and neither *Star Soccer* nor its later incarnation *The Big Match* ever showed Southend.[17] The good news was that careful twitching of the tuning dial eventually teased up some sort of picture from Southern and Anglia. The bad news was that watching a Southend match on Southern was akin to peering through a severe Arctic snowstorm, while watching on Anglia was positively ghostly, with ominous-looking spectral figures closely following the semi-transparent images of the actual players on the pitch. But, in the end, it was really our fault because we just weren't good enough to appear on *Match of the Day* or *The Big Match*.

It was so unfair because, in my totally unbiased opinion, Southend were far too good for the Fourth Division. As I saw it, everyone else in the division played the old-style kick and rush but we passed the ball from defence through midfield to the forwards with panache. After all, United had McMillan, Chisnall and Clayton, players with a First Division pedigree. On the wing we still had John McKinven. Up front we had Billy Best, the Scottish goal machine. We even acquired our own hardman in defence, a rangy Scottish warhorse named

---

17 We had to wait until February 1975 for Southend United's first appearance on *The Big Match* – and two minutes' worth of highlights. Preston North End were the visitors and included Bobby Charlton and Nobby Stiles in their line-up, so that probably explained it.

John Kurila, signed from Northampton Town and known to everyone as 'Joe' for reasons unknown to me.

The 1968/69 season seemed to promise so much. Off the pitch, I was just starting to harvest the fruits of increased independence and was allowed out on my own on weekday evenings to meet up with likeminded friends on my way to Roots Hall and catch the late bus back to Thorpe Bay.

Sporting a new outfit of Scotland-style navy blue shirts, United overcame a dose of opening-day jitters with a 2-1 victory over Halifax Town in the blazing August afternoon sun. Four days later came the challenge of a League Cup first round tie at Third Division Bournemouth. My expectations of success in any cup competition were already low, so imagine my astonishment when I read 'Bournemouth 1, Southend United 6' in next morning's paper. Then United signed the clever, fashionably long-haired Ian 'Chico' Hamilton from Chelsea. I had been at White Hart Lane when a very young Chico scored his very first league goal, against Tottenham, and never dreamed that he would end up at Roots Hall 18 months later. I'll bet he never dreamed it either. I saw Chico as the missing link, who would help Billy Best and the rest turn our panache into goals.

OK, so we have started the season of so much promise a bit slowly, but we aren't worried just yet. We have very nearly (but not quite) turned over First Division Wolverhampton Wanderers in the League Cup, the chants and songs on the North Bank are loud and tuneful and we enjoy our evenings out surrounded by crowds of around 11,000. It will all click into place as soon as Best finds his shooting boots again. And 'Johnnie Mac' is still on hand to 'give us a goal'.

A home match under the Roots Hall lights on Monday, 7 October 1968 and here comes McKinven, cutting in from the right wing with a lumbering Lincoln City defender in his wake. A clattering sliding tackle and I clearly hear the shriek of pain and the distressing crack of his leg giving way as he crashes on to the running track. And there, a few feet from me, are the physio, the doctor, the St John Ambulance guys, the stretcher and the end of McKinven's season.

Whatever else United have, we do not have a 'big 'un up front'. Most lower-division teams boasted a tall, muscled battering-ram. Alf Smirk, football correspondent for the *Southend Standard* and the voice of Southend United, used to plead the case on a weekly basis. But generations of United supporters have had a degree of ambivalence towards 'big 'uns up front' mainly because they have always regarded our Southend teams to somehow be above the biff and bash of the lower divisions. I've felt like that sometimes as well. United fans' treatment of 'big 'uns' has been an etymological study in popular abuse – 'pillocks', 'berks', 'cretins', 'twats', 'prats', 'wallies', 'dipsticks', 'dickheads', 'wazzocks', 'plonkers', 'muppets', 'numpties' and 'nongs' have been directed at Southend six-footers by the Roots Hall community.

We win the Lincoln match quite easily and then put six past Exeter City, but we have embarked on a journey of notable wins alternated with baffling defeats. We are there or thereabouts in the promotion stakes, albeit more thereabouts than there; which must have prompted manager Shepherd to get the chequebook out again.

If Billy Best buzzes, Gary Moore bludgeons. Signed from Grimsby Town in November 1968, he is very tall and very hefty and the answer to Alf Smirk's prayers. On his home debut against Doncaster Rovers, Gary rises high to plant a header of rare power and precision into the top corner of the Rovers net to the delight of the North Bank and, I dare say, Smirk too. And in front of the Southern Television cameras as well, so I can enjoy its snowy reprise the next afternoon. Maybe he's a bit clumsy, perhaps a bit off with his first touch, possibly a bit slow, but I'm not the only one who warms to Gary's heart-on-the-sleeve passion.

Despite Moore's arrival, the win-one, lose-one pattern persists, to the frustration of us diehards. One memorable lowlight was a Friday night visit to Layer Road, the home of Colchester United at the end of November. It was a school day so I didn't get a parental pass, but a couple of school friends bunked off early and made their way northwards. The Monday morning report from the bunkers made for sobering listening. Colchester had their own promotion aspirations, the crowd of 10,604 packed into their tight little ground felt like a full house and Southend's large travelling support was loud and tuneful – until Colchester's second goal went in. As another two goals hit the back of the net to seal a 4-0 hammering, those travelling Blues who stayed until the bitter end wondered why they'd bothered.

**

The FA Cup was different, however. The English Football League, for all its advanced age, is a mere youngster compared to the oldest football competition in the world. Sixteen years younger to be precise, when The Wanderers, an amateur team of upper-class sons and heirs beat the Royal Engineers, another amateur team of upper-class sons and heirs 1-0 in front of the 2,000 top hats, crinolines and officers' uniforms who turned up for the first FA Cup Final at the Kennington Oval cricket ground in 1872. Just 29 years later and 13 years after the launch of the Football League, the working-class professional footballers of Tottenham Hotspur drew with the working-class professional footballers of Sheffield United before 110,820 cloth caps and Woodbine cigarettes at the old Crystal Palace football stadium. The Premier League is 32 years old at the time of writing and the changes it has brought to English football are well documented, but they pale into insignificance against the seismic transformation in social and sporting history that the FA Cup and the Football League delivered in a shorter period of time.

When I was a kid, the FA Cup was THE tournament in England and the FA Cup Final was THE match. Kicking off at 3pm sharp on the last Saturday of the season in front of 100,000 spectators bathed (usually) in May sunshine at Wembley Stadium, royalty, T.P. Ratcliff, the big brass band, 'Abide With Me', 'God save the Queen' and all the rest, the FA Cup had real mystique.

Unfortunately, Southend United and the FA Cup has usually been a case of unrequited love, because the Blues all too often find inventive and unexpected ways of disappearing in the early rounds by losing to teams well below us: hello Harlow Town, Aylesbury United, Kingstonian, Dover Athletic, Boreham Wood. At other times, United can battle heroically through the early rounds, to be rewarded by the cup draw Gods with, for example, Rotherham United away.

Why Rotherham? In my first full season of watching and supporting Southend we drew them in the third round – away at Millmoor, a small stadium in South Yorkshire. We were struggling in the Third Division, while Rotherham were comfortably placed in the second tier; doable on a good day, but a tough nut to crack. And a nut too tough Rotherham proved to be as we were cracked 3-2 in front of a modest 11,000. Rotherham's reward was to be drawn away against Manchester United in the fourth round and they forced a 0-0 draw in front of 54,263 at Old Trafford. Manchester United finally scrambled through the replay 1-0 before a sold-out Millmoor attendance of 23,500. A bit of fame, a nice little earner for Rotherham, a lost opportunity for Southend, and a harbinger of things to come.

In the late 60s, we got our FA Cup draws the old-fashioned way. At one o'clock on the Monday afternoon following a round of cup ties the previous Saturday, groups of school kids and grown-ups across England huddled around transistor radios to hear the draw on the BBC, 'broadcast live from Football Association Headquarters, Lancaster Gate'. Cheers and groans spread up and down the land as the announcer melodiously but neutrally announced, 'Number 64, Southend United, will play number five, West Ham United.' In my dreams.

In the real world, lower-division clubs like Southend don't win big cups. No club from the third or fourth tier of the Football League has ever won the FA Cup, nor made it to the final. No fourth-tier club has even reached the semi-final, and the third-tier clubs getting to the last four total nine: well played Millwall (1937), Port Vale (1954), York City (1955), Norwich City (1959), Crystal Palace (1976), Plymouth Argyle (1984), Chesterfield (1997), Wycombe Wanderers (2001) and Sheffield United (2014).

**

Before Roy Wood's Wizzard and the Electric Light Orchestra there was a Midlands combo called The Move, the band which spawned those glam rock icons of the 1970s. Variously described as 'psychedelic pop' and 'psychedelic rock', The Move turned around a series of hit singles in the late 60s.

Their latest hit, 'Goodbye Blackberry Way', is a slow-tempo, bleak affair but is storming up the singles charts on Saturday, 25 January 1969. It is only 11 o'clock in the morning but the coach I'm sitting in, full of Southend supporters, has already heard Roy Wood's lugubrious strains more than once, courtesy of Radio 1. My teenage leap for freedom has not quite extended as far as a solo journey to the East Midlands, so Dad is with me. Some passengers are joining in the chorus, some quite loudly, but I'm not. I'm too keyed up.

We are halfway through the season of so much promise and this is my first long-haul away trip – and in the fourth round of the FA Cup, no less. Despite United's continuing travails in the league, our class shows in the cup. First round at home to non-league Kings Lynn: 9-0 to the Blues (Best three, Moore three). Second round at home to local non-league Brentwood: 10-1 to the Blues (Best five, Moore four). Now for the huddle around the transistor radio on a Monday lunchtime for the third-round draw, and the entry of the First and Second Division clubs. Oh, for Tottenham at home, please. Or Manchester United at home. Oh, all right, Arsenal at Highbury if you must. 'Number x, Swindon Town, will play number y, Southend United,' the BBC informs the world. Bugger. Swindon are only Third Division, but they are already looking like shoo-ins for promotion. They are also on a prodigious run in the League Cup, having already reached the final (where they ultimately overcome the Arsenal). And blow me down if Southend don't go down to the County Ground and defeat Swindon 2-0, with goals from Billy Best and Chico Hamilton.

Another Monday lunchtime, another huddle around the trannie, but with even more anticipation this time. West Ham at home, PLEASE! Or if not, Liverpool at Anfield would be OK, but maybe we would prefer Halifax Town at home because they're in our division and we have a good chance of marching on. 'Number x, Mansfield Town, will play number y, Southend United,' the BBC shamelessly announces. Double bugger. Mansfield are no great shakes but I have already identified them as a bogey team because of outrages not forgotten. In my first season of watching Southend, Mansfield beat us 4-1 at Roots Hall and 6-1 at their Field Mill ground. On the other hand, they are only Third Division, and look what we did to Swindon. That's why I'm sitting in an overheated coach on a cold, damp Saturday morning as our coach pulls off the M1 motorway into Newport Pagnell services.

Another new experience for me as we follow our fellow passengers into the special environment of an English motorway service area on cup day. Service areas are a mixing pot of football supporters, as southerners travelling north criss-cross northerners travelling south. Coaches, cars, motorbikes, many with team favours, populate the vast open-air car parks. Individuals and groups of fans, also wearing their team favours, mill around the cafes, shops and toilets.

Today, it looks as if Newport Pagnell is largely hosting Southend, Portsmouth and Watford supporters heading north, with a smattering of Leicester City, West Bromwich Albion and Wolverhampton Wanderers followers southward bound. The local constabulary maintain a discreet but visible presence. The more belligerent hordes from Chelsea and West Ham United will have mostly gathered at the more expansive Watford Gap services, 40 miles north, with a thicker blue line greeting their arrival.

But I am enthralled, from a safe distance, by my first pure-bred genuine skinhead, a tall, heavy, shaven-headed youth hunched over an electric pinball machine. His Crombie, a black, woollen, knee-length overcoat, has been adopted as a fashion statement by skinheads far and wide: with thick bare forearms sticking out from the too-short sleeves, the Crombie looks two sizes too small for him. A pair of skinny two-tone tonics, another fashion statement, have the appearance of normal grey trousers dipped in petrol. Beneath the two-tone tonics protrude an enormous pair of black Doc Martens, the fearsome bovver boots. The ensemble is completed by a thin, greasy nylon football scarf in gold and black wrapped tightly round the neck. A Wolves scarf, this one.

A picture of brooding menace stands before me, but today he seems more intent on inflicting injury to the pinball machine. He methodically feeds coins into it and the fascia tinkles and flashes. As the ball slides down to the flippers, he grunts 'baastudd' as he emphatically launches the ball back into play. Tinkle, flash, flip, 'baastudd'. Inevitably, his assault and battery end with a siren and the 'Tilt' sign lit up. A thud of hand on machine, one last drawn out 'baaasstudd' and off he stalks. Tottenham supporters had better watch their step.

Two hours later, our passage through the East Midlands ends at Field Mill. The stadium is close to the centre of Mansfield, so those of us who look old enough have the chance to find a pub for a couple of pints. I'm too young for all that so Dad and I grab some lunch from a cafe and take a walk around the Market Square, a rather grey place on a rather grey day. Then we make our way up a gentle slope to the ground, skirting the puddles. Local police on horseback await, the first time I've seen mounted police at a Southend match. We are bound for the Quarry Lane End, a smallish, shallow curved open terrace, the 'away end' for the day, although segregation was not such a major concern in January 1969. Ninety minutes before kick-off, we are among the first to arrive, so we have our pick of crush barriers as we watch the ground slowly fill up.

For a little while, the only sounds are our own voices, a crash from a slamming door, an echoing shout and laugh, the sporadic click-clack of a distant turnstile. The kind of disembodied noises you hear when you're in a football ground too early. To our left is the main West Stand, a modern concrete affair. To our right is a seriously small stand, an elongated bicycle shed which looks barely big enough for bicycles, let alone spectators. At the far end is a decent-sized covered terrace with a clock on its roof, Mansfield's version of the 'Popular End'. About an hour before kick-off, there is a brief rumpus when 200 likely lads from Southend find their way in and belt out a few choruses of, 'United, United, we are the Champions'. 'We've taken over their end,' I gleefully report to Dad. 'Not for long, I don't think,' he replies and, sure enough, the local constabulary in flat caps edged with black and white checks purposefully move in to escort the interlopers into our terrace.

Over the next hour, a healthy and noisy crowd of 16,160 has pretty much filled the ground, even the bicycle shed, generating an old-style cup day vibe of whirling rattles, jingling bells, honking tin trumpets and excited voices. A couple of Mansfield supporters are strolling around the running track sporting plastic antlers. This does not presage some archaic pagan ritual, but is a nod to Mansfield's club nickname of the Stags. 'Mooooosse', roar a few Southend comedians.

Enhanced by the brave efforts of about three thousand Essex citizens to drown out the home support, the atmosphere is unique to the FA Cup.

Mansfield are a division above us, but they play their football route one, long passes from defence picking out marauding wingers, crosses raining into the penalty area for their forwards to attack. In the meantime, United play in their customary style, moving the ball smoothly through midfield, low driven through balls for Best and Hamilton, Moore used as much to set up opportunities for others as to attack the goal himself. And it works. Southend, attacking the Mansfield home end in the first half, break down the left, the ball is driven low into the middle and there are two United players running in. Best accurately plants it low and hard into the Mansfield net and our terrace erupts. We are one up and deserve it, as our defence comfortably handles the Mansfield aerial barrage and our midfield trickery continues to traumatise their defenders.

Half-time and Southend are still 1-0 up. The floodlights are on and United are kicking towards the Quarry Lane End where we are standing. A good omen, perhaps. But not so good as it turns out, as Mansfield respond to the rocket they evidently received from their management and begin to take control. We don't seem able to get the ball up front as our forwards become midfielders and midfielders become defenders. Eventually, Mansfield score two goals to take the lead. Now it's time for the Mansfield supporters to raise the roof, 'We shall NOT be moved' and we are 'Just like a team that's gonna win the FA Cup'. And yet, as the match moves towards its closing stages, we start to reassert control ourselves and our terrace resounds with more insistent backing.

United have a corner; the ball descends into the six-yard box and a Southend head plants it against the underside of the bar. From what I can see, positioned directly behind the goal, the ball's dropped over the line. 'It's in!' I scream with excited prepubescent shrillness. A brief, frantic goal-line scramble follows, all flying boots and elbows. To my horror, the referee will not blow his whistle for a goal, the linesman will not wave his flag and the Mansfield goalkeeper ends up spreadeagled on the pitch with his head almost over the line, but his body in play, the ball grasped firmly into his midriff. No goal. Nobody will ever know if it really was. And that's the closest we come. A couple of late corners for Southend, a breakaway for Mansfield, where five against two somehow manage to squander the chance to finish us off. The referee blows for full time and Mansfield have nicked it 2-1. If the word 'gutted' had been in popular usage, it would have expressed my feelings. Devastated will have to do. I stand transfixed as the Mansfield supporters give the Southend players a generous round of applause and the ground slowly empties. 'Come on son, time to go,' says Dad, as he puts his arm around my shoulder.

To add insult to injury, we have to wait for 30 minutes in a sombre, quietened coach for a few cruel latecomers to retake their seats before we can escape from the accursed Mansfield to the blessed neutrality of the M1. Dad dozes off. Chin in hand, I stare wordlessly at the black shadows of trees and bushes rushing past. Raindrops streak the window, as Radio 1 and Roy Wood's voice drones around the coach for the umpteenth time. Nobody's joining in now.

Sometimes, one has to bow to the inevitable. In the next round, the cup draw Gods gave our dream away and rewarded the victorious Mansfield with West Ham United at home. This did not surprise me one bit. And the World Cup heroes Moore, Peters, Hurst and the rest of the First Division all-stars decided to play like pantomime horses and Mansfield thumped them 3-0. Then Mansfield scored a local derby, at home once again, to First Division Leicester City in the quarter-finals. Mercifully, Leicester put an end to the nonsense by winning 1-0 on their way to defeat by Manchester City in the final.

Blackberry Way, black and white, with 50 shades of grey thrown in. That's how I remember Mansfield versus Southend in January 1969. Rather like an old edition of *Match of the Day* with a musical backing track. The coach, Newport Pagnell services, the pinball skinhead, the town of Mansfield and its Field Mill stadium, the Billy Best goal, the goal that wasn't, all captured monochromatically in my memory. Friends say that Mansfield is quite a pleasant town and I'm sure it is. It's just that I have that gloomy black-and-white image of the place locked in my head. Maybe I'll pay a return visit, preferably not on a matchday. .

In the scrapbook that I scrupulously kept for that season sat a large black and white photograph cut out of the *Southend Standard* or the *News Review*. There's the Mansfield goalkeeper, straddling the goal line, face in the mud, ball gripped like grim death. Six feet away, an anonymous United player (Billy Best? Gary Moore?) is standing, knees buckled, hands to his thrown-back head, mouth open in dismay and frustration. All in grainy black and white, fringed with grey because of the floodlights. I wish I still had that photo, wish I still had my old scrapbooks.

How long does football grief and misery last for a dispirited 13-year-old then? Not as long as it might have done.

A city of the year-round raincoat. Central Liverpool as I first remember it in 1957.

Floods of tears at my first live football match. The pitch invasion after Liverpool's last-minute winner against Stoke City: Division 2 at Anfield, 23 April 1962.

Brash and, for the most part, very twentieth century. Southend as I first remember it. Peter Pan's Playground in the early 1960s.

The unexpectedly vast South Bank at Roots Hall in the early 1960s.

Billy Best in black and white, with fifty shades of grey. United's goal against Mansfield Town: FA Cup fourth round at Field Mill, 25 January 1969.

Manager Dave Smith and captain Derek Spence with the Fourth Division trophy, United's first significant silverware. May 1981.

Richard Cadette bringing the love back despite the deserted South Bank. Season 1985/86 at Roots Hall.

THE goal. Ian Benjamin's finish secures promotion to the Second Division for the first time in Southend's history. Bury vs United: Division 3 at Gigg Lane, 4 May 1991.

The laser-like intensity of Stan Collymore lights up his season at Roots Hall. United vs Newcastle United: Division 1 (second tier) at Roots Hall, 20 January 1993.

Sammy Bloody Shrimper in his Pink Period. United vs Hartlepool United: Division Three (fourth tier) at Roots Hall, 8 May 1999.

What a full house looks like at the 'new' Roots Hall. 11,735 for United vs Yeovil: League Two (fourth tier) at Roots Hall, 30 April 2005.

Duncan Jupp's goal clinches promotion to League One. United vs Lincoln City: League Two play-off final at Millennium Stadium, Cardiff, 28 May 2005.

Wayne Gray scores late and Southend United are 'Champeones' (sic). United vs Bristol City: League One (third tier) at Roots Hall, 6 May 2006.

Players, managers, heroes. Manager Steve Tilson and captain Kevin Maher with the League One trophy, 6 May 2006.

A goal that reverberated around the world. Freddy Eastwood's 30-yard free kick. United versus Manchester United: Carling Cup fourth round at Roots Hall, 7 November 2006.

A result that reverberated around the world. The shabby old scoreboard announces the score, pixels askew. United versus Manchester United at Roots Hall, 7 November 2006.

The lights go out on my most recent match experience at Roots Hall – but not for long, fortunately. United versus Millwall: FA Cup third round, 4 January 2014.

Dan Bentley's penalty save, cementing United's most recent promotion. United versus Wycombe Wanderers: League Two play-off final at Wembley, 23 May 2015.

Winter Wonderland under the lights: United's defence battle through the snow, Liverpool's Dalglish interested, referee Hackett vigilant. United versus Liverpool: FA Cup third round at Roots Hall, 10 January 1979.

Dad's railway odyssey ends with a ticket in the East Stand. United versus Liverpool: FA Cup third round at Roots Hall, 5 January 1957.

Stephen Humphrys' late winner, which provided the inspiration for me to write this story. United versus Sunderland: League One at Roots Hall, 4 May 2019.

Two weeks from the latest winding-up petition at the High Court. The time-honoured sign fronting the East Stand of Roots Hall: 12 June 2024. Had it really come to this?

What remained of the SUFC sign above the directors' box entrance, which somehow seemed to sum it all up. Roots Hall: 12 June 2024.

Never Never Land awaits its resurgence. Western Esplanade, Southend: 11 June 2024.

Chapter 8

So Much Promise: The Second Half

SOUTHEND'S FA Cup exploits have coincided with an inconvenient truth as far as the league is concerned. The Colchester United spanking has presaged the usual wobble around Christmas and new year, and the winning run I expected and hoped for hasn't happened as we continue our win-one, lose-one routine. Fortunately, you could say that about the whole of the Fourth Division. Nobody is walking away with the title or the other three promotion places this season, which looks to be shaping up as the ultimate dogfight. It happens. Despite everything, we are still within shouting distance of the top four. The goals have now arrived (at both ends, to be fair), the Roots Hall attendances are still around the 11,000 level, the chanting and singing of the North Bank remains exuberant.

Three weeks after the Mansfield calamity comes the evening of Saint Valentine's Day on Friday, 14 February 1969 and the Colchester return league match at Roots Hall. I am too young to have a girlfriend so I have no romantic complications, and apparently neither do the majority of the 12,849 fans present. We even have a decent showing of visitors from north Essex to ridicule, as Colchester are also in the promotion mix.

And, although it's had some competition over the years, this night stands out as the coldest I can ever remember at Roots Hall. From 30 minutes before kick-off to 30 minutes after full time we encounter, in no particular order: rain, sleet, snow, gale-force winds, freezing fog, rapier-sharp easterly blasts and a rock-hard, rutted pitch, laced with outcrops of ice sparkling under the floodlights. Steam from expelled breath mingles with the acrid eddies of cigarette smoke and drifts upwards into the glowering sky. It's the first time I have ever seen players wearing gloves on the pitch, although they're of the fingerless variety. Fair enough: I'm wearing two pairs, I'm buried inside a thick duffel coat and my pulled down bobble hat and pulled up scarf become much more than tokens of team loyalty. All the ingredients for the ideal Roots Hall encounter are there – except one.

It looks like the United of Colchester have won the toss because the United of Southend will have to play towards the North Bank in the first half. At least my group of friends and I are just about sheltered enough to avoid the icy water dripping from the roof and trickling down the necks of the suffering souls in front of us. After Southend open the scoring with a majestic header from the begloved Gary Moore, the elements conspire against us to the extent that we seriously consider abandoning our half-time change of ends for whatever limited protection is still afforded by the barely adequate roof. But we plod through the mud and slush behind the West Stand and take our frozen places on the frozen South Bank for the second half anyway.

After a half-time interval of community shivering, I can just about see Colchester search for an equaliser through the Arctic mist and wonder if we will find yet another way of throwing away a lead. However, propelled forwards by our whole repertoire of chants and songs now cascading from the North and South Banks – the East Stand does its bit with coordinated foot-stamping and even the West Stand offers up a few encouraging 'GAARRNNNS' – the Southend team, steam rising from their bodies, batters the Colchester defence into submission and Billy Best nips in twice to put us three up. We even have time to bemoan another two disallowed goals. I can vaguely discern Colchester scoring a late consolation from Danny Light, an incongruous name given the weather, but it's all too late. Roots Hall is dancing in the rain/sleet/snow; it's a way of avoiding frostbite but we are warmed by the knowledge that it's Colchester under the hammer. The stands and terraces tremble with United jubilation at the final whistle and my friends and I wander around to the car park behind the East Stand to gently taunt the disconsolate Colchester fans as they line up at their coaches for their own miserable journey home. It is three weeks since Mansfield, and it feels just great. Cold? Who's cold? I can always thaw out in the bus.

***

At last, my first trip to London as part of a travelling Southend support. On Monday, 10 March I leave school at four o'clock sharp and hop on the bus to meet Dad at Southend Central station. Into my duffel bag go the red and green tie and the green school cap. Out comes the blue and white scarf and bobble hat. The green school blazer is hidden under my trusty duffel coat. Only the regulation dark grey trousers and black lace-up shoes betray the fact that I'm straight from school. Dad, of course, is in tie, jacket and overcoat, the matchday outfit for adults of his generation.

A change at Barking for the District underground line sees us joined by smatterings of United fellow travellers for the Tube ride through a London rush hour. A few red and white scarves step through the sliding doors as we rattle westwards to Gunnersbury station. And then the march, surrounded by a surprisingly large number of City-suited types, toward the floodlights of Brentford's Griffin Park ground, just in time for kick-off. A commuter derby, no less.

Griffin Park bears a resemblance to Roots Hall, but it doesn't have a towering terrace like the South Bank and the crowd is smaller. With several hundred United supporters in a modest attendance of 6,030, the atmosphere is OK but the football is uninspiring. Fortunately, or unfortunately, there is a notable footballing memory to commemorate the occasion.

Even today, I can see Moore's well-directed header steered just inside the far post. Inexplicably, the ball ends up on the running track instead of the back of the net, and the referee does not blow his whistle and point to the centre spot. Prodding, poking and pulling of the net by the referee and players of both sides may or may not have identified a gap through which a football could have crept but it's not enough to convince the man in black, so the goal is chalked off. It looks like a valid goal to me and I'm not the only one, judging by the consternation of the other United fans. But I would say that, wouldn't I? The match ends up 1-1, not a bad result in itself, but that Moore goal would have made the long journey home so much more agreeable. That's west London for you.

The hoped-for unbeaten run has finally arrived, as United go seven without defeat and inch ever closer toward the promotion places as the season's sharp end approaches. We have an attack of the horrors with a humbling 3-0 home defeat by Scunthorpe United, an enduring bogey team. *The Southend United Chronicles 1906–2006* provides a searing insight into what happens when we face another notorious bogey team at the next home game. Having 'witnessed this sorry spectacle at Roots Hall ... I can honestly say, with little fear of contradiction, that this was one of the worst displays from a Southend side it has ever been my misfortune to have to sit through'.

Lest there be any doubt, the report goes on to describe United's performance as 'puerile and putrid'. The reporter is anonymous in the *Chronicles* but every Blues supporter of a certain age knows it is Alf Smirk.[18]

And Alf was right, as he so often was. I was at Roots Hall on Easter Saturday, 5 April and the 1-0 defeat inflicted by a very poor Grimsby Town was as bad as reported, if not worse. It wasn't just Alf's perennial campaign for the 'big 'un up front', his trenchant acerbity left every other Southend scribe at the starting post. I saw him a few times at Roots Hall, stalking towards the press box: trench coat, fedora, eyes hooded, vaguely sinister, just a hint of film noir about him, like Humphrey Bogart on a crash diet. I'm sure that other lower-division clubs have had their own Alf Smirks: shamelessly partisan, distrustful in success, implacable in adversity, suffering and rejoicing in complete sympathy with the supporters. That's why he was the voice of Southend United. That's why we liked him.

If Alf and a significant number of United supporters now believe that our promotion hopes have disappeared down the drain, the message has not filtered through to Billy Best, Gary Moore and Chico Hamilton. Here we go on one more unbeaten run and the Roots Hall faithful are finally treated to the long-awaited hatful of goals. Incredibly, we are still there with an outside chance of promotion as April, the month that Alex Ferguson, Manchester United managerial legend, so evocatively named 'squeaky bum time', unfolds.[19]

***

It may be my romanticised view of Southend's history, it may be the elusive charm of lower-division football 50 years ago, but the characters I grew up with don't seem to exist any more.

18 *The Southend United Chronicles 1906–2006* records Alf's analysis. Edited by Keith Rowe. Desert Island Books, 2006.

19 Ferguson was referring to the 2002/2003 Premier League title race, which Manchester United ultimately won, 'It's getting tickly now – squeaky bum time, I call it.' www.theguardian.com, 8 May 2013, and others.

Certainly, we don't see names like Rex Spittle and Alf Smirk – where did they all go?

Frank Gill, with his deep, middle-aged, Essex-accented voice, was the Roots Hall stadium announcer in the 1960s. But Frank's real name wasn't funky enough for me so I decided to nickname him Roots Hall Ron. In my early years of football fandom, Frank/Ron's communication style was characteristic of lower-division grounds all around England, differentiated only by change of accent: the pleasing West Country burr at Torquay United, the grating West Midlands whine at Walsall, the teeth-clenched Merseyside drone at Tranmere Rovers (more Lennon than McCartney), the irritating, teasing Farmer Giles soundalike at Colchester United.

In the time of the original Roots Hall Ron, the only electronically generated explosions were an occasional, unexpected 'BARRRFF!' echoing around the ground, presumably due to somebody flicking the wrong switch on the Tannoy console. Ron's scripted contributions were quite economical but could be laden with underlying meaning when he chose, not least when welcoming Rex Spittle.

On the evening of Friday, 28 April, the season of so much promise is approaching its climax. Southend are faced with their final home game, the must-win to end all must-wins. On a mild evening, my friends and I are taking in the setting sunlight on the South Bank, nerves tingling, as the usual pre-match stadium announcements float around Roots Hall: the teams, the officials, the ball sponsor. Unfortunately for us, our opponents are Newport County, a team who have recently made a habit of doing us harm (including a 4-1 thumping at Somerton Park back in August). To add to our misfortune, we have also lost the toss, which means we will have another unwelcome experience of kicking towards the North Bank in the first half, requiring a brisk trot to change ends before kick-off. The Colchester game aside, we hardly ever seem to turn it on in front of the more sedate, less atmospheric South Bank in the second half.

This is United's ninth game in a month and each game has had a 'last chance saloon' feel. To be frank, we look knackered from the start; laboured up front, lethargic in midfield, uncertain at the back. In a first half so devoid of action that I cannot remember a single significant moment, the match ambles to half-time. While we retake our places behind the South Bank goal for the second half, Roots Hall Ron continues with his neutral half-time routine, 'Tonight's winning Jackpot ticket numbers are blah, blah, blah.'

The floodlights are now on. United look more dangerous, the ball is pinging around the Newport penalty area more often, but the County defenders are big and stubborn and we can find no way through. Waves of resignation start to wash around, 'Oh well, we ballsed it up weeks ago'; 'There's always next year', the traditional Roots Hall mantras. Seventy-five minutes and Ron calmly informs us, 'Tonight's official attendance: 11,905.' Ten minutes to go and fans on the lower levels are starting to make their slow and steady way up the 72 steps to the top of the South Bank and a smart, disappointed exit when the final whistle blows. Two minutes to go, and even I'm starting the climb.

My watch tells me that time is up. United gave up one-touch football some time ago, and are now launching a series of aerial punts in the direction of the Newport penalty area. They are often called 'Hail Mary passes' nowadays, channelling the last-ditch desperate throws from an American football quarterback towards the endzone. From the latest of these, a Newport defender misdirects his clearing header and the ball rolls off for a corner. We all know it's not going to happen, so the South Bank response is muted. Southend's winger, John Baber, scurries toward the corner flag. A loud crackle from the Tannoy and 'COME ON, LET'S HEAR THE ROOTS HALL ROAR!!' howls from the loudspeakers to the astonishment of crowd and players alike. What the?? The Roots Hall what? The what roar? Guffaws of incredulity roll round the ground. In the meantime, Baber swings the corner into the six-yard box, someone knocks it down into the mixer and John Kurila slides in from three yards out to prod the ball past the Newport goalkeeper – his first and only league goal for Southend. That's a roar to remember all right. In the cacophony that follows, the referee's whistle ending the game is barely heard and the smart exit is delayed for a few ecstatic minutes; 1-0 to the Blues.

In five years of supporting Southend, I had never heard of the Roots Hall Roar. In all my 60 years of watching football, either in person or on television, I never heard a stadium announcer exhort a crowd to raise a racket while a match was actually in progress. Is it even allowed? (My understanding is that it is not.)

Not that it does us any good in the end. Realistically, United still have to win three of the final four games, all away, to secure a top-four finish and a path to the Third Division. We win the second and lose the rest. The promise of the 1968/69 season fizzles out ignominiously in the dustbowl that is Rochdale's Spotland ground in May, where the Dale beat us 3-0 and add insult to injury by pinching our promotion place as well.

Seventh place in the Fourth Division, five points short of promotion – again. If the play-offs had been around in the 1960s, we would have qualified three years in a row, with the chance of one last shot at the Third Division – but we had to wait another 20 years for play-offs. So much promise, 106 goals scored (and another 31 disallowed – including Moore's 'goal that wasn't' at Brentford and the 'in-off the bar' at Mansfield – a statistic that I diligently if pedantically compiled). What a shame, then, that we finished the season with nothing to show for it except memories. I was young but I was well on the way to protecting myself with a shield of stoicism which is a useful accessory when you support a lower division club. I would need the shield even more in the next decade.

Chapter 9

Life in the Doldrums

THIS IS what life was like for a football-daft-14-to-15-year-old around 1970. Into school early at 8.30am for a half-hour kickabout in the playground before assembly, fiercely competing over a little plastic ball with holes in it. On to the school playing field at lunchtime, weather permitting, for an hour's worth of head tennis, diving about on the grass in pursuit of a full-sized plastic ball with school blazers and satchels for a net. The weekly sports afternoon and a proper game with a real leather football on one of the school pitches, bemoaning the fact that my school mandated the playing of hockey on alternate weeks in winter, while the summer term was a cricket-only zone. Appropriately, all in sight of the Roots Hall floodlights.

Weekends and school holidays at the local park, commandeering an unused pitch for a three-man game: rotating goalkeeper, winger, and centre-forward for more heading practice; if four turned up, we'd have a centre-half as well. Seemingly endless warm summer evenings and scratch three- or four-a-side games on Shoebury Common, just behind the beach, with the legendary jumpers for goalposts. All this, and still I wasn't good enough to play for the school team. Useful in the air with all the heading practice. Decent right foot with all the crossing practice. Even half-decent in goal, with all the goalkeeping practice. But: a rubbish left foot, no matter how hard I tried, my enduring sporting achilles heel (or foot).

I had United and Roots Hall on Friday nights or Saturday afternoons. In front of the box for *Match of the Day* on Saturday night, *The Big Match* on Sunday afternoon, *Sportsnight with Coleman* on midweek nights. The odd visit to London and a queue of variable length, depending on the opposition, to see the 'London giants' in action: Arsenal at Highbury, Tottenham at White Hart Lane, West Ham at Upton Park, Chelsea at Stamford Bridge.

What goes around often comes around in football: at least when it comes to Workington FC, the club from a small town on the Cumbrian coast and recipients of the 7-0 thrashing in March 1968. Workington is about as geographically distant from Southend as you can be in England without falling off the edge. Nobody in their right mind would get up before six on a frosty Saturday morning in February 1970, spend seven hours in a stuffy supporters' club coach crossing a countryside locked into bleak midwinter to follow your struggling Fourth Division team, suffer in the cold as your team loses 5-0 in front of a sparse, taunting crowd of 1,790 and then spend another seven hours travelling back down south in the frigid dark, to finally return home tired, cold, hungry and hacked-off well after midnight. Not me: by February 1970, even I was not football-daft enough for that. However, a schoolfriend of mine did it and I remember thinking long and hard about joining him.

In case you were wondering, I was never one of those dedicated souls who faithfully criss-crossed the country, following their team to every single away game, but I had started to stretch my wings with the occasional foray to the local outposts of the Football League empire: Aldershot; the Uniteds of Peterborough, Cambridge and Colchester; Northampton Town; Gillingham; Brighton. I have journeyed to many Southend away games, some involving decisions as eccentric and as challenging as Workington in February.[20] Fanatical supporters of lower-division clubs do it week after week, season after season. Maximum commitment for minimum reward. I get it. I really do.

My sister Estelle gets it as well. Just never enough to bite the bullet and step into Roots Hall to watch the Blues. Which is why, when *The Southend United Chronicles 1906–2006* was launched at the Waterstones book store in Southend High Street, she not only picked up a copy for me, but also collected signatures from a selection of ex-United players who were also present. I asked Estelle what they looked like. 'A bunch of ageing bank managers' was the reply.

A couple of them predated my first appearance at Roots Hall. My only recollection of midfielder Bobby Kellard was the lament of long-term South Paddock inhabitants, 'Wish we still had him.' Ken Jones was an inside-forward in the days when being an inside-forward really meant you were a striker. He moved on to Millwall the season before I arrived on the Roots Hall scene – and was replaced by Bobby Gilfillan, my first United hero. Lou Costello was a nuggety right-back in the days when being a right-back meant that you crossed the halfway line on pain of death. There he was in his blue-and-white-striped number two shirt for my first visit to Roots Hall in 1964. Lou wore the shirt through the four United games I saw him in but, by the start of the next season, he was away to the dubious delights of non-league football after more than 250 outings for the Blues.[21]

And William James Blaikley Best, the icing on my autograph cake, who signed as plain old 'Billy Best'. Already

---

20 Workington FC failed re-election to the Fourth Division in 1977 and were replaced in the Football League by Wimbledon. And non-league they have remained, currently sitting in the seventh tier of the pyramid.

21 Costello's real first name is Mortimer and was presumably nicknamed Lou after the funny man in the 1940s and 50s film and radio double act of Abbott and Costello. He penned 'To Dave, Best Wishes, Lou Costello' on the autograph page in my copy of the *Chronicles*. Lou Costello it is then.

a Southend legend in 1969, he wasn't finished yet. Neither are the autographs in my copy of the *Chronicles*.

***

As my body grew into adolescence in concert with my hair, times they were a-changing in English football and Roots Hall.

For nerdy types like me with a budding interest in footballing cultural history, I can recommend videos of matches of pre-1965 vintage on YouTube. Quite apart from the supporters' attire (all those collars and ties!) the soundtrack reveals another world. As well as the absence of chanting and singing, the difference lies in the incessant 'clack-clack-clack' of handheld rattles mimicking the staccato din of the old mechanical turnstiles. I owned two of them: the first was a solid wooden affair which produced a rapid-fire, tenor-pitched salvo, guaranteed to grate on the ears of fellow spectators. After a year or so, I picked up a larger, heavier, metallic version second-hand, which growled its message in a threatening bass baritone. In addition to the irritation factor, life and limb were under threat if this noisy, whirling weapon contacted any part of your body, or anyone else's around you. Rattles were not a comfortable fit with the chanting and singing culture and were going out of fashion even before the football authorities banned them, much to the relief of the general public's ears, elbows and knees – and mine ended up in the bin.

More unwelcome changes were rearing their heads on the pitch. I didn't like United's new West Bromwich Albion-style outfit of blue-and-white-striped shirts. More importantly, Chico Hamilton left Roots Hall as expected, moving to Aston Villa where he lived his own version of snakes and ladders, descending to the Third Division and then rising back to the First Division in six seasons, picking up a League Cup winners' medal along the way. United didn't sign a replacement, but it didn't seem to matter too much as we started the new season in fine style, with Best contributing five goals in the first three games. Then he picked up an injury and the goals and the points dried up.

Roots Hall on Saturday, 27 September 1969 heralds a new reality, with empty spaces in the stands and terraces laid bare under the late summer sunshine. Following five defeats in six, Roots Hall Ron's solemn announcement, 'This afternoon's official attendance: 5,891,' is greeted with derisive jeers from our diminished band of believers as we witness the Blues bumble and fumble to a 1-1 draw against a Bradford Park Avenue side so bad that they ended the season in last place and suffered the ultimate pain and humiliation of failing re-election and tumbling into non-league – and non-league they have remained to this day.

After another dismal run of one win in seven games, United's attendances had reduced even further and the second-half North Bank crush receded further and further under the roof, like the ebb tide on Southend beach. It was as bad as I could remember and could have heralded a wave of disillusionment. Instead, I followed United to Colchester.

The town of Colchester has history seeping out of every pore. It is one of my favourite places in England. The Romans founded a city, but there is some evidence of a substantial settlement before that. Expanses of the old Roman wall still stand, together with other vestiges of the Roman legacy if you know where to look, a beautifully preserved early Norman castle and the town has more than a touch of mediaeval charm about it. Layer Road had a touch of the mediaeval about it as well, but was definitely not one of my favourite places. The home of Colchester United was a ramshackle assortment of poky half-sized terraces and higgledy-piggledy little stands hardly befitting a Football League club. Getting there was always a pain in the backside if you didn't have a car, being stuck way out of town and miles from the town's railway stations. The number 19 bus journey from Southend took for ever, so we never used it. Saturday, 8 November 1969 is not a day for sightseeing as our little platoon of travelling fans joins other platoons from south-east Essex on the trek from the station to the ground.

The crowd is only 6,021 but, given the size of the stadium and the surprisingly large turnout from Southend, the atmosphere is as crackling as 6,000 can manage. Instead of mingling with our own supporters, we decide to have a laugh and take our place with the locals on a covered terrace so minuscule that, by stepping up on a concrete block at the back, I can touch the roof with an outstretched hand. We manage to mildly annoy the locals, all the more because Southend improbably win 2-0, thanks to goals from ageing warhorses Clayton and McMillan. With some justification, Southend supporters would serenade the hapless Colchester fans for years with our version of the old nursery rhyme, *London Bridge*. 'LAYER ROAD is falling down, falling down, falling down; Layer Road is falling down, we hate Col U.'

Billy Best returns from injury, but United still can't get going. Into December, we moan in the ice and snow with 2,887 Roots Hall fellow sufferers as United fail to beat Aldershot, then squint through a cold, clammy mist as we finally manage to pinch a win against Swansea City to keep our place just above the bottom four.

It doesn't get much better after Christmas. January sees Gary Moore, standing virtually on the goal line, somehow sky a shot almost vertically over the bar – the ball is still rising as it clears the North Bank roof. In mortification and disbelief, he sits on the ground for a moment shaking his head, then gets up and kicks the nearest goalpost – the one that Best shinned up two years previously – and damn-near uproots the thing. As the rest of us groan 'Jesus, Gary' one fellow North Bank inhabitant, who had developed his own opinion on Gary's prowess and was not afraid to express it frequently and loudly, thunders, 'Moore, MOORE! You are a TOTAL. WASTE. OF. BLOODY. SPACE!!' Shortly afterwards, in another Roots Hall encounter, Gary's in a similar position. This time the ball ends up in the back of the net, as does Gary, the opposition goalkeeper and a defender. If the referee had been close enough, he would have ended up there as well. How we loved it on the North Bank.

And we needed all the inspiration we could get. It wasn't until March that United finally turned a corner and ended their season in 17th place with a string of decent results, undoubtedly helped by a flourish of 11 goals in the last eight matches by the ever-reliable Billy Best.

United's position in the depths of the Fourth Division saw the departure of manager Ernie Shepherd and Geoff Hudson, Ernie's erstwhile assistant, after a short but painful experience in the managerial hot seat. The board of directors then turned to the footballing legend that was Arthur Rowley. Rowley had scored a remarkable 434 goals in 619 appearances in a career spanning 20 years and encompassing all four divisions of the Football League. Incredibly, he never pulled on an England shirt (possibly because his scoring record in the First Division was patchy) but, if anyone knew to inspire goalscoring heroics on the field, then surely it would be our Arthur.

But the goals stubbornly refused to arrive. Yet another change of kit, this time to Chelsea all-blue, didn't help either as a second season in the doldrums followed. Clayton, McMillan and Kurila were gone, Moore was in and out of the side and Chisnall was getting on a bit. Bill Garner had arrived from non-league Bedford City but hadn't exactly set the Thames alight with a string of very average performances as part of a very average team. A poor start was succeeded by a truly terrible middle which was only partly alleviated by a semi-revival at the end to finish in 18th place, at that time the lowest league position in Southend's history.

It was all so nondescript that I retain virtually no memories of the 1970/71 season, apart from Billy Best's mop of curly hair, long bushy sideburns and downturned Mexican bandit moustache. He now looked more predatory than ever, rising above the dross around him and weighing in with his customary 20 goals plus.

Other things in life were starting to get in the way as I clattered into adolescence. It wasn't just United's underwhelming exploits. As the product of a boys' high school, joining the Wednesday evening youth club at the local Methodist church hall and meeting girls at close quarters for the first time was a gamechanger for me and a handful of other Roots Hall devotees. We played energetic games of badminton in the main hall, drank coffee and Coca-Cola and awkwardly chatted up girls in the kitchen. We played table tennis, manned the record player and awkwardly chatted up girls in the large room next to the kitchen. In the quiet room behind the large room, we made our awkward clandestine forays into the world of beer and romance with the young ladies we had successfully chatted up. Not very Methodist perhaps but, hey, it was the 1970s.

None of my early girlfriends had the slightest interest in Southend United or any other football team. At least one was the embodiment of the oldest of old football jokes, 'She knows nothing about football, she thinks Sheffield Wednesday is a bank holiday.' And Friday night at Roots Hall occasionally clashed with Girlfriend Night so I gave a few under the lights experiences a miss. If it wasn't Friday, then Girlfriend Night would definitely be Saturday, which effectively took most away games out of the equation, unless they were very local (and very local rivals to United have always been few and far between).

I am less nostalgic about the arrival of skinheads at Roots Hall. Resembling the 'Pinball Wizard' I had observed at Newport Pagnell were legions of shaven-headed, Doc Martens bovver boot-wearing troublemakers with braces who rapidly spread across English football grounds and society at large like a malodour, trailing hooliganism in their wake. The teasing, tuneful ditties that used to ring out from our second-half vantage point were replaced by discordant growls of grinding hostility. The American military themes and protest songs gave way to 'We want a riot [clap-clap-clap-clap-clap]' and 'You're going to get your fucking heads kicked in [clap, clap, clap-clap-clap]'. Even the innocuous hit from Chris Montez, 'Let's Dance', got the treatment:

> *We are the boys in blue and white,*
> *We love to sing and we love to fight,*
> *So let's fight…*

I didn't fancy a riot or a fight, kicking people's heads in was definitely not my style, so I tended not to join in. Skinheads had no hair at all and listened to reggae. My cohort and I had long hair and listened to progressive rock: Harry J and the Allstars, Dave and Ansell Collins, Desmond Dekker and the Aces against Deep Purple, Led Zeppelin, Emerson Lake and Palmer. Not much common ground there.

The fabled leader of the North Bank, 'Pak', was the ominously nicknamed Harry Hatchet. I never got to meet or even see Mr Hatchet, so I'll never know whether he really existed or really had a hatchet. But you get the message. Even so, 'Hairies' like us (because that's what we called ourselves, not bloody hippies, no way, no matter what the skinheads said) never felt particularly threatened on the North Bank. We were cheering for the same team after all, and a fair number of the follicly challenged were our schoolmates, so Roots Hall was a kind of demilitarised zone. The DMZ had its limits, however, and did not extend very far past the floodlights as we gritted our teeth, made ourselves as invisible as possible and sprinted past skinhead strongholds of the Tavern in the Town on High Street and the Criterion on Marine Parade.

Skinhead girls laboured under the collective name of 'Doris', presumably a self-conscious nod to the working-class vibe with their cropped hair, skinny jeans and two-tone tonic skirts. I only knew one Doris. She was smart, well-spoken and lived with her posh parents in their posh Thorpe Bay house, so what you saw was not always what you got.

If skinheads were short on style compared to the Mods, Greasers were short on motorbikes compared to the Rockers. They all paraded about in their leathers but, for the lucky few with wheels, they tended to be of the Honda or Yamaha variety, rather than the stately British machines of the 60s. Skinheads and Greasers didn't like each other either, as evidenced by the flailing bovver boots and swinging bike chains along Marine Parade on Saturday nights. The only thing they had in common was an active aversion to Hairies, so the Foresters joined the Tavern in the Town and the Criterion as places best avoided by the likes of me. A few of them were at my school but I don't remember any of them turning up at Roots Hall. Just as well. The competing subcultures were confronting to behold, but at least you knew what to avoid. It was the sullen, lank-haired sociopaths of no identifiable sartorial allegiance that posed so many problems for football and society in years to come.

Whether it was the disappointments on the field and/ or the associated fall in attendances and/or the rise of the skinhead, the half-time migration from South Bank to North Bank had lost its lustre somehow. By a fortunate coincidence, those in charge solved the problem by building a fence across the muddy track behind the West Stand to block the half-time passage. I and many others simply moved to take up new places in the West Stand because, in the 1971 West Stand, we were still able to stand and change ends. Not behind the goal, of course, but roughly in line with the opposition penalty area, and under cover as well, so I considered that a fair deal. So: I suppose I became a 'moaning old git' at the tender age of 16. But not really – the new inhabitants changed the demographic of the West Stand and a younger, noisier band of fans permanently transformed the atmosphere.

***

The new season marked my departure from the North Bank. Hopes were not high and we started the new season with more of a stagger than a swagger. Then Billy Best scored a clinically efficient hat-trick in a 3-1 win over Grimsby Town and off we went, with virtually the same team as the one which had so richly deserved our derision just a few months earlier. Up the league we marched, crowds doubled and the goals rolled in; which is as good a time as any to introduce another *Chronicles* autograph.

If Gary Moore occasionally resembled a bomb-laden Lancaster and Billy Best was the in-your-face Spitfire of the six-yard box (I hardly ever remember him scoring from distance), the tall, majestic, clever Bill Garner revealed himself to be more of a Stealth Bomber. Billy terrorised defenders with a startling change of pace and forensic finishing; Bill so often seemed to glide undetected into goalscoring positions; headers, long-range shots, short-range shots with either foot, the net bulged all the same. Bill's Yin to Billy's Yang.

Garner and Best combined to sweep all before them. If Bill didn't get a goal, Billy would; and vice versa. But they weren't the only ones as the four-pronged United strike force demolished opposition teams with a devil-may-care *élan* I hadn't seen before. Gary Moore proved himself the rough-cut jewel in Southend's attacking crown. He didn't score that many goals – we had another short, moustachioed predator called Terry Johnson who scored more – but Gary Moore had the happy knack of scoring important ones and, when he didn't, he battered opposing defenders into submission, enabling Garner and Best to take advantage of the carnage.

United followers really start to believe on Saturday, 20 November 1971 when we play Aston Villa, Chico Hamilton and all, in the FA Cup. Chico and co are suffering their brief, painful spell in the Third Division so it's only a first-round tie; but it is Villa after all, which explains is why I'm in the

West Stand nice and early to marvel at the stands and terraces filling around me to make up a crowd of 16,929, the largest attendance I have experienced at Roots Hall.

I also marvel, but with less pleasure, at the first concerted bout of 'aggro' I have seen at a home game, even before the teams come out. The attempted pitch invasion by travelling Villa 'bovver boys' on the South Bank is countered by a similar contingent of United skinheads from 'The Pak' and the thinnest of thin blue lines representing the local constabulary. Result of pitch invasion: a short standoff followed by a mutual retreat, no heads kicked in, but a sign of the times.

Aston Villa are a better side than us and it shows, but they're not that much better and we battle their superior style with a gritty resilience that powers us to a splendid 1-0 victory.

As if to underpin United's new resolve, our winning goal is assisted by a very gentle nudge by Bill Garner on the unfortunate Villa goalkeeper, who drops the ball for the head of ever-ready Billy Best to nod in amid a roar that must have resounded all the way to Colchester. Ten years later, Villa would be First Division champions and European Cup winners, but we won't go into that, thanks very much. Our cup run lasts until a 2-0 defeat at Bournemouth in the second round and we won't go into that either.

But in the league, United march on regardless. We delight in a crowd of 15,434 turning up post-Christmas to see United beat Lincoln City 2-1 at Roots Hall, a match we would probably have lost in previous seasons and a result of some import as it turned out. Even the traditional Christmas and new year hangovers are put on hold as we continue to grind out results. When the hangover eventually arrives at the end of January 1972 (which includes a 4-1 mauling at home by a merciless Colchester United), Moore weighs in with his little run of vital goals and he begins to win over some of his more vocal detractors, exasperation and fury giving way to tolerance and forgiveness. The 14-game unbeaten run helps.

On Good Friday, 31 March, Bill (Garner) scores the first and Billy (Best) scores the second as we inch past Doncaster Rovers 2-1. Even the habitual fatalists in the huge bank holiday crowd of 15,814 can see the Promised Land. Three wins and three draws put Southend one win from promotion.

***

Nothing could be more beguiling than a balmy Friday evening, as day turns to night under the lights on 21 April 1972. Apollo 16 is on the Moon and I'm at Roots Hall for the visit of mid-table Cambridge United. Approaching the end of only their second Football League season, Cambridge must be a soft touch for the two points we need to clinch promotion and: who knows? Maybe a late dash for the Fourth Division title.

The strike force of Best, Garner, Johnson and Moore are all fit and raring to go. Also in United's ranks, warming the substitutes' bench tonight, is a 19-year-old local signed for £100 from Canvey Island Town, the diminutive but highly promising winger Peter 'Spud' Taylor. In seven starts, Taylor has contributed three goals and we expect bigger and better things from him next season.

Home from school, a quick, expectant dinner and off I go with Dad, nice and early, to meet friends and pass long, snaking queues around the ground on the way to our own long, snaking queue for the West Stand turnstiles. All the seats in the East Stand are taken and even the South Bank looks busy. A small knot of Cambridge fans has innocuously made the journey south, perhaps slightly intimidated by the biggest crowd they have ever experienced: 17,059 Essex enthusiasts in festive mood.

I am still a couple of years too young to legally buy a beer. But I can pass for 18 on a good day and not many bar staff troubled themselves to ask in those days. They certainly didn't ask in a small hostelry at the top of Pier Hill. The Royal Stores (colloquially known to us as the Rod and Reel) is almost directly between the no-go areas of the Tavern in the Town and the Criterion, but its laid-back atmosphere exudes a quiet, cosy and safe skinhead-free ambience. This is the venue we choose for our modest promotion celebration after the match, just in time for a couple of celebratory pints before closing time. And Dad, bless him, has given me a free pass to enjoy the triumph without his magisterial presence.

The North Bank still wants to 'get your fucking heads kicked in', but the rest of Roots Hall resounds to the more wholesome encouragement of 'We shall not be moved' and 'Southend United, Southend United, we'll support you ever more; we'll support you ever more'. 'Southend [clap-clap-clap]' rumbles from the seats as Best buzzes, Moore bludgeons and Garner lurks. Twenty-five minutes gone and the score is still 0-0, but we're all over them and our first goal can't be far away. Then United's goalkeeper Derek Bellotti crashes into Cambridge's Greenhalgh and collapses to the ground clutching his arm. Five minutes in a hushed Roots Hall and one stretcher later, Bellotti exits to a sympathetic ripple of applause overladen with a familiar sense of foreboding.

In 1972, only one substitute is allowed and no team would ever put a spare goalkeeper on the bench. We've lost our goalkeeper and, Houston, we have a problem. Enter Peter Taylor, all 5ft 7in of him, to don an oversized green jersey and take his place in goal to general astonishment. 'WHY-WHY-WHY??' is my anguished lament to Arthur Rowley when he overlooks all our on-pitch six-footers. And yet we soon start to see the logic as Taylor shows an unexpected skill in anticipating danger and stopping shots; so long as we don't rely on him for corners and free kicks, of course. It's 0-0 at half-time.

As if written in the stars, Best passes and Garner lashes the ball into the net two minutes into the second half. Now Roots Hall is bouncing all right. Every United attack and defensive clearance, every stop from Taylor is greeted with raucous cheers. We are holding on quite comfortably and there's less than 20 minutes to go. Brian Albeson is one of our overlooked six-footers in defence and it's he who clatters heavily into the unfortunate Taylor, enabling the fateful Greenhalgh to steer home an equaliser. Twelve minutes to go, and Greenhalgh does it again after another piece of defensive mayhem; 2-1 to Cambridge.

Roots Hall resounds to the pleading and increasingly desperate 'Come on Southend'. Rowley finally moves full-back Alex Smith into goal to let Taylor have a go at the Cambridge defence in the last few minutes, as United transition to a front five. But a front ten wouldn't have been enough tonight. Cambridge hold out and the referee blows the final whistle to a communal sigh from 17,000 despairing souls.

My group is feeling a little weak and nauseous with disappointment. But we say 'Oh, sod it' and off to the Royal Stores we go, taking care to skirt the Tavern in the Town, where the atmosphere is unlikely to be quiet, cosy and safe. Deep into our second pints, we are still reprising our sombre assessment. Can we cock it up from here? What do Lincoln need to do? Who's going to Scunthorpe next Tuesday? Stark realism, based on several years of practice. The beer helps, but not much.

Desolation lasts less than a day. Fidgeting nervously in front of the teleprinter's 'clack-clack-clack' and Len Martin's intonation of the results the next afternoon, I take note of Lincoln's failure to beat Aldershot, meaning that United need one point from the last three games to be safely promoted. That Christmas win came in handy after all. And redemption duly arrives four days later when Billy Best scores THE goal which secures a 1-1 draw at Scunthorpe's Old Showground and nudges Southend over the line for our first promotion in 52 years. I wasn't there (school night still ruled), but the *Daily Telegraph* told me all I needed to know the next morning and I got the jubilant details from a few bleary-eyed travelling Blues as they made their way into school the next day.

I'd already committed to the last two matches of the season. Now freed from anxiety, I immensely enjoy the five-hour return journey to Priestfield, courtesy of three railway trains to Gillingham and three back, though Gillingham is but a few miles up the River Medway, the mouth of which is visible from Southend seafront even on a hazy day. I could almost have walked it if Old Father Thames wasn't in the way. I don't even mind the 0-0 result. Also enjoyable is the visit of Gillingham for the final outing under the lights at Roots Hall the following Wednesday, where the rejoicing of the 15,854 spectators belies the fact that we only draw 2-2. As I and, it seems, half of Southend run on to the pitch at the final whistle to register our appreciation for the players crowded into the East Stand directors' box, I spend a (very) little time pondering how close we have been to winning the Fourth Division trophy, just three points adrift of Grimsby at the end. But so be it; we don't do silverware, do we?

People who don't get it, that is to say people who aren't a bit football nuts, sometimes ask me why it all matters in the big scheme of things. What if your team was rubbish last season? Relegated? Missed promotion? Knocked out in the first round of the cup? There's always next year. And I suppose in the real world they are right. At any particular time, triumph or disaster may be a few short months away. I gave up trying to analyse it years ago. It matters; it just does.

Chapter 10

Snakes and Ladders

CALL IT simple nostalgia, call it a generational thing, but I loved English football in the 1970s. Yes, hooliganism was all around – I could read about it and see it on the TV – but, in my personal experience, it always seemed to happen somewhere else. In all my years of watching football, I can count the instances of direct exposure to significant 'aggro' on the fingers of one hand.

And yes, attendances at matches continued their slow decline, but the big clubs could still pack them in now and then with 50,000 or 60,000 filling the ageing cathedrals of English football: Goodison Park and Anfield in Liverpool; Old Trafford and Maine Road in Manchester; White Hart Lane, Highbury and Stamford Bridge in London; St James' Park and Roker Park in the north-east; Villa Park in the Midlands. By the time Goodison finally closes its doors in 2025, half of these cathedrals will be fondly remembered history and those that remain have changed beyond all recognition.[22] English football has moved with the times.

It was also the end of an era when English league football was at its most egalitarian, before the Liverpool ascendancy from the late 70s, succeeded by the Manchester United and now the Manchester City dynasties with the big bucks of American

22 The lost cathedrals are Maine Road (Manchester City), White Hart Lane (Tottenham Hotspur), Highbury (Arsenal) and Roker Park (Sunderland).

franchises and Middle Eastern oil sheikhs. Derby County and Nottingham Forest could seize the First Division title; Sunderland, Southampton and Ipswich Town could lift the FA Cup; Manchester United, Chelsea and Tottenham Hotspur could manage to find themselves in the Second Division, even if only briefly. Older heads would recall Arsenal's hegemony in the 1930s before the intervention of the second world war. Younger heads would point to the probability of a Manchester United dynasty in the 1950s and 60s, if not for Munich. But we didn't expect to see the rise of a new dynasty for most of the 1970s and it wasn't just about the money. With due respect to the coaching genius of the Bill Shankly, Bob Paisley, Joe Fagan and Kenny Dalglish regime at Liverpool, Alex Ferguson at Manchester United and now Pep Guardiola at City, it was still possible for the mercurial Brian Clough to weave his managerial magic around the relatively unglamorous East Midlands strongholds of Derby and Nottingham.

***

And Southend United could pull in gates of over 10,000 to Roots Hall. Back in the Third Division after an absence of six years, we could dream of United climbing to the Second Division, if not this season, then maybe next.

In my eight years of support, I have never seen United play a First Division team. Early in the season of 1972/73, the glamour boys of Chelsea hit town for a second round League Cup tie. Roots Hall is more crowded than I have ever experienced as 24,160 fans pile in, making it impossible to change ends at half-time. We suffer an agonisingly close 1-0 defeat while Bill Garner gamely resists the attempts of hardman Ron 'Chopper' Harris to rearrange his physique, only to join Chopper in a Chelsea shirt a few days later for the (then) significant sum of £100,000.

As for Billy Best, we had the pleasure of his company at Roots Hall for just one more season. Having lost a yard or so of pace, a rapidly balding Billy contented himself with a modest 11 goals in 40 appearances. After teasing us with a parting flourish of five goals in his final four games, he returned to Northampton Town to be reborn as a midfielder and, incredibly, a part-time defender. In six years at Roots Hall, Best went about his business and endured four changes in football kit as I evolved from snotty-nosed schoolkid to bolshie college student-to-be. A total of 123 goals in 246 games for Southend United. Precisely one goal for every two appearances. Immaculate and symmetrical, as you would expect.

As for me, beer and romance had to be paid for somehow. In my last year at school, I forsook my Saturday afternoon spot in the West Stand for ten hours of shelf-stacking at the Tesco supermarket in High Street. I could have added another three hours on Friday evenings but, hell, I had to get to Roots Hall sometimes. The weekly Tesco endeavour earned me a whole £2 to add to my pocket money: not a fortune but not to be sniffed at when a pint of bitter cost 15 new pence. But it cooled my ardour, as United meandered towards a safe mid-table position and I frantically revised for the A-level examinations.

Partly forgotten in my old autograph collection, possibly because his scrawl does not appear in my copy of *The Chronicles*, was another big 'un from the 1970s. I don't know why it was partly forgotten, for Chris Guthrie was front and centre of my generation.

A Geordie born and bred, tall and lean and only two years older than me, Guthrie may have seen himself as the true successor to the tall and lean Geordie icon 'Wor' Jackie Milburn, Newcastle United's spearhead of 20 years earlier. Unfortunately for Guthrie, Newcastle spoiled the narrative by signing the stocky Malcolm Macdonald, born and bred in Fulham and acquired from Luton Town – just about as un-Geordie as you can get. Consequently, Guthrie ended up at Southend shortly after Bill Garner's departure.

Around this time, the immovable object of my long hair finally met the irresistible force of the hair stylist armed with the layer and feathering scissors. Goodbye to the collarless Henley shirts, the Levi corduroys and the desert boots.[23] Now the shirt collar would be worn outside the wide lapels of the jacket as I climbed into my platform-soled shoes. We could all be six foot two now. My change in persona would not have guaranteed safe passage from the skinheads and Greasers rapidly going out of fashion, disappearing almost as quickly as they had appeared, so their diminishing strongholds still needed to be carefully bypassed as I stepped out into the not inconsiderable nightlife of early 70s Southend and its collection of discotheques: Zero 6 next to the airport, Scamps opposite the old Odeon cinema, Zhivago's buried in the concrete ugliness of the Victoria Shopping Centre, the venerable Alexandra Yacht Club on the Cliffs for Thursday night Hard Rock and the Talk of the South (better known as ToTS), an atmospheric nightclub-cum-disco perched behind the seafront pubs and amusement arcades.

The yacht club aside, the music was not generally to my taste, but sweaty headbanging to Purple and Zeppelin was not the object of the exercise. The girls sipped Cinzano Bianco or Dry Martini and lemonade, the boys downed pints of Younger's Tartan or Carling Black Label. The girls danced around their handbags and the boys danced around the girls in a circular courting ritual, in hope of a friendly collision for the slow dances. Among the regular *habitués* was local sporting celebrity Chris Guthrie and I obtained his signature at one of these venues.

Guthrie could put himself about when he chose and was certainly no slouch in the goalscoring stakes. Somehow, he always seemed to leave us wanting just a little more. Every now and then he would wander around the Roots Hall pitch as if

---

23 Henley shirts were better known as Hippie vests or Grandpa vests back in the late 1960s and early 1970s.

in wait for a number seven bus after the final whistle. A wag from the West Stand once yelled 'See you at Scamps, Guthers!' to the chortling amusement from those of us in the know. A forgiving lot, United fans. To slightly misquote a classic Deep Purple lyric, Chris Guthrie stands out as a child in my time.[24]

***

My A-level results worked out more or less according to plan and proved good enough to send me off to the University of London. I waved a non-tearful farewell to Tesco and spent the summer of 1973 working for the Joint Credit Card Company, a large local banking organisation responsible for a green and red bit of plastic known to the rest of Britain as the Access credit card. Much of my princely wage of £30 per week was squirrelled away to supplement the woefully inadequate state student grant which would, on its own, have not quite funded the lifestyle of a typical impoverished undergraduate.

Attending a London college meant that I could still get along to Southend matches but not as often as usual. Some of my old Roots Hall pals also departed for their own universities so their visits were even less frequent, making Christmas, new year and Easter catch-ups on the terraces all the more precious.

Incongruously, I also paid the odd visit to the home of Leyton Orient, then in their Orient FC phase and punching above their weight in the Second Division. Orient's Brisbane Road ground was on the Central underground line, almost equidistant between my college campus in Mile End and the college halls of residence in South Woodford. It was interesting to see how the other half lived – good practice for United's years to come in the second tier, I thought – and the Orient didn't steal my heart, I'm happy to report. In revenge, they have made a point of spoiling Southend's day with distressing regularity ever since.

24 'Child of my time' appropriates the title of my favourite Deep Purple song 'Child in Time' from the iconic 1970 album *Deep Purple in Rock*.

Another season came and went, but the Second Division was as elusive as ever. Part-time goalkeeper and full-time winger Peter Taylor was on the way to realising his potential, so he was off to Crystal Palace for £120,000. Gary Moore finally reached the end of his United journey and I forgave him when he went out on loan to Colchester, scoring a brief flurry of goals for the north Essex rustics before decamping to Chester. Nobody could replace Billy Best but Stuart Brace, late of Grimsby Town, buzzed with purposeful intensity for a couple of years. Nobody could replace Bill Garner but Peter Silvester, signed from Norwich City, was well capable of ghosting his way into goalscoring positions. United were always close, but never quite close enough for a promotion challenge and we had to settle for another mid-table position. Never mind. Guthrie, Brace and Silvester would see us climb the ladder to glory next time. It was a hopeful time to be a Southend supporter.

It was even more hopeful in 1974/75 – for the first month. A Friday evening match against Crystal Palace at Roots Hall in September 1974 is memorable because United are top of the Third Division and it coincides with my 19th birthday. It's also the first United versus Palace match for years and the first I've ever seen. Palace have suffered the trauma of two successive relegations, but still have the charisma attached to a 'big' club with a 'big' away support. And they have Peter Taylor. Optimism is sufficiently high for 17,394 to turn up, including the diaspora of my United-supporting friends still on college holiday. It didn't take much back then. Unfortunately, the Roots Hall multitude, the diaspora and my birthday celebrations are somewhat subdued as Taylor and Palace pinch it 1-0, kicking off a cataclysmic tumble down the table which nearly sees us relegated.

Having contributed 35 goals in 108 appearances, Chris Guthrie hustled off to Sheffield United and most of us mourned his departure: he was not the first Southend star to tread that path and not the last either.

Painstaking and painful research for this story has revealed an enduring truth. When it comes to Southend, clean slates are rare events. In other words, our failings at the back end of one season tend to follow us into the next too regularly for comfort. In gazing up at the ladder which would take us to the bright lights of the Second Division, we missed a scaled reptile hiding in the shadows.

In 1975/76, the scaled reptile revealed itself to be a long, sinuous snake. A dreadful start was compounded by an awful finish. The middle wasn't that clever either. It wasn't necessarily a failure to score goals or a propensity to let them in, it was United's inability to capitalise on short-term advantage and overcome short-term adversity that cost them dear, as they slithered to a 23rd position and relegation. Attendances fell below 4,000 and even I didn't turn up as often as I should have.

Ironically, the FA Cup provided a few pinpricks of light in the gathering gloom. United beat Swansea City, Dover Athletic and Brighton & Hove Albion, all at home, to make a rare excursion into the fourth round. After Stuart Parker rises to power a last-minute header into the South Bank net and seal a 2-1 victory against Cardiff City, I and most of the crowd of 12,863 stay in Roots Hall to enjoy the novelty of hearing the fifth-round draw from the Roots Hall PA system. Loud cheers accompany the announcement of United's reward: a clash at the old Baseball Ground, home of Football League champions Derby County.

The cup run had been great fun, but the Derby match took place in my absence. I still can't remember why I wasn't there, but the upcoming university finals and the parlous state of my finances must have had something to do with it. My place was taken by old school friends and United optimists from the universities of Liverpool and Exeter who reported that Derby probably deserved their 1-0 win and the late disallowed 'equaliser' for Southend, which caused me a great deal of angst at the time, was probably offside.

It was a brave try but all to Noah Vale, the malevolent mythical character who haunts Southend's misfortunes across the ages and, indeed, the misfortunes of football teams all over the English-speaking world. Derby ended the season fourth in the First Division while we ended up back in the Fourth Division and struggled to understand how United could hold the league champions to 1-0 and then lose 5-1 at Preston North End ten days later.

***

Another season in the Fourth Division, another ladder to climb, minus Arthur Rowley – well, he'd taken us down, but the sack wasn't always a given in 1976. Our Arthur was replaced by Dave Smith who had done good things at Mansfield Town, fortunately post-our 1969 FA Cup calamity. One more difference: United's best spell came over the Christmas and new year period for a change. Despite this welcome relief, an indifferent start and an indifferent finish meant that we quickly resigned ourselves to an indifferent mid-table position.

Now I had a degree, a job and a fiancée. I found a girl with more than a fleeting interest in the whys and wherefores of Southend United Football Club and knew that Sheffield Wednesday wasn't a bank holiday. Of course, it wasn't the prime reason why we got together, but it didn't do any harm. Hilary had already joined the United caravanserai to who-knows-where as we embarked on 1977/78 as a married couple with a mortgage.

Confidence in the new campaign was limited, with a sprinkling of new faces but no 'big 'un up front'. What a pleasant surprise, then, to find United in top spot at the end of September. After the inevitable hiccup, when we forgot how to win at home, runaway leaders Watford fell to earth as we secured a 1-0 win at Roots Hall.

On Friday, 9 December 1977 third-placed Southend welcome fourth-placed Newport County to Roots Hall. The

Southend public is in pre-Christmas mode so only 5,840 hardcore supporters have turned up on a cold, misty evening under the lights. County are on my lengthy personal list of bogey teams, so I can feel the nerves tingling as I take my place in the West Stand. I'm not the only one either, judging by the uneasy atmosphere.

In the first half, our best efforts are denied by the visiting defence and we find inventive ways to miss decent chances. An old lower-division warhorse named Brian Clark puts Newport ahead and a nifty little finish from defender Tony Byrne doubles the lead early in the second half. With 17 minutes to go, we're still 2-0 down and going nowhere. The exit gates are open in the West Stand as I reluctantly trudge up the terrace steps and out into the wintry night, and I'm not the only one.

As the hunched shoulders of the disgruntled early departures disappear into the mist, I take a moment to survey the modest Edwardian terraced dwellings of Shakespeare Drive, similar to numerous roads alongside numerous stands at traditional football grounds. Was ever a street name more out of kilter with its next door neighbour? How many lunacies have these old bricks and mortar witnessed? Something doesn't feel right, so I turn on my heel and march back into the ground just in time to see Hadley head United's first goal. Five minutes to go: a surge down the right wing, a pinpoint cross and Derrick Parker rises to level the score.

If there'd been anyone on the South Bank, they would have raised the roof – if there'd been a roof. The East Stand feet are rhythmically stamping. 'We love you Southend, we do; we love you Southend, we do; we love you Southend, we do; ohhh Southend, we love you!' Three minutes left. Another cross and Gerry Fell launches himself, nose brushing the turf, to crash in a diving header as spectacular as it is unexpected. Almost straight from the restart, Fell collects the ball in midfield, sprints up the pitch and arrows a vicious drive into the County net; 4-2 to United at the final whistle and the kids are on the pitch in amazed excitement.

Ninety minutes of raw emotion condensed into five. There were other notable performances that season: another tilt at Derby at the Baseball Ground in the FA Cup and another narrow defeat, this time 3-2; a useful 0-0 draw at promotion rivals Swansea; a 2-1 victory over Brentford, another promotion rival, on Good Friday, the winner coming from an own goal which makes Roots Hall resound with uproarious laughter for its sheer silliness and a 1-1 draw at Watford in April which effectively pushed United over the promotion line in front of *Match of the Day* cameras for the first time. And we finished the season in second place, ahead of Swansea and Brentford, albeit miles behind Watford. But none of these matches, notable as they were, stick in my memory after 47 years as much as Newport at Roots Hall, December 1977. In the end, maybe that's what it's all about.

For anyone who cares to ask, my single piece of advice to any supporter of any football club high or low, anywhere in the world is: don't ever leave the ground before the final whistle. And I never have.

***

Argentina's victory in the 1978 World Cup Final was followed by the arrival of the overseas vanguard of Osvaldo Ardiles and Ricky Villa, who joined Tottenham Hotspur and helped to change the character of English football. No such distractions for Southend, but Dave Smith recruited a full-back from Tottenham, Micky Stead, and a centre-back from Sheffield Wednesday, Dave Cusack, for £50,000 apiece. That was quite a lot of money for a club newly promoted from the Fourth Division. As we renewed our acquaintance with the third tier United made a sound enough start, not pulling up any trees but on the outer fringes of another promotion challenge as the dangerous month of December loomed.

There is no better time to return to Tommy Smith, the 'Iron Man of Liverpool'. Tommy was one of a select bunch of high-profile hardmen who adorned the First Division in the 60s and 70s. Every big club had one: Tommy at Liverpool, Nobby Stiles at Manchester United, Peter Storey at Arsenal, Ron 'Chopper' Harris at Chelsea. Leeds United, being Leeds United, had two: Billy Bremner and Norman 'Bites Yer Legs' Hunter. Even soft-centred Spurs had Dave Mackay, one for the ages. Hardmen were as old as football but, like brass bands, rattles and the *Football League Review*, the concept is history. I struggle to think of a single current Premier League player who would fit the bill. Footballers are more subtle now; they have to be, otherwise the plethora of red and yellow cards flung around today would leave them semi-permanent residents of the stands.

When Tommy uncharacteristically rose high into the Rome sky to power a near-post header deep into the Borussia Mönchengladbach net for Liverpool's second goal and collected his winners' medal in the 1977 European Cup Final after a 3-1 win, it surely couldn't have occurred to him that, 18 months later, he would be turning out for a Swansea side peppered with Liverpool old boys in a Third Division Friday match at Roots Hall. 'From the sublime to the 'cor blimey,' as Dad used to say.

Still, here he is on the evening of Friday, 8 December 1978. So is a crowd of 8,969, and so am I. From the start, Tommy is booed without malicious intent every time he touches the ball, but he must be used to that. Then, about 30 minutes in, the ball bounces off the pitch and into the West Stand for a Swansea throw. Tommy trots over to collect it but, with an astonishingly impromptu meeting of collective minds, several hundred of us regale him with, 'We all agree, Tommy Smith is a WANKER!' The recipient of this extempore masterpiece grins broadly as he slows to a walk. A few feet away from the ball, a croaky adolescent voice pipes up, 'And a fat, spotty old wanker he is too!' Tommy's grin turns wolfish as he makes a joking attempt to reach into the stand toward the direction of the young miscreant. Then he shakes his head, picks up the ball, takes the throw and off we go again. For the rest of the match, the West Stand breaks into loud cheers and applause every time the ball comes within spitting distance of Tommy, even though Swansea go on to beat us 2-0. Sometimes, you just have to love this sport.

It is ten days before the FA Cup replay with Watford.

Chapter 11

The Breathless Year

FOR ME, the start of a new football season is the conjunction of hope and uncertainty, with expectation running some way behind.

Take August 1979. Following a Third Division season of two halves, even I had no idea of what awaited Southend United: maybe a slide down the snake of relegation. Or a scramble up the promotion ladder. Or another season in between. I was now well-versed in each scenario. The first two league games: two wins, two clean sheets. First round of the League Cup: home and away wins against Brentford, aggregate score 6-2 to United, including a 4-1 trouncing at Griffin Park. A trip to Burnden Park, the home of First Division Bolton Wanderers in the first leg of the second round, and a famous 2-1 victory for the Blues, thanks to a double from tricky winger Colin Morris. Flipping heck! And we're not even out of August yet.

Early September sees Bolton at Roots Hall for the second leg, where our loud celebrations at the final whistle belie the reality of the 0-0 result; the 2-1 win on aggregate means that we are in the third round all of a sudden. Our reward is West Ham United – at last; but away – obviously. To their great credit, the West Ham diehards treat little old us with the bristling hostility specially reserved for genuine local rivals, rather than the patronising disdain for hicks from the sticks.

United battle to a 1-1 draw at Upton Park, maybe because West Ham are only a Second Division team this season but maybe also because Southend are determined to give it a real go, on the first occasion we have played the Hammers in my lifetime.

Then it's off to Roots Hall for the replay on Monday, 1 October 1979 and the prodigious noise generated by a crowd of 22,497, boosted by a sizeable contingent of east Londoners in their claret and blue regalia (with a few local turncoats in their midst, no doubt). The atmosphere is mutually and spikily disrespectful. West Ham's traditional rendition of 'I'm Forever Blowing Bubbles' is hijacked and misused by Southend's consistent theme for many years, 'They fly so high, they reach the sky, then like WEST HAM they fade and die', a Roots Hall staple, irrespective of the opponent. It gets a special airing tonight. West Ham's response is of a more contemporary stamp. 'You're shit and you know you are', a new song adapted from the Village People single 'Go West'. The encounter on the pitch between West Ham's Billy Bonds and Southend's Ron Pountney is also spiky enough, despite the disparity in height, to keep the crowd entertained. The silky skills of West Ham legend Trevor Brooking, and his up-and-coming protégé Alan Devonshire, are nullified by the close attentions of the Southend defence and midfield as the two Uniteds cancel each other out in a watchable but ultimately inconclusive 0-0 draw. A worthy performance over two legs and an away goal to boot.

Well done Southend, and into the fourth round draw we go. Er, no, because this is 1979 and the Football League has not yet got round to the concept of away goals counting double in the League Cup. Celebrations at Roots Hall are put on hold while we wait for the lottery of the coin toss to decide the venue of the second replay – which we lose, to the raucous jeers of 5,000 West Ham fans and disappointed groans of 17,000 Southend supporters. And it is back to Upton Park, where we flatter to deceive in holding West Ham to a 2-1 deficit at half-time, only to collapse in the second half and lose 5-1. Over a two-week period, the euphoria of the 1-1 draw was dampened by the goalless replay, drenched by the coin toss, and finally drowned in the second replay. Cost me a fortune as well. Be careful what you wish for.

In the meantime, the West Ham saga proves to be the catalyst for a dismal run of draws and defeats which sees us locked in the relegation zone by January. The alarm bells are ringing and manager Dave Smith can hear them. We have a decent side, but just can't put the ball in the net. Colin Morris, arguably our best player, is infuriatingly but symmetrically sold to Blackpool for £111,111. Coming the other way is classy Derek Spence, a tall, sinewy striker of some distinction and a current Northern Ireland international. In short order, Spence is supplemented by the on-demand biff-bash of Keith Mercer, veteran of December-on-Sea, who has seen the light and joins United from Watford.

Neither of our new acquisitions are prolific in the goalscoring stakes at first but their presence seems to add a bit of oomph, as United finally start to pull a few results together. A tight 2-1 victory against Millwall at the old Den followed by an even tighter 3-2 win at home to Brentford set the tone. We stay just outside the dreaded bottom four as April, Easter and the squeakiest of all 'squeaky bum times' loom.

And Sheffield Week. A Saturday afternoon match against Sheffield Wednesday with their blue and white horde, when Roots Hall outsings the visitors and United outplay their promotion-bound opponents, deserving better than a 1-1 draw. Good Friday and the visit of promotion-chasing Sheffield United with their red and white horde. One down at half-time, the Blues battle back to win 2-1, with goals from Pountney and Mercer accompanied by an incessant barrage of support for the entire second half. Easter Monday and Millwall at home, followed by their own blue and white horde. Skill and endeavour aren't enough today in the claustrophobic atmosphere at Roots Hall. Not for the first time during my years in the West Stand, I wish that I could levitate above the suffocating anxiety under the double-barrelled roof and the war of attrition on the pitch as the toiling United players fight to hold on to a half-time 1-0 lead. But hold on we do until the final whistle, to release the tension I could have cut with a blunt knife.

I never remembered much animus with the infamous Millwall supporters at Roots Hall. My recollections are of small groups of them mixing harmlessly with United fans in the West Stand. As I celebrate the final whistle and dare to breathe again, a passing Millwall supporter remarks, 'I hope you lot stay up ...'

'Thanks.'

'...and send Brentford down, I hate the bastards.'

'Why?'

'Because I live there.'

There are no geographical boundaries to the tribalism of London football rivalry.

United's heroics at home have kept us out of the bottom four, just. All roads now lead to United's final fixture on Saturday, 3 May 1980. Another away game. At Hull City. In my first full season as a supporter, City beat us 1-0 at their Boothferry Park ground in May 1966 and dispatched United to the Fourth Division. Fourteen years on, the portents are not encouraging. It's a good job I'm not superstitious. Ha-ha-ha!

I could spend the week before the match fretting in my spare time, but statistical analysis is a key component of my job so I decide to get out the pen, paper and calculator. This season, the race to the bottom is even more convoluted than usual. Entering the final weekend, Wimbledon are already down and Mansfield Town all but down, which still leaves five teams trying to avoid the two remaining relegation places.

Brentford, Blackpool and Bury are in jeopardy. But so are Southend and Hull.

I spend some time working through the permutations: goal difference (Hull and Brentford have the worst, United and Blackpool the best). Games in hand: Hull, Bury and Blackpool still have two to play, while the rest of us are on our last game (that doesn't happen any more, to ensure a level playing field for the season's climax). Then it's down to who's playing who in their last game.

An hour of careful calculation reveals the simple truth: if Southend beat Hull, we are safe and they go down (barring a cricket score in their last match). If Hull beat Southend, they are safe and we go down. If it's a draw, we are both in the morass with the three 'Bs'. Trying to work out the possibilities nearly fried my brain so, if you're wondering how my memory could possibly retain all this stuff after 40-plus years, it doesn't. In writing this story, I dug out a well-thumbed *Rothmans Football Yearbook* and repeated the laborious exercise.[25]

***

I will not be making the northward journey on this fateful Saturday. Not many others are present in the cavernous Boothferry Park ground either because the city of Hull is also home to two major rugby league teams, Hull FC and Hull Kingston Rovers. It so happens that 3 May is the day of rugby league's Challenge Cup Final and they are playing each other at Wembley in front of 95,000 Humberside citizens. I am told that the city streets of Hull are almost deserted and only 3,823 round-ball supporters turn up for City against United, with everything at stake.

The statistical analysis is on my lap while I sit down at home with teeth clenched in front of the telly and fitfully watch the rugby league final on *Grandstand*. Kingston Rovers

25 I repeated the analysis with the help of the *Rothmans Football Yearbook 1980/81*. Queen Anne Press, 1980.

win 10-5; good luck to them, but I don't care. I could try and pick up score updates from the radio but prefer not to do so because they make things worse. I am fidgeting on the edge of my seat waiting for the BBC's *Final Score* at 4.40pm. The pitiless 'clack-clack-clack' of the teleprinter eventually informs me that Hull have beaten Southend 1-0, keeping them up and sending us back to the Fourth Division. Brentford have also saved themselves by winning their last game 1-0 at Griffin Park; their victims are Millwall, which must have impressed my Brentford-hater no end. And unlucky Bury realise that a remarkable 2-1 win at promoted Blackburn Rovers has not been enough to save their bacon.

Three tumultuous seasons for three different reasons. At the end of it all, I sat back and exhaled a long, whistling sigh of disappointment. With the benefit of hindsight (it didn't occur to me at the time), United's late-season collapse in 1978/79 with seven defeats in the last nine games and the clean slate rule made our demise predictable. A decade of snakes and ladders ended with Southend back where they started, in the Fourth Division basement. It was a mixed bag overall and a minor tragedy at the end, but at least it wasn't boring. What would the next decade bring? Up or down? Up and down, and up, and down?

Chapter 12

How I Lost the Love

ENGLISH FOOTBALL in the 1980s seems to be the enduring subject of a grand, media-induced nostalgia trip. This is possibly because most of the commentariat in print, on the TV, on the radio, even on the internet are of a certain vintage; the 40-to-50-somethings. They grew up as kids and teenagers in the 80s, and the game in those days was what they knew and where they got the love. You don't get to choose your generation.

Being a few years older, my memories are of old-style football grounds decaying by degrees and beset by hooliganism, attendances on an accelerating slide overseeing an air of dreary pragmatism on the pitch. At the top of the tree, Liverpool were in the middle of a seemingly endless cycle of league championship wins spanning 15 years, briefly interrupted by Nottingham Forest, Aston Villa and Everton – plus the European Cup in three of the more forgettable finals. The FA Cup was left to other teams who aspired to but could never quite emulate the juggernaut from Merseyside: Tottenham, Manchester United, Everton again.

It all seemed so predictable. For a legion of kids, the football world revolved around Alan Hansen, Terry McDermott, Graeme Souness, Ian Rush, Kenny Dalglish, John Barnes and co. All brilliant players, right enough. And I know all about Manchester United's 20-year epoch of success in more recent years; some people may scream special pleading at me if I make the case for my second team. Hansen, McDermott, Souness, Rush, Dalglish, Barnes against Ryan Giggs, David Beckham, Eric Cantona, Dwight Yorke, Cristiano Ronaldo, Wayne Rooney. If I come across as slightly biased, consider me guilty as charged.

Two events define the era for me. In April 1982, Dad and I were at Anfield for the visit of Stoke City, 20 years on from my first live football match. This time we were standing on the Kop, a rare and, as it turned out, final visit to the terraced colossus. Liverpool were back on top of the First Division and walking it, but the crowd was only just over 30,000 and we could see quite a few sparsely populated islands around the ground, even one or two in the Kop itself. The Reds did their business and put Stoke to sleep 2-0, but the atmosphere was soporific. 'I don't remember it ever being this quiet,' commented Dad.

Then there was Old Trafford in December 1983 and a short-lived, ill-fated experiment with live First Division matches on the TV: Manchester United versus Tottenham, the gold standard top-flight fixture of a few short years earlier, and a great game won 4-2 by the Reds. Fewer than 34,000 fans turned up in a stadium that could hold 60,000. What was that all about? Football had changed, but not in a good way.

* * *

It was also changing closer to home. Dad was now more of a bank holiday visitor to Roots Hall (Boxing Day, New Year's Day, Good Friday, Easter Monday; and 'special occasions'). My fellow United-lovers from school had scattered themselves around England. Fortunately, my return to the home of the Access card (at a much higher salary than I had commanded in 1973) produced a new group of adherents even though, as a proud new father, my own visits to Roots Hall were less frequent than they had been. Back in the Fourth Division for the 1980/81 season, Southend footballed their triumphant way to the Fourth Division trophy, the first significant silverware in our history. We started at the top and stayed there to the end, with barely a blip to cause us concern. With not a single point dropped at Roots Hall until the end of January, an ultimately unbeaten home record, winning away for fun, I loved that season, revelling in the 79 goals scored and the miserly 31 conceded.

Derek Spence and Keith Mercer made real the potential they had hinted at the previous season. Terry Gray revealed a playing style reminiscent of Billy Best as he buzzed his way to 17 goals. Two attacking full-backs, Mike Stead and Steve Yates, provided the ammunition for Spence, Mercer and Gray. Our stylish centre-backs, Alan Moody and Tony Hadley, complemented the more rugged Dave Cusack in keeping the opposition out, backed by the nerveless competence of Mervyn Cawston in goal. Ron Pountney was just immense and ably supported by our tricky midfielder, West Yorkshire's own Anton Otulakowski.

After a couple of false starts, Roots Hall Ron triumphantly succeeded in pronouncing his name in the proper Polish style, carefully and correctly enunciated as 'Anton Otula-Koff-ski'. Stadium announcers elsewhere tried their best, with a few of them playing safe and opting for the American variant 'Otula-Cow-ski'. However, at one stadium (rendered anonymous to save embarrassment, but it was north of Watford), the announcer nervously intoned 'Number 11 – Anton, oh, Anton Ott – Ottool – oh, Anton,' to the delight of our small band of Essex sophisticates on the away terrace, who knew what his name was and sang it with gusto to educate the home fans.

No 'squeaky bums' this season. Saturday, 11 April is a 'special occasion' as United play their closest rivals, Lincoln City, in the bright sunshine of Roots Hall. Me, Dad, and 11,953 other supporters have turned up, including a couple of thousand noisy Lincoln fans in red and white. The West Stand

and North Bank are expectant and confident, an emotion we don't often experience at Roots Hall.

Spence nearly scores in the very first minute but the City goalkeeper pulls off a stunning save. We are up in the air when Hadley's header hits the inside of the post, but the ball ends up in their keeper's grateful arms instead of the back of the net. My most vivid memory is the cross from Yates which Mercer somehow manages to scream over the bar from close in. The howl of mortification from the crowd is epic and Mercer's miss would, on another day, draw loud criticism from those Blues fans who, as always, are not enamoured with 'big 'uns up front'. But today we shrug our shoulders with acceptance.

Lincoln keep it tight for their own reasons and the match ends in a 0-0 draw, but we don't care. The point is just about enough for us and will prove to be enough for City as well. Celebration rings around the ground and the Lincoln travellers generously applaud the United players gallivanting around the pitch. All that's needed now is a nutcase with a set of wailing bagpipes in the West Stand and we have him for our last home match against Rochdale with the trophy safely secured. It was all very marvellous, but I was not oblivious to the fact that our average crowd was barely 6,000: ten years earlier it would have been double that and more, no problem.

Back in the Third Division, United weren't too bad for a year or two, but not good enough to excite the terraces. Crowds were routinely below 4,000 now. It was all the same to me. I was once again a regular in the West Stand as I suffered the pain of separation and divorce, clinging to Southend United like a blue and white life raft. There were another two football-loving colleagues at work, one a Liverpool supporter from Liverpool and one a Motherwell supporter from Glasgow. In my one-man mission to arrest the decline, I managed to cajole them into a few Friday nights at Roots Hall, hoping and half-expecting them to catch the United bug. They were politely and mildly enthusiastic but Roots Hall was not contagious.

Meanwhile, things got worse and worse still on the pitch. Garry Nelson was a turbo-charged winger who went to my old school; but then he left for Swindon Town. We had another shining star for a little while: Danny Greaves, son of the great Jimmy. Crafty, razor-sharp in front of goal, devastatingly quick over five yards, Danny WAS his dad to my eyes. A cascade of goals in the short-term, promotion to the Second Division, a big-money transfer down the track; everything was possible. Then he suffered a career-threatening injury and the possibilities faded away with the United support base (although Danny later joined the coaching staff). Crowds dropped to levels previously unseen and there were few sights or sounds more depressing than the old Roots Hall with fewer than 2,000 voices echoing around it.

Off the pitch, United embarked on a boardroom changing of the guard which introduced a new owner, one Anton Johnson. Almost the first thing he did was to dismiss Dave Smith, replacing him with Peter Morris who lasted six months. Johnson also oversaw an increase in club debt from £250,000 to £700,000 in just over a year.

I had no detailed access to the Roots Hall financial machinations – none of my West Stand contemporaries did – but we picked up snippets, some of them likely to be apocryphal, that we absorbed with a combination of horrified fascination, resigned cynicism and a growing sense of unease. *The Centenary History of Southend United – A Century United* details 'our darkest hour' admirably and I can't be bothered to recount the minutiae behind the whole meltdown but, suffice it to say, the club was in deep financial doo-doo which we could all see for ourselves.[26] Just what you need when you're back in a relegation dogfight with an average gate of 2,000 and falling.

---

26 The financial meltdown is detailed in *The Centenary History of Southend United: A Century United*. Written by Peter Miles and Dave Goody. Shrimper Publishing Limited, 2007.

In September 1979, United announced themselves as giant-killers by beating First Division Bolton Wanderers in the League Cup. Less than five years later, Bolton had found their own snake to slide down and now both teams face each other in the Third Division at Roots Hall on Monday, 6 February 1984. The attendance is 1,594, at that time the smallest crowd for a Football League match in United's history. Against Bolton, for Heaven's sake. Count them; I almost could. And we lose 1-0. Now is the winter of our discontent.

Into the maelstrom stepped an English footballing legend: Bobby Moore, captain of England's 1966 World Cup-winning team. His persona was inspirational in itself; his managerial credentials (non-league with Oxford City and a spell in Hong Kong) less so. United's perilous league position on Bobby's appointment in February 1984 rapidly turned into a crisis as we continued to slide down the table. Even a brief flurry of three wins in six games was not enough to climb away from danger as we found ourselves back in the relegation zone at the sharp end of the season.

***

Like beauty, bogey teams in football are in the eye of the beholder. I reckon I could put ten Southend supporters in a room, ask them for their number one bogey team and get ten different answers. I could wax lyrical with my views on the contenders: Newport County, Grimsby Town, Scunthorpe United, Mansfield Town, Leyton Orient, Gillingham. And then there's Hull City.

I like the big old English cities spawned by the Industrial Revolution; it's because of my Liverpool roots as well as my love of British history. I have been to the east coast city of Kingston upon Hull several times and I've always enjoyed communing with the Victorian grandeur of Queen Victoria Square and Queen's Gardens, wandering around the deliciously atmospheric Old Town at night. I don't even mind Hull City

AFC all that much. But to my mind they are *the* bogey team for Southend. United's penalty for putting the mockers on City's promotion challenge in my first season of supporting the Blues was repaid by them sending us down to the Fourth Division one year later. Then they sent us down to the Fourth Division again in 1980.

Saturday, 5 May 1984 is another rugby league Challenge Cup Final day at Wembley. Widnes against Wigan, for those who are interested. But it's Hull against Southend and this time I am making my own way to Boothferry Park. United are in imminent danger of relegation again. City, by contrast, have different fish to fry and are sitting just outside the promotion places with four games to go.

I am visiting football-phobic friends with a care factor well below zero. They are deeply suspicious of my motivations for choosing this particular weekend to descend upon them. It's obviously a coincidence, but their teasing wind-ups suggest that they know better; and they're kind of right, of course. As I arrive at Boothferry Park for my first and only time, I approach three representatives of the local constabulary and ask, quite politely I think, for directions to the stand or terrace housing the United fans. The oldest representative thinks for a moment, looks me up and down and declares, 'There's no away section here, sonny.' (I was 28 years old). 'Tell you what: you go through that entrance there,' indicating over his shoulder, 'and they'll look after you if you behave yourself. If you don't, you'll see me again and you don't want to do that. All right?'

I nod dumbly. That's me told, then.

That is how I end up in the Kempton Stand, a cramped, smoky and not-very-full covered terrace as part of a not-very-crowded crowd of 6,758. The Kempton architecture strongly reminds me of the West Stand at Roots Hall, as do the home supporters, who I find are almost as adept in the dark arts of moaning as their Essex counterparts. Same abuse, different objects, different accent. I also find that the local constabulary have been economical with the truth and there are, in fact, a few United supporters occupying the surreally small terrace to my right with a new supermarket hiding behind the advertising hoardings – the shared fate befalling several proud old football grounds in the 1980s.

The City fans are friendly enough but I choose to keep incognito. It's easy enough to do, because there is little for me or the other United supporters to shout about. Most of the action is in the first half, which closes with City 2-1 up. In the second half, United huff and puff with some degree of desperation, City are hanging on a bit, but we can't force our way back into the match. It ends 2-1 to Hull. The home fans celebrate in relief as their promotion hopes remain alive for another week but we are down, barring a miracle. And miracles don't crop up very often for Southend.

My disappointment was only partially relieved by the soothing balm of John Smith's Yorkshire Bitter and chicken vindaloo in the Old Town that night. Hull ended the season in fourth place, just missing out on promotion on goal difference to Sheffield United in those pre-play-off days. As for Southend, our miracle was missing in action and relegation was duly confirmed a few days later. Rugby league Challenge Cup finals give me the willies to this day, but I had more immediate concerns. For the first time as a United supporter, I felt a tidal wave of disillusion break over me.

When the first home game of a new season attracts 1,902 spectators, public dissatisfaction with the United becomes self-evident. Our standing joke was that the Roots Hall coppers should have been outside the ground chucking people *in*. The team was poor and demoralised, but other disquieting things were happening off the pitch. Another round of boardroom upheaval brought the accession of Vic Jobson to the joint challenges of owner and chairman of the board at the end of 1984. Chairman Vic inherited a veritable train wreck of a club.

Volcanic activity at Roots Hall coincided with seismic rumbles in my life. I was too young for a mid-life crisis, but I was presiding over a failed marriage, the distress of an intense subsequent relationship gone wrong and a grumbling dissatisfaction with my career. As with United, things had to change. I decided that I needed a new job, a new home and a new, deep, lasting relationship – not necessarily in that order.

As far as career was concerned, I cast my net across opportunities as diverse and exotic as Witham in rural Essex (insurance), Central London (marketing consultancy), Edinburgh (bank), Rome (United Nations), New York (bank) – and Halifax (West Yorkshire, not Nova Scotia – building society). Only two of these options guaranteed regular visits to Roots Hall, but that was not central to my thoughts.

Because even I was getting fed up with Southend United. The 1984/85 season was the worst yet, with a mediocre strike force in front of a defence which looked OK on paper but hopeless on grass. Tuesday, 29 January 1985 is a chilly night under the lights at Roots Hall. United are sliding down the Fourth Division table after three successive defeats in which we have scored two goals and conceded 11. I am stamping my feet to keep warm in the whisper-quiet West Stand for the local derby against Colchester United. And I am soon stamping my feet in frustrated rage. Three down at half-time, we capitulate to a woeful 5-2 defeat. There I am: cold and pissed off as part of a paltry crowd of 2,190 (most of whom leave before the end), the mockery of the small coterie of Colchester supporters ringing in one ear and the derision of the few remaining Southend fans in the other, encapsulated in the time-honoured anthem of the disenchanted, 'What a load of rubbish, what a load of rubbish.' I stand on my own in the now completely deserted West Stand and wonder, 'What the hell am I doing here?'

That night, I concluded that supporting Southend was a burden too many in my endeavours for a change in personal direction, so I decided that I'd had enough and parted ways with the Blues. For the rest of that appalling season, the thinly populated Roots Hall was not favoured with my presence. Apart, that is, from the final match where Southend faced a battle to avoid the drama of applying for re-election to the Football League and exposing the added trauma of all those financial shenanigans before the critical eyes of the people who make decisions on these things. My final goodbye, all dues paid and an amicable *decree absolut*, I was thinking.

On that Saturday, 11 May 1985 we need to beat Torquay United at Roots Hall in the last game of the season to avoid ending the season in the bottom four of the Fourth Division and having to rely on the good offices of our Football League peers, which is not guaranteed if your club is on the verge of going broke. Torquay are already entrenched in rock-bottom position and condemned to ponder their own re-election fears. But we are coming off five defeats in a row, and we have not troubled the scoreboard in any of them. In the glare of a sunny spring afternoon, there is no disguising the empty spaces around the ground. From my usual location in the West Stand, I have a crush barrier entirely to myself. That's what an attendance of 1,704 looks like at the old Roots Hall.[27]

Not surprisingly given the circumstances, the two Uniteds serve up quite prodigious awfulness as they woofle their way through 44 minutes of thud and blunder. Just before half-time, we win a penalty from our only coherent forward movement of the entire first half. Diminutive lead striker and the only silver lining in Southend's dark cloud, Steve Phillips, strikes the penalty well enough but against the inside of the post, from where the ball 'trickled tormentingly along the line before rolling into the net'.[28] From where I'm standing, looking

---

27 Season 1984/85 registered United's lowest ever average home attendance of 2,103. Source: *Potted Shrimps*. Written by David Goody and Peter Miles. Yore Publications, 1999.

28 Source: *A Century United*.

almost directly across the line of the penalty spot, it takes an age of slow-motion to get there. As the ragged cheers echo around the wide-open spaces, I let out a long breath.

The second half is only marginally better and, although Torquay don't look like doing much, we don't either, apart from a couple of opportunities that Phillips wallops against the woodwork. After a few nervous minutes of added time, we finally stagger over the line for a 1-0 win to escape the re-election imbroglio on goal difference. At the final whistle, I see a few youthful Southend enthusiasts running on to the pitch and dancing in celebration. I also later read that a few more cavort about in the East Stand car park, but I am already on my way to the exit; I've done my bit by turning up. I amble home in the late afternoon sunshine, relieved but not euphoric.

My insouciance lasts as long as the 'on' button on the TV remote control. Then, to my goggle-eyed disbelief, I see the dilapidated wooden main stand at Bradford City's Valley Parade ground burning down at the cost of 56 lives. Then I see the pitched battles between Birmingham City and Leeds United 'supporters' on the field at St Andrew's, which result in the death of a teenage Leeds fan and injuries to 200 spectators and police. Eighteen days later comes the Heysel Stadium disaster in Brussels, a perfect storm of crumbling stadium architecture and hooliganism at its zenith, where more crowd trouble and a collapsed wall result in the death of 39 Italians at the European Cup Final between Liverpool and Juventus.

All within three weeks of each other. English football: May 1985.

Chapter 13

How I Got the Love Back

NOW DETACHED from the Southend United scene, I registered the departure of Ron Pountney before the start of the 1985/86 season with mild regret, because he had been around for ever. Chris Guthrie's departure in 1975 had more or less coincided with Pountney's arrival in the first team, but a striker he most certainly was not. Another Roots Hall Ron (though not related), this short and skinny dynamo could out-buzz Billy Best. His busy, scurrying warm-up routine on a matchday foreshadowed his feisty and focused demeanour from the first whistle as he anchored United's central midfield for ten years. With the ball at his feet Pountney already had his head up, looking for the surging run or the killer pass, be it a three-yard sideways poke or a 20-yard slider to the wing. When he didn't have the ball, no opposing midfielder was spared his close attention. Ron Pountney must have been the opponent from Hell.

Ron was intensity made flesh. He was an integral part of some of United's greatest days, and some of the worst ones too. Over ten years, he strapped himself into the Southend rollercoaster with the rest of us as we celebrated two promotions and mourned three relegations. Snakes and ladders were no stranger to him. He was the curly haired bloody nuisance who suffocated the Watford midfield on the night we turned them over to earn our FA Cup third round tie against Liverpool in

1978. He was the snapping and growling martinet that drove Southend towards the Fourth Division championship in 1981.

You wouldn't hold your breath for a Pountney goal: just 26 in more than 300 starts, but I was there for 17 of them. Ron it was who scored the late winner to beat Tranmere at Prenton Park in March 1979 and then a sneaky second-half winner three days later against Watford, when we fleetingly thought we could reach up to the twinkling lights of the Second Division. Ron was the indefatigable midfield general with the receding hairline on that 1985 day when United beat Torquay to avoid the humiliation of re-election. But Torquay was the last competitive match that Ron Pountney ever played for the Blues. Bobby Moore's decision to release him mystified me. Apparently, it mystified Ron as well. Poor old Bobby didn't get many things right as Southend manager, and he got that one wrong too.

I remember a night at Roots Hall when we are chasing the game, as so often during the Pountney years. The ball bounces over the wall into the West Stand, in front of a thinly spread group of Southend lifers. We try to grab it as it ping-pongs around the deserted terrace steps. Ron has already sprinted over for the throw-in, all sweat and heavy breathing. 'Gimmee the ball,' he gasps as he approaches. 'Gimmee the ball.' We are laughing at our clumsiness, but Ron isn't. As we make another hash of retrieving it, he roars, 'Just gimmee the ball, will you?' His arms gesticulate impatiently. Eventually, someone sheepishly delivers it into his hands and he grinds out a sarcastic 'Thanks a lot' before taking the throw and play moves on. We aren't offended; that's what he was all about. 'Super, Super Ron, Super Ronnie Pountney,' as the old song went.

* * *

Three months after Heysel brought a new season, but no league football on the TV, live or recorded, due to some dispute or other between the Football League and Independent Television. I have nothing better to do on the Friday evening of 23 August 1985 and decide to rock along to Roots Hall for United's first home match against the Orient; more out of curiosity than desire. Up front for Southend and playing against his old club is a new signing, a short, stocky striker I've never heard of.

Ninety minutes later, Richard Cadette has scored four goals on debut for a 5-1 win in front of a delighted crowd of 3,643, our biggest attendance in nearly two years. In 90 minutes, I am hooked once again and the divorce is rescinded for good, as simple and as complicated as that.

In all honesty, United did not play much better than they had the previous season. After a strong start, when we are unbeaten in our first eight games and crowds soar at Roots Hall, 8,120 fans (including me, of course) receive another salutary slap-down from Colchester United in October, this time a 4-2 defeat. And that sparked off a decline in performance and attendances that was no less disappointing for being half-expected. It made little difference to me; once again I was stuck with it.

I am even there on a miserable Wednesday night in March 1986 when we beat Halifax Town 2-1 in front of an embarrassing and embarrassed congregation of 1,006 under the unforgiving lights. The smallest crowd for a league match in Roots Hall and Southend United history stays in my memory for all the wrong reasons as a football match unfolds in virtual silence, punctuated with sporadic catcalls.[29]

United ended the 1985/86 season in an anonymous ninth place, never quite in the promotion race. Crowds were up; not by much but still reversing a six-year decline and comfortably confounding the Football League statistics which reported the lowest average attendances since the advent of the four

29 www.european-football-statistics.co.uk records 1985/86 as the lowest average attendance since the advent of the modern Football League.

divisions in 1921. Cadette scored 25 league goals in his first season. If a corner hadn't been turned that season at least it felt as if we could actually see a corner ahead and a cautious – very cautious – waft of optimism was abroad.

By the end of that season, I had bought a new home and landed a new job (I played safe and went for the Central London option). The deep, lasting relationship took a while longer, after a false start or three. But, without a doubt, it was the understated genius of Richard Cadette who brought the love for Southend back to me. It was not an unconditional return. I reserved the right to pay occasional visits to other football grounds, and I did. White Hart Lane, Highbury, Upton Park, the City Ground, Villa Park, Hillsborough, Anfield, Goodison, Maine Road, Old Trafford; all the big arenas took my money. But without Richard I might have ended up as one of those home counties Manchester United enthusiasts so unfairly derided as 'plastics': impoverished by travel and ticket costs, hollow-eyed from early morning and late-night encounters with the M1 and M6 motorways, a sad husk of a human being with no mates and no girlfriends. That's why I will always thank my lucky stars for Richard Cadette.

***

Ninth place and Richard Cadette were not enough to save poor old Bobby Moore, who vacated the manager's office at the end of the 1985/86 season. Mum, as usual, nailed it. 'The trouble with Bobby Moore is that he's too nice to be a manager, he won the World Cup and everybody loves him,' she remarked. 'What Southend need is a tough old bugger like Jack Charlton.' Well, Charlton had some tough old bugger credentials, and he'd won the World Cup as well, but the Republic of Ireland had got there first. Instead, Moore's replacement was a tough young bugger, David Webb, who arrived from unfashionable Torquay and transformed the atmosphere immediately.

To collective shock and horror, Webb departed in March 1987 with two months of the season still to run and United battling for promotion. Apparently, a furious dispute with Chairman Vic over transfer funding culminated in Webb walking out, claiming that he was being 'treated like a dirty rag'. Webb's words of wisdom inspired much hilarity among my Central London work colleagues, none of whom had any sympathy.

In Webb's place, Chairman Vic appointed a caretaker manager, but what a caretaker. He couldn't point to any previous management experience, but he knew the club from top to bottom, right back to the mid-1970s. Welcome Paul Clark, United defender, captain and fixer-upper of other people's messes.

Chairman Vic was busy in other areas too. Noises about a new stadium were starting to emanate from the boardroom. Initially, the noises were about moving the club to a new stadium in another town 15 miles west of Southend and well on the way towards London. Bollocks to that. 'We'll never go to Basildon' (and other, less than complimentary, observations about the chairman and the board of directors) rang around Roots Hall until common sense prevailed.

Yet another Friday night at Roots Hall, 24 April 1987. A season-best crowd of 10,369 is assembling in the mild evening air; just as well, as my train from London is delayed for reasons unexplained and not for the first time on match night. As a result, I sheepishly take up my West Stand position in City suit and tie having walked directly to the ground from the station – and I'm not the only one. A light haze lies over the ground mingling with the smoke of nervous pre-match ciggies, the floodlights casting a haloed glow over the South Bank and the 1,000 or so away supporters tightly gathered in its centre. We are sitting in a handy third place with four games to play and tonight, in another throw of the dice on the Snakes and Ladders board, we are playing the fallen giants

Wolverhampton Wanderers, who are only one point and one position behind us. The match matters even more than it would have done in times past, for this season has seen the introduction of the Football League play-offs, and finishing fourth does not guarantee automatic promotion any more. Instead, it gets you the stress of an extended season as you battle your way through a two-legged semi-final and then a two-legged final. Hence the biggest attendance at Roots Hall for six years; hence the strong and vociferous turnout from the Black Country.

Wolves have only just started on the road to recovery, following a rapid and catastrophic slide down the longest snake in league football from First Division to Fourth. To be honest, Wolves are better than us, their team including the human battering-ram called Steve Bull ('Bully' to friend and foe alike), a ferocious amalgam of speed, technique and brawn, topped with a throwback skinhead blade one haircut. We don't have anyone like that. And indeed, for most of the first half, Bully is putting himself about with gusto. Southend defenders bounce off his frame as he careers towards goal with the steely eyed intensity that was, in my opinion, later so woefully underused by England in the 1990 World Cup. Surely, it's only a matter of time before Wolves score. But there is a goal, and it doesn't come from Bully. United break free down the right, the ball is floated across, the unmarked Martin Ling drifts in from the left wing, leaps to connect from 15 yards out and his header describes a teasing parabolic arc over the Wolves goalkeeper before the ball lands securely in the South Bank net. Our resident cheeky chappie, the mop-haired Ling gallops past the stranded goalie, arms outstretched, and then wheels away past the Wolves fans behind the goal, waving benignly. The Wolves fans wave back, less benignly.

Into the second half and suddenly it's the old Watford FA Cup replay all over again. This time it's the Wolves who are pressing, with the Southend defence and midfield struggling to hold the line. Bully is running amok, as if on a one-man kamikaze mission. Tonight, it's Roy McDonough who can't 'hold on to the bloody ball', it's Shane Westley who needs to 'stop poncing about and get rid', it's Glenn Pennyfather who finds himself with 'Man on!' and invokes 'oh, Jesus Christ' as his attempts to regain control are frustrated by the Wolves snapping at his heels. But, despite the flash-bang-wallop around the penalty area that characterises a team with Steve Bull in it, once again United are keeping them out, and 'Come on you Blues' begins rolling around three sides of the ground in a raucous, beseeching wave.

The screech of premature whistles from the crowd, because we still have no way of knowing how much added time there is, is finally answered by the only whistle that matters and we Southend fans are weak at the knees with jubilation and relief. Nobody invades the pitch, because the local constabulary don't allow that any more. The silence from the South Bank is palpable, until some Wolves players make their way over and applaud their travelling faithful. The applause in return is less than rapturous, as the denizens of the Black Country contemplate their four-hour journey home empty-handed. I live closer to Roots Hall than that and can walk home; I don't even have to climb the South Bank to retrieve the car. I can walk out of the West Stand into Shakespeare Drive and adjourn to the nearby Plough Hotel for a couple of calming beers amid curious looks from the clientele, because I'm still wearing my suit and tie. Are there better ways to spend a Friday night and welcome the weekend? I can think of a few, but not many.

With all due respect to the Wolves supporters, a comparison between the excited 10,369 crowd at Roots Hall in April 1987 and the forlorn 1,006 who had turned up for the Halifax embarrassment 13 months earlier tells of a corner being turned. Certainly, the size of the Southend following for the final, promotion-clinching match at Stockport County's

Edgeley Park matched the Halifax game turnout. Cadette's 24th goal of the season was our second in a 2-0 victory and would have made the long journey home all the more worthwhile – if I'd actually made the journey. Stockport on a Friday night was just too hard.

But the main reason I remember Southend United versus Wolverhampton Wanderers 1987 is Martin Ling's looping header and his cheeky, regal wave to the Wolves fans. To sentimental old me, Ling was also waving a metaphorical farewell to the immense 72-step, 15,000-capacity South Bank, on the last occasion it had anything like a crowd standing on it. Just over a year later, Chairman Vic found a way to mitigate his Basildon stadium setback by demolishing virtually all of the South Bank to make way for Priory Court, a few blocks of medium-rise apartments, leaving behind a sad, 15-step remnant of what had once towered over the whole stadium.

If we thought that the good on-field times were already back, we had another think coming. Richard Cadette was stolen by Sheffield United for a derisory £120,000 (some reports suggest even less), and it took us a while to find a replacement. For reasons unknown to me and my fellow nonplussed West Standers, Paul Clark's caretaker position was not formalised as Chairman Vic decided to appoint Dick Bate, intriguingly named but shockingly inexperienced and ultimately useless who lasted less than three months in the management hot seat. Our start to the new season was so dire (an 8-1 defeat at Gillingham followed by a 6-2 defeat at Notts County were not the only shockers) that recalling the early season fiasco still makes me shiver.

Quite rightly, Paul Clark returned to his personal player-manager labour of Hercules. In Clark's first match back, United defeat First Division Derby County 1-0 in the first leg of the League Cup second round at Roots Hall, to universal amazement. We beat Brighton 2-1 at Roots Hall to register our first league win of the season. Then we cemented an aggregate win against Derby with a barely believable 0-0 draw in the second leg at the Baseball Ground. Life was never meant to be this easy, and it wasn't. United were still all over the place and the Great Storm of 15 and 16 October 1987 stands out to me as a metaphor for the latest turbulent period in the club's history.

On the Thursday night, I was rudely awakened by the howl of the wind, the shuddering of the foundations of my home and the shattering crash of slates ripped from the roof and cast to the ground. Unable to sleep, I sat quietly in the bay window of the lounge as uprooted trees and bushes tumbled past and my roof disintegrated, slate by slate. When the attic door started rhythmically banging open and shut, I knew that the roof was gone. The hurricane, because a hurricane it was and not the breezy night forecast by the BBC, wiped out the rail services to London the next morning. As I wandered around, surveying the wreckage that littered the power-cut Westcliff-on-Sea on my impromptu day off, I was stunned to discover that Roots Hall had secured an electricity generator and the match was still on.

So it is that, on Friday, 16 October 1987, I leave home and the billowing tarpaulin that is my roof for the next few days to pick my way around the fallen greenery and scattered brickwork towards Roots Hall, with the floodlights blazing above the dark streets below like four upright beacons of defiance. With 2,217 similarly defiant folk who have somehow made their way to the ground, I see Southend grind out a 1-1 draw with Rotherham United, by no means our worst result at that stage in the season. Dunkirk spirit under the lights from clubs, players and intrepid supporters.

It all started to unravel again with a 7-0 defeat at Sunderland bringing us back to the real world. But Paul Clark had a plan. Midfielder Glenn Pennyfather trod the Peter 'Spud' Taylor path to Crystal Palace for a sizeable fee and some of this cash was used to entice seasoned striker David Crown from Cambridge United. Defensively, we were a disaster; up front, we were operating with one and a half strikers. Fortunately for us, Crown had a more than decent scoring record at Cambridge and took to his task almost immediately. Neither short nor tall, neither thin nor fat, he couldn't stop scoring as we started ever so slowly to turn the tide.

In a season of the unexpected, we saw the return of the dirty rag to the role of general manager, while Clark continued as team manager. How the David Webb and Paul Clark duo would work was anyone's guess, but at least we managed to win more than we lost, keeping us in touch with safety. But April Fools' Day 1988 coincides with Good Friday and we are still in the relegation zone. I've thought about giving it a miss, but I've managed to talk an old friend into forsaking the pub and making his once-in-a-decade trip to Roots Hall.

It serves me right, because United are 2-0 down to Wigan Athletic with not very long to go. The friend is in merciless wind-up mode, 'Excuse me, what are we doing here … Good job I only turn up once in a blue moon,' and so on. Out of the blue comes a penalty for United, emphatically converted by our resident 'big 'un up front', Roy McDonough. With time running out, an equaliser comes out of the blue by Martin Ling. The Easter holiday gathering of 5,003 is making big noise as the clock ticks down and then Crown thunders towards the penalty area, ball at his feet. We know what's going to happen, it's happened so often, as David hammers his trademark drive low into the net. Roots Hall explodes. United have nicked it 3-2 in the final minutes and we move out of the relegation zone for the first time all season.

Of course, it wouldn't be Southend if there wasn't another spanner or two chucked into the works, but in the last match against Blackpool at Roots Hall, we wallop them 4-0 without major drama and reach safety. Crown scores the nerve-settling second goal just after the break and celebrates by performing a cheerful, quirky little dance in front of a sad, deserted little terrace overlooked by an even sadder mound of grass, weeds, dirt and a few rusting crush barriers; all that remains of the partially demolished South Bank.

With Paul Clark and David Webb at the helm, a recovery on the pitch finally slotted into place and we just about got away with it. But if it hadn't been for the goals of the reliable David Crown, a late scoring flurry from the sprightly Martin Ling and the acquisition of a new midfield terrier in Peter Butler, an immediate return to the Fourth Division would have been inevitable. All the while, the Southend public remained largely unconvinced, despite early signs of a recovery in attendances across the Football League as a whole. Average home crowds of 3,700 did not a fortress make.

On the afternoon of Saturday, 15 April 1989, I was enjoying a leisurely walk around Chalkwell Park in the warm spring sunshine and in a good mood. The previous evening, I had seen United turn over Reading 2-1 at Roots Hall to Crown (pun intended, because David scored both goals) a fourth successive win and a climb out of the relegation zone. A friend's wedding and a big overseas holiday were a few days in the future, so I would miss the next two home games in a part of the world where news of Southend would be non-existent. But I would be home just in time for the last match against Chester City, hopefully to celebrate another great escape.

In the park, I overheard news of a commotion somewhere from the blare of a passing radio. I rushed home and tuned into a live TV broadcast from Hillsborough, where there was supposed to be an FA Cup semi-final between Liverpool and Nottingham Forest in progress. This was strange, because the semi-finals were not broadcast live in 1989, otherwise I would have been watching it. There was no match in progress either, which was also strange. In the brilliant sunshine of Sheffield were spectators, police, medical crew with stretchers, civilians with makeshift stretchers fashioned out of advertising hoardings, ambulances and bodies laid on the pitch in front of the fences fronting the terrace at the Leppings Lane End still crammed with Liverpool supporters. There were 94 dead bodies on the day, to be 95 shortly afterwards, 96 by 1993 and, finally, 97 in 2021.

The inquests, commissions and investigations of the worst disaster in England's football history have been ongoing for more than 30 years. I can only add my own emotions as I surveyed the carnage on the day: horror and sadness, sometimes anger, and these are still my feelings today. My intense distaste for football post-Hillsborough didn't last for long and I knew it wouldn't, but it took a close-season for the intensity to dissipate entirely.

It could have happened to any of us. Maybe we'd been getting away with it for years. The dilapidation of old football grounds laid bare by Valley Parade, the long-standing issues with crowd control culminating in the Heysel disaster and the inadequate attempt to resolve Heysel by planting high fences in stadia like Hillsborough not designed for the purpose, meant things had to change. And change they did, but it took a while. In any event, English football has not suffered any Valley Parades, Heysels or Hillsboroughs for the past 35 years and, for that, we should be grateful.

Chapter 14

The End of the Beginning

ON THE final day of the 1988/89 season, United had to beat Chester City at Roots Hall and Blackpool had to lose at Cardiff City. Blackpool saved themselves with a 0-0 draw and our 1-0 win was all for nought. I didn't go. Typically, we went down with a total of 54 points, a league record in the three points for a win era and one we share with Peterborough United. It wasn't David Crown's fault: with 25 goals, he scored virtually half our total for the season, giving him a scoring record of 42 goals in 72 games from the day he arrived at Roots Hall. Impressive, but now we needed him more than ever. And was he ready?

***

A new season, a sensational two-legged win over Colchester United in the Littlewoods Cup (this year's version of the League Cup) and, for a change, Southend have received the second-round draw they deserve. It's early evening on Wednesday, 4 October 1989 and I am in suit and tie, sitting in the fast train from Fenchurch Street, sharing a carriage with a substantial number of well-behaved Tottenham Hotspur supporters. My eyes leave the evening paper I am fitfully reading and gaze out at the remains of a livid crimson sunset fading over Pitsea Marshes, a flat, darkening expanse of nothing much heading out towards the ultramarine line of the distant River Thames.

I may be showing my age, but I can remember when the self-designated 'pride of north London' were universally called 'The Spurs'. That quaint moniker went out of fashion around 1970, about the same time as the word soccer was finally and rightly superseded by the word football in Britain. Spurs and soccer; Tottenham and football; there's a kind of social and cultural historical symmetry about it. The Spurs they were when they knocked Southend out of the FA Cup way back in 1921 on the way to a victorious conclusion in the final and then again in a 1936 replay at Grainger Road, following an improbable 4-4 draw at White Hart Lane, but, by the next time we play them more than 50 years later, they are definitely Tottenham. Forget about different planets; Tottenham are in a different universe.

As the train stops at the outer suburbs of Southend, other besuited commuters leave the train and are replaced by small groups of youthful, nervous-looking United supporters, who make themselves inconspicuous. Thankfully, there are no challenging glares, no taunting banter, no flying boots, because Southend are not Arsenal and Tottenham are not West Ham. Public transport could get a bit feral on matchdays back in the late 80s. On one late train ride home, I witnessed the unedifying spectacle of a few 'supporters' of Arsenal and West Ham knocking seven bells out of each other in my carriage; and Arsenal hadn't even played West Ham that night.

I have the ticket for the second leg securely in my jacket pocket, just in case the trains go on the blink and I have to walk directly to Roots Hall from another late-running train and stand self-consciously under the bright floodlights in suit and tie. Network SouthEast behaves itself tonight and I leave the train at Westcliff, my local station, in good time to get home and plunge into jeans, jumper and light jacket. I pick up the old blue and white scarf I reserve for special occasions, drape it over my shoulders (not wound around the neck, not ever) and step out of the front door into the mild, still autumn night. And if Southend United against Tottenham Hotspur is not a special occasion, I don't know what is.

* * *

For Tottenham, Paul Gascoigne has arrived from Newcastle United and is already embarking on his road to the England national team and Italia 90 World Cup immortality. Gary Lineker, already an English living legend from his exploits in the 1986 Mexico World Cup, is plying his trade as Tottenham's attacking spearhead. To my mind his hat-trick against Poland in that World Cup, which saved England from an abysmal group stage elimination, kicked off the slow recovery of English football from its post-Valley Parade and Heysel malaise. Lineker has returned from Barcelona, from the Camp Nou to Roots Hall in a matter of months. The world of football turns in mysterious ways.

Tottenham are a leading light in the First Division and clear favourites tonight: an indifferent start of the season to be sure, but we expect the Spurs to turn it around, as they normally do. United are back in the Fourth Division, but we have started off the new season in good nick and currently sit top of the league, which may explain why we managed to keep Tottenham down to 1-0 in the first leg, leaving the second leg alive and kicking. I don't expect us to win tonight, but I hope that the Blues will put on a performance we can be proud of.

As I take my usual place in the West Stand, I can feel the buzz of a big Roots Hall night. Presumably as a result of the Hillsborough disaster and a stringent risk assessment from health and safety bureaucrats or the local police, or both, Roots Hall has an imposed crowd capacity of 10,418. I can see Tottenham fans packed into the South Paddock, a block of seats in the East Stand and, perversely given the recent Hillsborough experience, squeezed in behind a fenced-off partition on the remains of the South Bank. Meanwhile, we fortunate 8,000-plus home supporters luxuriate in the half-empty expanses of the West Stand and North Bank. Even so, tonight's attendance is the biggest at Roots Hall for eight years.

Tonight, the stadium is entertained by a pipe band, complete with kilts, sporrans and tam o' shanters. Although both teams hail from somewhere south of Hadrian's Wall, the skirl of bagpipes and the thud of the drums add to the sense of occasion. As the band marches off, the United players canter on to the pitch in their royal blue shirts and garish yellow shorts; no way am I ever going to buy a pair of those. 'Yellows, Yellows,' bay the home supporters, weirdly singing for the shorts, not the shirt. A moment later, the Tottenham players emerge and run towards the South Bank, giving their adoring supporters a quick but purposeful round of applause.

From the first kick, it's clear that both teams have decided to go for it. With a more direct playing style this season than we Southend purists are used to, United have tall and hefty Gary Bennett up front, operating down the right. David Crown has a roving commission across the front line. Tall and hefty Roy McDonough is playing just off Bennett and Crown down the middle – what might now be called a 'false nine', but wasn't in 1989. Five minutes gone and a corner for United: in it comes and tousle-haired defensive midfielder David Martin leaps above the Tottenham defence and emphatically directs his header downwards into the corner of the net. He wheels away in a characteristic, crouching, scurrying sprint of delight, pursued by his team-mates; 1-0 to United after just five minutes – and level on aggregate. 'Yellows, Yellows!' booms around three sides of Roots Hall.

Bennett is playing the game of his United career, marauding down the right wing in front of the West Stand and torturing Tottenham's left-back, Mitchell Thomas. McDonough is winning more than his fair share of high balls and Crown is all over the pitch with danger in his boots. Left, right, centre, blink and you'll miss him. Lineker and Gascoigne miss in quick succession, Crown drives the ball low into the middle and McDonough hits the bar. It's end-to-end stuff and we're breathless. On 40 minutes, Crown latches on to a loose ball on the left: another low driven cross and Bennett loses his marker to steam in and lash the ball high into the net. Two up and we are now ahead on aggregate. In the West Stand, we are incredulous at the sheer cheek of it all. 'Here we go, here we go, here we go, here we go,' Roots Hall gleefully sings at the stony-faced Tottenham supporters. Of course, it can't last; Paul Allen plays a one-two with Lineker and tucks the ball away to bring the score back to 2-1 just before half-time and level the aggregate scores. Even then, there is still time for McDonough to find the net, but the 'goal' is disallowed for a slightly unlucky offside. Half-time arrives to give the crowd a chance to catch its breath and for some of us in the West Stand to change ends, because we have plenty of room in which to do it.

In 1989, I don't recall that a particular derogatory term to describe Tottenham Hotspur was around. The consensus definition of 'Spursy' is the desire to play football as it should be played, with style and *élan*, 'push and run' like the stylish Spurs teams of the 50s, exponents of 'the glory game' as espoused by Tottenham's 'double'-winning captain Danny Blanchflower in the early 60s; but all too often accompanied by the lack of end product and a tendency to wilt under pressure. Other definitions include more prosaic words, involving 'guts' or 'spine'. In the 1987 FA Cup Final, Tottenham had gloriously pushed and run their way to a 3-2 defeat by fearless, robust and resilient Coventry City, a performance that could have written the rule book for Spursiness.

How Spursy are Tottenham tonight? Well, McDonough is dominating England centre-back Gary Mabbutt, Bennett is murdering Thomas, Crown is making the whole Tottenham defence look statuesque and Lineker is subdued. And the scoreline tells its own story, perhaps. But there's nothing Spursy about Terry Fenwick, a well-known hardman of the

80s. Nor about Paul Stewart, a bustling in-your-face forward. Early into the second half, the United right-back Paul Roberts ends up in a heap right in front of me, with Stewart in close, wild-eyed proximity. 'Off, off, off' chimes 80 per cent of Roots Hall, followed by a mighty cheer as the referee produces the red card. Nothing Spursy about Nayim, a nuggety Spanish midfielder, who dummies the entire United defence to make space and bury a drive into the corner to equalise and put ten-man Tottenham ahead on aggregate.

Nor is there anything Spursy about Gascoigne – never Gazza – who takes over the match from midfield, winning and holding the ball, incisive short passes, visionary longer passes sprayed to all corners, and powering forward with the sharp turn of pace often missed by the TV cameras. 'We are Tottenham, we are Tottenham, super Tottenham, from the Lane,' rings out from the South Bank, to the tune of Rod Stewart's 'Sailing'.

And yet – McDonough wins the ball in the air for the umpteenth time, Bennett loses his marker again and slips his shot under the Tottenham keeper for United's third goal. Bennett performs a joyous slide towards the rejoicing North Bank, fists in the air, shouting his head off. Level on aggregate once again. 'You're not singing, you're not singing, you're not singing any more' crows the West Stand, North Bank, most of the East Stand and even a segregated section of the South Bank, taunting fingers pointed at the Tottenham fans, who look stunned. But nothing stuns Gascoigne; two more near misses from him. Then, with minutes remaining, United's Ron Pountney-esque midfield terrier, Peter Butler, wins the ball in midfield, where it breaks off a Tottenham defender and releases Crown, who is in the clear. With the expectant roar of the crowd building in his ears, a characteristic galloping run, a characteristic low drive past the keeper and United fans are aghast as the ball hits the post and bounces away instead of ending up in the net. And then 90 minutes are up, to another ovation from all sides of Roots Hall. Crowd and players are running on adrenalin and there's still 30 minutes of extra time to go.

In the first period, Tottenham are kicking towards the North Bank and are on top again. Lineker hits the post with a bicycle kick of serpentine agility, then Nayim breaks clear of the United defence, rounds the keeper and scores with aplomb; 3-3 we think. But I have changed ends for the second time and I crane my neck to see the referee striding to the linesman. A brief discussion and the 'goal' is disallowed. Handball. Offside. There's no knowing from my position but it's struck off anyway. How we laugh; how we cheer.

Second period of extra time and I've changed ends for the third time. Ah, Roy McDonough, another polarising presence in the United forward line. Gary Moore reincarnated, apart from the mullet and moustache and I never got his autograph. Sometimes thoroughbred, sometimes carthorse, sometimes both within a few seconds, he has also made a career of collecting red cards. Therefore, it is no great surprise that a mistimed sliding tackle and a tumbling white-shirted figure right in front of the Tottenham hordes is followed by the ominous chorus of 'Off, off, off'. Here comes the red card and Roy is walking towards the players' tunnel to jeering farewell waves from 2,000 fans in white and a standing ovation from 8,000 in blue. It's not quite all over; a sharp, late chance for Crown is blocked by the keeper. And that is that. Shortly afterwards, the referee blows for full time. We've seen a high-speed, helter-skelter game: full-blooded, feisty, sometimes a bit rough, exhausting for players and supporters alike and ending 3-2 to Southend.

Ten years and four days before this night, I had seen United draw 0-0 with West Ham at Roots Hall after a 1-1 draw at Upton Park. Away goals didn't count double in those days and we ended up losing the toss for the venue and collapsing in the replay. So: what's it to be tonight? A replay? Penalties?

Neither. Inevitably, the away goals rule was introduced to the League Cup the season after our West Ham marathon and Tottenham's two at Roots Hall are enough to secure their onward passage and United's elimination. Another egregious appearance by Noah Vale.[30]

What we've got is a final standing ovation and a few kids streaming on to the pitch, dodging the dogs leashed to the local constabulary. And the memory of United's performance brimming with excitement, passion, grit and no little skill. Viewed in retrospect, the Tottenham match kicked off a new wave of hope and confidence in us world-weary supporters. To slightly misquote Winston Churchill, Southend United versus Tottenham Hotspur, October 1989, was not the end. It was not even the beginning of the end. But it was, perhaps, the end of the beginning.[31]

**

Seven months later, on Saturday, 5 May 1990, I am sweltering under the roof of the Moy's End terrace with around 1,000 Southend supporters at a sun-baked London Road, the home of Peterborough United. After a strange season in which fleeting florets of wins have alternated with brief tumbleweeds of defeats, we have still remained in the promotion frame and the last match has arrived with a simple equation: we have to win to guarantee promotion back to the Third Division and Peterborough have to win to secure a place in the play-offs. Today, we are in our all-yellow away kit, but there are other differences between now and the Tottenham game. Raw-

---

30 The away goals rule was abolished for the League Cup (or the Carabao Cup as it is now called) in 2018 – only 30 years too late.

31 The actual Churchillian quotation is, 'Now this is not the end. It is not the beginning of the end. But it is, perhaps, the end of the beginning.' From Winston Churchill's speech to the London Lord Mayor's luncheon at the Mansion House on 10 November 1942. Churchill was referring to the Allied victory at the second Battle of El Alamein, which helped turn the tide of the second world war.

boned Gary Bennett, the hammer of the Spurs, has left for Chester City and big Roy McDonough is now an infrequent inhabitant of the substitutes' bench. Thankfully, we still have David Crown who retains his roving commission as a defender's nightmare. We also have the cool, elegant and athletic Ian Benjamin in our ranks. He was well known for his habit of regularly driving a spoke into United's wheels during his own Cook's tour of the lower divisions, especially during his time at Northampton Town, but has now become poacher turned gamekeeper and signed from Exeter City to join Crown up front.

Nerves are jangling at kick-off, but United settle quicker. With 15 minutes gone, Benjamin heads forward, Crown picks the pocket of a home defender and bears down on goal. A shot with his left foot, driven low as we have seen so many times, a dreadful misfield by the Peterborough goalkeeper and the ball crawls into the net. Twenty-one minutes gone and a long ball out of defence finds Crown unmarked on the right. Another driving run, another low drive from his right foot this time and the ball is in the net to put us two up and comfortably in charge.

But comfortable and supporting Southend are not mutually inclusive. A 2-0 lead at half-time becomes 2-1 within a few minutes. More fingernail damage for me as Peterborough are pressing. But as the game opens up, we have our moments on the break as well. Crown bears down from the left, ball at his feet. A last-ditch challenge in the penalty area and down goes David. The United fans bellow, it looks like a clear penalty to my eyes (not that I am always the most objective of observers), but the referee waves our appeals away and Crown thumps the ground in anguish.

The Peterborough left-back hoists the ball into the United penalty area, it bobbles around dangerously and goalkeeper Paul Sansome makes a kamikaze dive at the feet of the Peterborough striker to block. As the ball continues to bounce around in the area, Sansome puts his body on the line for a second time and barges through a morass of attackers and defenders to fist clear. After a period of added time that seems endless – still no added time signs or stadium announcements – the referee finally blows his whistle; 2-1 to United and the Southend players sprint *en masse* towards their jubilant fans. Some of them strip off their yellow shirts and throw them to the crowd. I didn't get one, I left them to the kids but my euphoria lasted through the three-hour journey home.

David Crown scored the two goals that sealed our triumph and he completes my autograph collection. Nineteen league goals for the season (despite an inconvenient dry run of one in 16 at an awkward time). In total, 61 goals in 113 games – an amazing return, considering what he had to work with.

The Southend United Chronicles with the scrawled autographs on the title page in black and blue biro sits in front of me as I write these words. One little page encapsulating the snakes and ladders of three decades in the club's history and a significant part of my personal history as well. Kellard, Jones, Costello, Best, Garner, Pountney, Crown. Slips of paper with the signatures of McKinven, Moore and Guthrie from other sources. Nobody seems to collect autographs any more, not when you can get a selfie. I don't care; selfies don't mean the same to me. Even now I still pine for the old coloured cardboard team line-up with the autographs of England World Cup heroes Bobby Moore, Geoff Hurst and Martin Peters that I somehow managed to lose when moving house in 1979.

There is one autograph I didn't lose and treasure to this day. I'll see your Moore, Hurst, Peters and raise you. In late 1996, Kim and I were at a restaurant just off Kings Road in Chelsea with a small group of friends. To our astonishment, the front door opened and George Best ambled in, sharing a laugh with Rodney Marsh. Rodney the footballer was a famous and much-loved cheeky chappie of the 60s and 70s, starring for Queens Park Rangers, Manchester City and not often enough for England. George and Rodney had enjoyed a brief sojourn at Fulham in the twilight of their careers, delighting Craven Cottage and the TV viewing public with pure Hollywood football. Then Mark Lawrenson, stern and stalwart defender from Liverpool's golden years, strode in. He never did Hollywood football.

There was a TV sports social event going on in the back room. I was too starstruck, so Kim made the request. Not only did we get the precious signatures on the back of a bar tab, George and Rodney joined us for a drink or two and the opportunity to shoot the breeze on things football for 30 minutes of pure magic.

George Best and Billy Best: footballing contemporaries, same surname, but a universe apart. Snakes and ladders in a name: priceless.

***

Another decade had passed. There we were; back in the Third Division, exactly where we had arrived in 1981. Charles Dickens was thinking about Britain and France in the late 18th century and was certainly not thinking about United when he put pen to paper thus, 'It was the best of times, it was the worst of times, it was the age of wisdom, it was the age of foolishness, it was the epoch of belief, it was the epoch of incredulity, it was the season of light, it was the season of darkness, it was the spring of hope, it was the winter of despair.'[32] He didn't know it, but Dickens could have been writing an allegory of Southend United in the 1980s. Given our past history, what the next decade would bring was anyone's guess. But for both of us, United and me, the next decade would be different from the 1980s and, indeed, all the decades before that.

---

32 The Dickens quote comes from the first paragraph of *A Tale of Two Cities*, written by Charles Dickens, originally published in 1859. Sourced from my Dickens collection, published by Octopus Books, 1986.

Chapter 15

The Dream

SUPPORTING A lower-division team confers heroic status on those who take up the burden. The eternal optimist, the irascible old moaner, the amateur comedian, the silently suffering stoic, the red-faced ranting loony: yes, I've been all of these people, though not necessarily in a single game. Some fans, however, seem to have particular character traits embedded in their DNA. I've seen endless examples at Roots Hall.

A few terrace steps away from my second-half position on the West Stand in the late 1980s and early 1990s stood a distinctive-looking couple. The overgrown schoolboy in me christened them Sid and Doris Bonkers after the supporters of the fictional and serially unsuccessful Neasden United FC from the satirical magazine *Private Eye*. Some of my West Stand chums called them Mr and Mrs Average, but they weren't. Sid was tall, wafer-thin and ramrod-straight. His matchday outfit consisted of a long overcoat, a tartan scarf, a beanie and hiking boots for the wintry days we learned to expect at any time between October and April. Doris was a full head and shoulders shorter than Sid, loyally kitted out in blue and white scarf and bobble hat, always well and wisely wrapped up in a black anorak autumn, winter and spring.

Rarely raising their voices for the West Stand songs and chants, Sid greeted United goals with a reserved, haughty semi-enthusiasm, while Doris managed a more animated response which involved vigorous bobbling of the bobble hat. He was also prone to delivering a stentorian bellow of disconcerting volume but uncertain meaning at unexpected times, leaving those around him temporarily dumbstruck. At half-time, Sid produced a Thermos flask from the small rucksack he used to carry (I'm not sure if Thermos flasks are still allowed at football grounds), and they toasted each other with tea, coffee, Bovril; whatever Sids and Dorises put into Thermos flasks at football matches 35 years ago. To my mind, it was being outwardly so uninteresting that made them so interesting.

Sid and Doris Bonkers, an intriguing addition to the rich tapestry of United fans across the ages as they take their place, with all the others, as heroes. Be honest: for those who support lower-division teams, there's a bit of Sid or Doris in all of us, isn't there?

**

Southend United have celebrated the start of the 1990s by trumping the season of so much promise and returning to the Third Division, albeit by the skin of their teeth. As the 1990/91 season approaches, their exploits in the transfer market are, as usual, a mixed bag. Roy McDonough has left for Colchester United, just as Gary Moore did 15 years before, and goes on to achieve great things as player and coach. I forgive him, especially as Colchester languish in non-league for a while. But United have inexplicably failed to retain the icon that is David Crown and he departs over the Thames and up the Medway to Gillingham. This makes me quite unhappy for quite some time.

Fortunately, we have kept most of our best players and made some key signings. Paul Sansome, who never gets injured and never loses form, is entrenched as our goalkeeper. Dean Austin, who arrived late last season, is our busy, stylish full-back on the right. Chris Powell, just as busy and stylish as

Austin but on the left side of defence, has joined from Crystal Palace. David Martin, our marauding defensive midfielder from the Tottenham match, is joined by the towering Spencer Prior, a young local lad who has just recovered from serious injury. Paul Clark is still the rock holding the back line together. Steve Tilson, a strong-limbed, hardworking left-sided midfielder who knows where the goal is, has just broken through after a couple of years under the radar. I'd seen him score his first goal for United, a storming effort, against the Wolves back in March 1989 and couldn't work out why he wasn't an automatic starter. Peter Butler, who really could be Ron Pountney in disguise (*sans* bubble cut) is orchestrating the play from central midfield. Andy Ansah, a fast, tricky goalscoring right-winger, joined from Brentford last season and has shown enough promise to secure a starting position. Ian Benjamin has already shown his class in a blue shirt and is still with us. Even our supporting cast is encouraging. Adam Locke is a ready-made replacement across our front line because he knows where the goal is as well. John Cornwell has joined from Swindon Town and can stand in as defender or central midfielder. Christian Hyslop, another tall defender, is a local boy at the start of his career with the unfortunate nickname of 'Sloppy' awarded to him by the West Stand. Andy 'Eagle' Edwards, yet another young, towering central defender, awaits his chance.

To soothe my David Crown angst, we have acquired an authentic 'big 'un up front'. Brett Angell was last season's Fourth Division Golden Boot winner for Stockport County and we have snagged him for the significant fee of a hundred grand. Angell is not your common or garden lower division centre-forward, however: good in the air he is, not averse to putting himself about, but he is also quick, clever and has magic in left and right boots. A powerful striker spearheading a potentially powerful outfit in all positions. Sammy, Deano, Chrissie, Marts, Spenno, Clarkey, Tilly, Butts, Andy, Benji,

Lockey, Corny, Sloppy, Eagle, Bretty. A squad of nicknames reflecting a new era of familiarity and the dawning realisation that all of my current on-field heroes are now younger than I am. And the whole ensemble is managed by the one we never called Webby: the talismanic David Webb.

* * *

After five games, we have five wins and crowds are edging above the 5,000 level for the first time in years, but a reality check is due and is duly provided by fallen giants Stoke City, who thump us 4-0 at their Victoria Ground. Not an ideal prelude for a cup tie against a First Division team, especially when that team is Crystal Palace.

It's second round, first leg day in the Rumbelows Cup (as the League Cup is known this year) on Tuesday, 25 September 1990. I am at Palace's Selhurst Park ground, with the anthem 'Eagles, Eagles' droning around me, but I'm not with 'David Webb's Yellow Blue Army' on the Holmesdale Road terrace as I should be. Not even with the small group of United supporters seated in one corner of the Arthur Waite Stand. Instead, I am sitting with the home supporters a few yards away from my normal comrades next to a good friend, a staunch Palace fan. Plus, I have bought the tickets because it happens to be my friend's birthday. First Division against Third, sitting with the enemy, purchase of both tickets, birthdays, Crystal Palace – the balloons are gathered and a bloody great pin is waiting.

At half-time, we're two down and not really in it, but Palace aren't out of sight yet. Maybe we'll nick one in the second half, maybe we'll keep it tight and not let any more in – with the second leg at Roots Hall to come. But Palace's dual strike force of Mark Bright and Ian Wright have been a problem and, after the break, they take off and so does the scoreboard. Bright, Wright, Wright, Bright; ah, shite. Resignedly accepting my friend's mocking banter (a lifetime's practice in stoicism), I applaud politely as each goal hits the back of the net.

This evening also marks the first time I have heard the biting sarcasm of a new taunting anthem to the tune of 'Knees up Mother Brown'. 'You're not very good, you're not very good, you're not very, you're not very, you're not very good' is loudly offered by the Palace fans, accusing fingers pointed in unison. I can even raise a rueful laugh at the satirical high-pitched 'oohs' and 'aahs' of the Palace fans around me, cruelly mimicking the 'oohs' and 'aahs' of the Holmesdale Road end when a very rare assault on the Palace goal goes for nought. A hat-trick each for Bright and Wright and 8-0 to Crystal Palace.

If I was with the appalled United following that night, even I might be tempted to do what most of them do and leave well before the end. But I'm not and I don't; I grit my teeth until the final whistle and finally weave around the high-fives and joking hilarity of the local fans into the night.

Something has to be done. The experience needs to be purged and relieved as soon as possible. Fortunately, the answer lies in a nearby curry house, where I order chicken phaal (a meaner and spicier relative of the vindaloo) for the only time in my life and consume copious amounts of Kingfisher lager to stop my airways from exploding. The purgative qualities of the phaal are satisfactorily dramatic, the lager-induced relief less so, but it all helps. I find something else – anything else – to do on the night of the second leg at Roots Hall, where we lose by a more respectable 2-1.

**

News of United's imminent demise is premature, however. We win the next three games, including the acid test of a 1-0 success at Mansfield's Field Mill. Even a crunching 4-1 defeat at Wigan Athletic doesn't slow us down. Another three consecutive wins follow, including a rare victory over Brentford at Griffin Park. I watch the match with the home supporters after a run-in with a touchy steward for my cardinal sin of accidentally joining the wrong queue. My entreaties fall on deaf ears. 'Enjoy the game,' the steward dismisses me with a smirk, as I am dragooned into the New Road Stand. United win 1-0, so I do enjoy the game; more than the Brentford supporters around me, actually.

Talking of west London, our record of home wins is brought to an end by Fulham who burgle two points from us when hanging on for a 1-1 draw at Roots Hall. Then our FA Cup challenge is stymied at the first hurdle with a 3-2 defeat at the Orient. Some things never change, but we compensate with another two away league wins as we enter December and a home match against our closest challengers, Grimsby Town. In front of an exuberant Roots Hall crowd of 8,126, we score two first-half goals – a 30-yard piledriver from Tilson and a diving header at ground level from Martin – and end the day seven points clear at the top. Eighteen games played, won 14, drawn two, lost two and even long-term sceptics like me are beginning to believe in the Second Division dream. I'm starting to work the numbers: I can hypothesise that mid-table form from now on will comfortably see us to promotion. Even relegation form should get us in the play-offs.

As if to test the hypothesis, United proceed to win one of the next seven matches, starting with a 1-0 defeat at Chester City. On Boxing Day, my family welcomes visitors from the United States and Southend welcome Bolton Wanderers to Roots Hall. One of the visitors is sitting with me in the East Stand, just about sheltered from weather of near Biblical proportions for only his second English football match: a howling gale blows directly from the Thames with torrential rain gusting in horizontal blasts over the South Bank, into half of the West Stand and into the faces of the poor sods huddled under the North Bank roof. My visitor is entranced by the culture shock and bemused by the frequent and vehement use of one word. 'Look – wanker. What does this word mean exactly?' He's thrilled to bits when someone below us wails 'Oh, Spenno!! For fuck's sake!!' as Prior's weak backpass is compounded by a slip in the mud, allowing a Bolton forward to negate the slender lead we have so painstakingly built. Another 1-1 home draw follows and then a 3-1 defeat at Tranmere Rovers on New Year's Day, where we manage to concede a goal ten seconds after kick-off. That's how you fritter away a seven-point cushion, but we are still leading the table – just, thanks to Grimsby, who take the opportunity to have a little festive wobble themselves.

David Webb can clearly see what the fans can also clearly see, namely a worrying touch of naivety in central defence. He celebrates the new year by bringing in the tall, no-nonsense Pat Scully from Arsenal to steady the ship. It takes a while, though. We are doing it the hard way as we move into freezing February, but successive single-goal wins away at Shrewsbury and at home to Stoke ease us back into first place, offset by a 2-1 home defeat by Reading under the frigid lights shining on the snow piled on the running track, the only home league match I miss all season, thanks to the weather and Network SouthEast. But I am at Fulham's Craven Cottage four days later, in the right queue this time, to see United produce one of their best performances of the season to walk away with an easy 3-0 win.

And off we go again with five victories in the next six games. Most satisfying are successive home wins after being one down at half-time against Mansfield Town, which is always satisfying in its own right, and Birmingham City. After a first half of alarming vapidity and 1-0 down, United come out swinging in the second half. An equaliser quickly arrives, courtesy of another Martin header from a corner, one of many this season. Now we are moving the ball through midfield at breakneck speed, Chris Powell is streaking down the left wing and the West Stand is heaving, literally bouncing with excitement. In comes the cross, in steams Brett Angell to climb outrageously high and meet the ball with a perfectly executed, perfectly placed header down and into the net with the City goalkeeper nowhere. In my lifetime, I have rarely heard a roar like the explosion from the vast majority of the 6,328 spectators present, have very rarely witnessed the leaps of exultation on the stands and terraces of Roots Hall.

***

After the Lord Mayor's Show, anyone? Time to gather one point from the next three games as we enter April, Ferguson's 'squeaky bum' time, and United drop off the top. That's why I have brought a change of clothes to the office and navigated through the London rush hour on the trusty Central line to Brisbane Road, home to the frequently problematic Leyton Orient, on the evening of Tuesday, 9 April 1991. As I leave Leyton station, Southend and Orient supporters are mixing in perfect harmony; most fans of both persuasions have probably arrived via the Central line as well. As I am nice and early, I can stroll through surroundings familiar from years ago towards the floodlights and the ground, which is quite old-fashioned; even more so than Roots Hall. This time, my polite enquiry of the local constabulary is met with a helpful answer. Tonight, I can choose between standing with the eponymous 'David Webb's Yellow Blue Army' on the South Terrace or sitting in an adjacent section of the Main Stand allocated to Southend. I choose a seat, more for the view than anything else, because the South Terrace is not huge and is likely to be distinctly busy.

Not surprisingly for a clash between teams only 40 miles apart, half of the 6,306 spectators inside Brisbane Road are of the blue persuasion and this is reinforced by the barrage of encouragement and 'Yellows, Yellows'. United need all the help they can get, as we are struggling for goals. With 25 minutes gone, Andy Ansah breaks clear of a static Orient defence, rides a last despairing tackle and calmly slots the ball under the advancing goalkeeper and into the net. Half of Brisbane Road goes potty as Andy celebrates with his usual understatement, but we can't quite snare the additional goals our pressure deserves and the communal anxiety around me becomes more intense as the second half drags interminably. The final whistle and the roar of triumph from the United fans is once again mixed with gasps of relief. In our section of the Main Stand, we are on our feet in concert with the South Terrace, feet stamping, hands clapping, blasting out our favourite chant for the season, 'We are top of the league; I say, we are top of the league.' As I walk down Leyton Road, strains of 'Going up, going up, going up' follow my passage to the tube station.

Another 1-0 nerve-shredder, but we have achieved the impossible: three away league matches in London, three wins, in one season. Now there are only seven games to go, five of them at home. As I stand on Liverpool Street station waiting for the train home with a Casey Jones burger in my hand, the only meal I'm having tonight, I can almost touch promotion, I can almost smell it and – sorry, Casey Jones – yes, I can almost taste it.

Four days later, another Friday night under the lights, a visit from Tranmere Rovers on their own late run for promotion and cascades of noise from the 8,622 fans in Roots Hall. Andy Ansah has the answer again, this time with an outrageous overhead kick into the top corner of the net from close in. In the second half, United win a penalty. After an age of protest and procrastination from the Tranmere defenders, assisted by the histrionics of veteran goalkeeper Eric Nixon, David Martin strokes the penalty too close to Nixon who promptly dives to his left and turns it aside – but too quickly by half for the referee, who orders a retake. More protest and procrastination, more histrionics from Nixon and Martin trots up for a second go: same stroke, same direction, same turn aside from the goalkeeper, but no retake this time. Despite

Martin's aberration, we do enough to edge another 1-0 victory amid more raucous celebration.

An unexpectedly tentative home defeat to Wigan keeps us on our toes. A hard-fought win at Exeter and Southend are back at Roots Hall for a crucial match against the route one brigade of Cambridge United, Dion Dublin, Steve Claridge *et al*, who are now our nearest challengers. Some 10,665 supporters peek nervously from behind their fingers at a match which simmers but never really comes to the boil and finishes 0-0, although even I have to concede that Cambridge are probably the better side. If we'd won, we could have just about secured promotion that night (depending on results elsewhere), but that would be too easy. The material point, however, is that we didn't lose. Getting there, inch by inch.

***

I had decided not to go to the Bury match. After all, it was only a matter of time. United's wobbles in March and early April were behind us and we were back on top of the table. Promotion was inevitable. Our last two matches were at home. What could go wrong?

Long experience has told me otherwise and a feeling of deep apprehension starts to build, culminating in a largely sleepless Friday night. We are having problems winning at home and goals are hard to come by. There is another reason. In parallel with our league campaign, we have also navigated a decent run in what I dismissively used to call the Also-Rans Cup (officially called the Leyland DAF Trophy this year and reserved for teams in the bottom two divisions of the Football League). We've destroyed Aldershot 10-1 in the group stage and monstered Torquay United 7-0 in the knockouts to earn a home tie in the southern section semi-final against Brentford. We lose 3-0, and Brentford's third goal is shamelessly tapped in from two yards out by Richard Cadette, the man who had restored my love affair with the Blues. And our final league match of the season is – Brentford at home. Therefore, by six o'clock in the morning of Saturday, 4 May 1991, I just know that I have to be at Gigg Lane.

One hour later, I have grabbed coffee and doughnuts from the local 7-Eleven, chucked the well-thumbed *AA Road Atlas* used for away games too many to mention on the passenger seat and off I go for pastures north. I know the way for about 200 miles to the junction of the M6 and M62 motorways. After that, it'll get a bit tricky; I am used to frequent left turns towards Liverpool, no stranger to right turns towards Manchester, but Bury is somewhere north of Manchester and I've never been there in my life.

I am making good time, though. Enough time to stop at Hilton Park services, north of Birmingham on the M6, grab another coffee and phone with apologies to break a date for that evening. As it turns out, the motorways provide an easy transition and the turn-off to Bury is clearly signposted, easing my concern at having to weave through the sprawling northern suburbs of Manchester, where once I disappeared into a Bermuda Triangle trying to find Oldham. As a result, I am driving into Bury just after 11. Nice and early; not half, this is early, even for me. The football ground is easy enough to find, a place to park less so, but I am at the Gigg Lane ticket office when it opens. I'm not wearing any gear indicating my club allegiance, my accent has always been difficult to place and I've chosen not to take the mickey by asking for a ticket with the United supporters, who will be mostly occupying what is ominously known as the Cemetery End. Instead, I buy a ticket for the Main Stand, an anonymous everyman from somewhere in England; just as I had intended.

I am only a 30-minute walk away from the centre of Bury, so I do what I have done many times when following the Blues to far-flung places I am visiting for the first time: a wander around the town centre to see what's there and a pie and a pint in a pub with a bit of character. It is sunny but there is some residue of winter in the chilly, gusting wind swirling around the streets. Bury as a town is OK, more than a touch of Industrial Revolution about it, and I am taking my seat before two o'clock, where I can relax with the matchday programme as spectators, including the vociferous Southend contingent, take their places. We had hopes of Tilson being fit, despite having missed the past few games due to injury. As the Roots Hall Ron of Bury drones out the line-ups, Tilson's name is not announced. But Adam Locke has more than played his part in recent times and we are just about at full strength.

Bury Football Club has a unique place in history: two victories out of two FA Cup finals around the turn of the 20th century with an aggregate winning score of 10-0, a record unlikely to be broken. Fittingly then, Gigg Lane is an English football ground of a bygone age: terraces behind each goal, a smallish, old-fashioned stand down each side. As many as 35,000 spectators had squeezed into the place as recently as 1960 – how, I don't know. Today's attendance of 4,254 is somewhat lower, and nearly half of them, like me, have made the trip up from Essex. I appear to be the only United supporter in my section, but the locals are friendly enough, as they generally are in the lower divisions, recognising fellow-sufferers. 'Yellows, Yellows' rises up from the Cemetery End as the teams take the pitch.

From the start, we can see the effect of the wind gusting from behind the Cemetery End. United have the advantage of possession and the wind in the first half but can't make the most of it, stray passes drifting harmlessly away, while the home side can't seem to master the conditions at all. The first half is a stop-start affair, with a bad miss from Ansah early on, and a miscue from Angell when well-placed. On 42 minutes, United win a free kick, 25 yards out, dead centre. Austin's shot is blocked by the defence and a break is on for Bury. One of their midfielders hurdles one tackle and encounters Pat Scully, who attempts a typical Arsenal central defender's tackle, except that it's totally mistimed: sliding, scything, late, the ball an afterthought. Down goes the poleaxed Bury player and the hitherto quiet home supporters around me are on their feet, incandescent. 'Oi!! Oi!! Oohh, you dirty bastard!! Whaddabout it, ref? Whaddabout it?? Off, off, off!'

'What about that?' someone pointedly asks me. 'He's off; got to be,' I reply quietly – there's nothing else I can say. And in all honesty, it's a shocker of a tackle. It takes the referee an absurdly long time to complete his lecture and fish out the inevitable red card as another chorus of 'Off, off, off' dins in my ears. Scully doesn't have far to walk to the fenced-off players' tunnel, boos and ferocious abuse in his ears. Then it's half-time, greeted by another barrage of boos from everyone around me.

Things gradually quieten down over the break, always a good opportunity to check out the loves and hates of our opponents as the PA system churns out the half-time scores. Manchester United 1 Manchester City 0: cheers and boos in equal measure. Second team syndrome is alive and well up here, it seems. Oldham 0 Notts County 1 amid loud cheers, and it's not because County are so popular in this part of Greater Manchester. Bolton 1 Swansea 1, Rochdale 0 Burnley 0: sullen silence.

I keep my head down, admiring the way some Bury fans can still find ways of changing ends at half-time and wonder how the hell we're going to get a result against the wind with ten men. But United show signs of getting to grips with the match – the half-time team talk must have been interesting – whereas Bury are still struggling with the conditions. Ansah tries a shot from distance: it's well wide, but it inspires a short burst of pressure; a couple of corners go nowhere in particular but the Blues fans are also getting the taste for it. The match finally starts to open up with 20 minutes to go as Bury have a spell. Paul Sansome tips a speculative shot from distance on to the crossbar as I rise from my seat in concert with the Bury fans and stay standing, barely able to look, as a header from the ensuing corner flashes just over. Come on Blues, why do you keep doing this to me?

Seven minutes to go: Clark wins the ball in the air and it falls to Ansah again on the right wing. Off he goes, weaving past a couple of defenders. A heavy touch loses the ball but, somehow, he wins it back and continues down the wing. A pause, a pull back and a low, bobbled cross into the centre where Ian Benjamin gathers, swivels and strikes a low left-footed shot as sweet as you like past the Bury keeper's dive and into the net. The Cemetery End goes mad and so do a few Southend fans dotted around the stand I am in, but I hadn't noticed until now. I jump up, shout 'Yes!' once, applaud briefly and sit down again. An ovation of one. The Bury supporters around me have been perfectly decent, but I'm not going to push my luck.

'Going up, going up, going up,' sing the United faithful as the match draws to its close and the visitors play the ball around safely with Bury nowhere in sight. The final whistle blows, it's 1-0 to Southend and we are promoted to the Second Division for the first time in our history. Everyone around me is on their feet, but the locals are getting ready to make their exit and I'm the only one applauding. 'Well done, lad,' says the guy who had enquired, 'What about that?' one hour earlier, in an emollient tone. I am slightly stunned, I think most of the United fans are, not to mention the players and coaching staff as they leap and dance in front of the leaping and dancing Cemetery End. I move as close to the Cemetery End as I'm allowed and pay my own respects. After 30 minutes of euphoria, the United players and staff finally leave the pitch and I leave the Main Stand of Gigg Lane, the wind beneath my wings.

I've often wondered why so many important Southend games end up 1-0. My personal conspiracy theory is that it's to keep us on the edge of a nervous breakdown. But when you leave the venue of a triumph like today and you walk to the car, with the delightful prospect of BBC's *Sports Report* on the radio for an hour or more, even the four-hour drive home is designed to allow you to savour the day. A takeaway from the magnificent Mitalee curry house, a cold bottle of white and *Match of the Day* await my return. Manchester United 1 Manchester City 0 is the final score, United's goal scored by a youth scheme graduate called Ryan Giggs. First I've heard of him: wonder how he'll get on?[33] Ryan Giggs, Gigg Lane; my mind is trying to take it all in. Shame about the broken date, but Manchester United win the derby and Southend United win promotion to the Second Division. There aren't many things to beat the feeling, there really aren't.

***

Two home games to go and two points are needed to secure the Third Division championship trophy. Orient and Brentford, as we might have expected, haven't read the script. A late equaliser, a quite brilliant lobbed effort by Locke, salvages a point against the Orient, which leaves us needing just a draw against Brentford, who have already done the dirty on us in the Leyland DAF and need a positive result to cement their place in the play-offs.

A warm but rather dull afternoon on Saturday, 11 May 1991 and an expectant flag-waving crowd of 9,666 is in Roots Hall to celebrate United's coronation. Richard Cadette is not playing for Brentford today, allaying our fears that he would repeat his Leyland DAF outrage. But in the West Stand, we are more than slightly unnerved at losing the toss and having

33 The Ryan Giggs medal tally: 13 Premier Leagues, four FA Cups, three League Cups, two Champions Leagues, one FIFA Club World Cup, one UEFA Super Cup, one Intercontinental Cup. Ryan Giggs did all right.

to kick towards the North Bank in the first half which, as we know, is not historically good news. It doesn't look so bad when Locke breaks into the penalty area and is comprehensively upended for a clear penalty. Up strides David Martin, with a building commotion in his ears. The Brentford goalkeeper may have been studying the Tranmere video because the dive to his left emulates that of Eric Nixon while Martin firmly strokes his penalty in the other direction this time – and six feet wide of the post. Roars of jubilation are choked at birth, the North Bank surges down the terrace and sways back in disappointment as Martin slowly bends over and stares at the ground, but he's been monumental for us all season so is soon forgiven. Not to be outdone, Brentford have a spell which results in a 'goal' disallowed for a handball that I didn't see. Not surprisingly given their need, there seems to be more urgency about Brentford's play, while the Blues look as if they are coming to the end of a long, hard season.

It's the same in the second half as Brentford snatch the lead. As we chase the game harder and harder, Brentford still look more likely to score as successive breakaways end in great saves from Sansome. The final whistle blows and the score is Southend United 0 Brentford 1, to the delight of the visiting fans gathered in the south-east corner of Roots Hall and the disappointment of the United fans everywhere else. Brentford have the result they need and, by now, we also know that Cambridge United have won their last match 2-0 to secure the Third Division title by a single point.[34]

I take the opportunity to stroll slowly around the hallowed turf breathing in the atmosphere of the old Roots Hall, which will never look quite the same again. I also mull over the missed opportunities against Orient and Brentford. The feeling of anticlimax is real but not devastating because we don't do silverware, do we? The title of my old VHS video

34 Brentford ended up playing Tranmere Rovers in the play-off semi-final and lost 3-2 on aggregate.

recording the second part of that magical season says it all – *The Dream Realised* – and that will never change. And three short months will elapse before it all starts again, this time in the giddy heights of the Second Division.

Chapter 16

One More Rung on the Ladder

ON SATURDAY, 17 August 1991 I'm standing at the back of the West Stand of Roots Hall, proud owner of the first season ticket I have ever bought in my life. Southend United are now members of the Football League Second Division for the first time in their history. As my gaze wanders around the old ground, taking in the pristine emerald-green turf and the new blue paint glistening in the blazing summer sunshine, it's easy to see the transformation of the close-season.

The North and South Paddocks are no more, with rows of new seats amalgamated into the East Stand. The West Stand is now all-seater as well, which is why I walk down the steps, ticket in hand, to locate the uncomfortable plastic seat which is now mine for the next nine months. No more changing ends at half-time for me or, indeed, any of the United faithful. No major feats of engineering were required, as rows of seats were bolted directly on to the old terraced steps, but it sure looks and feels different. The North and South Banks have retained their terraced crush barriers and stubbornly remain as standing areas behind their nasty new security fences. No Sid and Doris Bonkers in sight: their seats must be elsewhere, unless they preferred to stand and migrated to the North Bank.

The new season has seen the final demise of another Southend United institution and the passing of an era: Friday night football at Roots Hall. From now on, United experiences under the lights are almost exclusively on Tuesday or Wednesday evenings; better than nothing I suppose, but not quite the same if you have to crawl out of bed in the darkness of an English winter's morning and go to work. I always missed Friday night football at the Hall; always will.

Like all diehard football fans of lower-division clubs before the world wide web, I eagerly followed the pre-season transfer merry-go-round through local media and the rumour mill that grinds away around all football clubs, large and small. For Southend, the inevitable transfer market churn has produced yet another jaw-dropping outcome. Paul Clark, our own Captain Marvel, sometime player, sometime captain, sometime coach, sometime manager, sometime all four, the finger plugging innumerable dykes during our years of struggle, has crossed the water to join David Crown at Gillingham. The politics and economics of contract negotiations, outside interest, dressing room tensions and the like leave me cold as a rule, but honestly. On the other hand, David Webb has added midfielder Andy Sussex and winger Kevin O'Callaghan, both players of note. They start in our first match against Bristol City, as well as our attack force from last season, Andy Ansah, Ian Benjamin and Brett Angell, with Steve Tilson on the bench, all still here at Roots Hall despite some scurrilous rumours to the contrary. But Peter Butler is injured and we will miss his bristling intensity for most of the season.

Last season, despite our success, average attendances at Roots Hall were only just over 6,000, pretty much identical to ten years previously in the Fourth Division. I'm expecting a full house for our first home match against Bristol City and the actual turn-out of 6,720 is somewhat underwhelming (although it looks bigger than that). Despite a strong contingent of Bristol City supporters in red and white behind the South Bank fences, I can see gaps in the new seats where our new adoring fans should be and some thinly spread areas in the North Bank. I'm also wondering whether the seats will dilute the old West Stand atmosphere, but it's ebullient enough and 'Yellows, Yellows' rings even more loudly than usual as the teams take the pitch together.

It must be kismet because our hero from Gigg Lane, Ian Benjamin, continues his record of history-making goals by scoring our very first in the Second Division. Angell shoots, the City goalkeeper parries and Benjamin nips in to steer the ball into the net. He leaps prodigiously and reaches for the sky while we patrons of the West Stand have the unfamiliar experience of jumping up from, and celebrating within, the confines of our seats.

Amid a wave of appreciative applause, it's 1-0 to United at half-time and we are good value for it as well. United start the second half strongly and Ansah breaks down the middle but his hard, low effort is turned aside by City's goalie at full stretch. Maybe we could win this thing.

But Bristol City are no mugs, and a free kick at the edge of our box catches the United defence napping and Taylor buries the equaliser. A very late City chance well saved by Sansome gives us a scare but the match ends up 1-1. Roots Hall gives the Blues players a much-merited standing ovation and goes home happy; we were more than a match for City. To me, it feels like the excitement and trepidation of buying a new house and finding, to our relief, that the roof doesn't leak and the central heating works.

Equally, it sometimes takes a while to find the light switch for the attic. It takes United some time to settle in; a win here, a defeat there, reasonably comfortable in mid-table – then Angell takes wing. Brett's goals in seven successive matches, each seemingly better than the last, makes our position look a bit more interesting. It's not just the season ticket, nothing – not even Network SouthEast – is going to stop me getting to Roots Hall for a Tuesday night match under the lights against Kenny Dalglish's cashed-up and born-again Blackburn Rovers. My train finally expires somewhere deep in Southend western suburbia so I end up doing what quite a few fellow frustrated commuters do. Accompanied by the crackles, hoots and zooms of fireworks, occasionally illuminated by the brilliant flare and boom of high-flying rockets (for this is 5 November, Guy Fawkes Night), I jump out of the carriage to briskly and irresponsibly march two miles up the railway track to Chalkwell station, where I get hold of a cab. In City suit, tie and raincoat, I am a few minutes late but just in time to see Brett direct in a far-post header for the first in what proves to be an emphatic 3-0 win. Four days later, he scores a wonder goal, an absolute screamer of a volley against Swindon Town to inspire another win. And, hell, we beat Sunderland at Roker Park. Another transfer coup saw attacking midfielder Keith Jones arrive from Brentford (he had created havoc at Roots Hall back in May) and his pure inventive class provided additional momentum behind United's upward surge.

In the meantime, I had embarked on a relationship with Kim, an Anglo/Aussie or Aussie/Anglo, whatever, who actually liked football as much as I did. She'd grown up in Sydney but was a Manchester United supporter, she'd been to an FA Cup Final, and had been to a West Bromwich Albion match at The Hawthorns (which was more than I'd ever done). She also lived in west London, so her trips to Roots Hall were infrequent in the early days, which was probably just as well. Her first Roots Hall appearance against the Wolves saw us well beaten 2-0, with Kim's antipodean peals of encouragement accompanied by her first experience of my resigned gloom – not her last – and initiating her legend as the Jinx of Southend United.

New Year's Day 1992 and a home match against Newcastle United. After a heavy New Year's Eve in west London, even I wasn't stupid enough to hazard the drive home for a noon kick-off, so I let it go, one of the few home games I missed that season. The majority of the 9,458 supporters enjoyed the spectacle of the United of Southend dismantling the United of Newcastle 4-0, helped by another double from Angell. After

I had crawled home from London, I immediately switched on the TV and my bleary eyes saw the league table in the pixelated, multi-coloured script of Ceefax. Southend United: top of the Second Division, two points ahead of Ipswich and Blackburn. If I'd had any film in my camera, I would have taken a photo for posterity, because it didn't last long. Ipswich and Blackburn both won their matches later that afternoon, dropping us back to third place, but it had happened and I'd seen it, just not in the flesh, sadly – just six years and seven months after Torquay United and our re-election near-death experience.[35]

A 1-0 home win over Watford at the beginning of February saw United in second place and Roots Hall, to its delirious surprise, could see the ladder to another, bigger dream. But then reality hit with a solid thump with successive away defeats at Charlton Athletic, Barnsley and Grimsby Town. Then our home form dried up as well and we faded away to just two victories in our last 17 games. More bad news arrived in March. After what we understood to be yet another dispute with Chairman Vic over transfer funding, David Webb announced that he would leave the club at the end of the season. Definitely not something United supporters wanted to hear, and another stick with which to beat poor old Jobson, as we always did.

United ended up 12th, respectable but ultimately disappointing, given our position at the turn of the year. As for the one and only Roots Hall season ticket I have ever possessed, I might have needed to rely on it two, maybe three times as we ended up with a higher average attendance than the previous season, but not by much.

***

35 Ipswich Town and Blackburn Rovers won promotion to the Premier League at the end of the season. Ipswich won the title and Blackburn won the play-off final. Typical.

All Southend United ever wanted was to be a Second Division club, the story goes. And we finally achieved it for one season and one season only because the old First Division of the Football League became the FA Premier League and the old Football League Second Division became the new Barclays First Division for the 1992/93 season. But supposing we had managed to climb one more rung and found ourselves in the newly minted top tier?

What if David Webb and Chairman Vic hadn't fallen out once too often and Webb had been freed of the distraction that an impending departure must have caused? I recently looked back at the participants for that inaugural season of the Premier League. Many things have changed, some haven't. Eleven of the original 22 teams are still there after 30 years, five of them comfortable long-term residents like Manchester United, Liverpool, Tottenham, Arsenal and Chelsea. Everton have also managed to keep their place despite more than one flirtation with the tumble to the second tier. As for the rest, they have experienced the intervening years enjoying or suffering their own snakes and ladders. Aston Villa, Crystal Palace and Middlesbrough have shuttled between first and second tiers. Norwich City, Blackburn Rovers, Queens Park Rangers, the Sheffields of Wednesday and United, Ipswich Town, Nottingham Forest, Leeds United, Southampton and even Manchester City have tasted the bitter fruit of the third tier. Coventry City paid the price for their own brand of financial incontinence with one season in the fourth tier. Oldham Athletic, bless 'em, fell through the trapdoor to non-league in 2022 – the first and so far only Premier League team to suffer that indignity. Wimbledon don't even exist any more. The over-achieving little club from leafy south-west London renowned for its 'Crazy Gang' generation of wild, cheeky and robust footballers did a very crazy thing and moved itself 60 miles north to Milton Keynes, the city of dreaming roundabouts.

In today's big TV money world, every club winning promotion to the Premier League pockets £170m plus, according to financial gurus like Deloitte's Sports Business Group. They get it even if they're rubbish and only last one season, thanks to parachute payments which soften the short-term financial blow of losing Premier League status. Therefore, your club is never quite the same any more. This is why the Championship play-off final is the most valuable club match in world football – and that includes the Champions League Final. Nothing like that sort of money was around back in 1992. I'm not sure if Southend United Football Club has seen £170m cross its path in its entire existence. So, to have climbed that final rung may not have changed United for ever; but it would have been nice.[36]

36 The estimated financial implications of promotion to the Premier League are based on TV, sponsorship, merchandise, etc. Some estimates are higher still, which may explain the modern phenomenon of a handful of clubs being habitually just too good for the Championship but not quite good enough for an extended stay in the Premier League. Recent examples include Norwich City, Watford, Sheffield United and West Bromwich Albion.

Chapter 17

A Man for Half a Season

WHEN YOU'RE in the First Division (even if it's the new First Division) and close to the big time, what did every Football League club need in the early 1990s? A decent ground, a board of directors who weren't completely deranged, good playing squad, good management, a few quid in the bank. Southend United could tick some of the boxes but not others. But what we do have is a cuddly mascot to delight the kiddies and wind-up opposition supporters.

Southend had their own mascot from the late 1960s; a cheerful, chubby hand-drawn crustacean with a football in his hand called Sammy Shrimper, who took pride of place in the matchday programme promoting an East Stand cubbyhole called the Shrimpers Club. I was the lucky owner of an enamel Sammy Shrimper badge and was a member of the Shrimpers Club for a few years.

We had to wait ten years for the first appearance of a living, breathing Sammy Shrimper (or Sammy Bloody Shrimper as he was often known). There he was, strutting his stuff in front of the West Stand before the Swansea City match in December 1978 when we all agreed Tommy Smith was a wanker. Immaculate in top hat, tails and spats, complete with supercilious grin, the only obvious resemblance to a shrimp was some helpful padding around the midriff. All in all, not an ideal role model for young supporters. The

Penguin in the old *Batman* television series bore some kind of similarity to Sammy, although he waddled more than swaggered. However, Sammy was star quality when it came to teasing opposition supporters, who greeted his pitchside histrionics with two-finger and fist-pumping salutes and a range of vocal accompaniments. The trouble was, he inspired similar emotions among some of his own supporters. Sammy's first incarnation didn't last long.

The early 90s saw a new manifestation. This version had decided to dress down, sacrificed a few inches of height for a few additional pounds of weight and emerged as something more akin to his cartoon ancestor. With a dopey grin plastered across his otherwise featureless face, the new Sammy had stubby legs, a broad stomach and a narrow chest, tapering to an even narrower head and finishing with a sharp peak at the top. A pair of bulbous eyes and a United football kit completed the ensemble. Although more child-friendly than the creepy Penguin lookalike, the second Sammy also inspired highly vocal disdain from opposing supporters who might have been provoked by the hint of mischief in his otherwise relentlessly sunny demeanour. Not every local was convinced either. Sometimes pink, sometimes white, he was a Roots Hall fixture for nearly 30 years.

***

Whatever boardroom ructions may have transpired during 1992, David Webb always came across to me as a man of few words, some of them unprintable. By contrast, his successor was a flood of eloquence, some of it misplaced. I remembered Colin Murphy and his flailing battles with the English language from tortuous television interviews as coach and then briefly as manager of Derby County in the 70s. When he disappeared below the mass media radar, his unique writing style had earned him local legend status in a broadly successful spell managing Lincoln City.

As soon as he joined Southend, he revealed his house style. *A Century United* records the remarkable circumlocution of his very first programme notes at Roots Hall. A torrent of motivational *non sequiturs* included, 'Enough has been written about the past. Wonderment and disenchantment pondered about its motives. Philosophies expressed about repairing and planning for the future.' Now who could argue with that?

Whoever sat in the manager's office at Roots Hall, the clean slate rule was always waiting in the wings. And history repeated itself in season 1992/93, as United started with four straight defeats and two wins in our first 16 matches. Brett Angell was injured for most of the season and it was left to Ian Benjamin, our Mr Reliable, to contribute the lion's share of our meagre goal tally. However, to my consternation, Benjamin left for Luton Town, another entry in the thickening journal of unbelievable departures.

But Colin Murphy had a plan, or a 'philosophy expressed about repairing' as he might have put it. Some reports said £100,000, others £150,000, still others £250,000 but Murphy secured the services of Stanley Victor Collymore, an occasional stand-in for the famous Ian Wright-Mark Bright axis at Crystal Palace. Tall but not mountainous, muscular but lithe with it, great in the air, genuinely two-footed, Collymore also possessed a laser-like intensity; but we haven't seen that before his debut on the chilly, damp Saturday afternoon of 21 November 1992 at Roots Hall, in front of a depressingly small and sceptical crowd of 3,219. A *tour de force* of controlled attacking aggression follows: a right-footed volleyed piledriver high into the roof of the Notts County net and a head-down charge to a through ball, culminating in a rasping low drive into the corner with his left; two goals for Stan in a rare 3-1 win and a new United star is born.

I'm not saying that Collymore scored in every match, but his physical presence, especially at the Hall, seemed to inject a spark into the whole team as United started to pull things around. 'Ohh, Stanley, Stanley; Stanley, Stanley, Stanley Collymore' we sang, a cover version of an early 70s venture into techno pop called 'Son of my Father' by a band called Chicory Tip. Not many football songs have featured the word 'Stanley'. Even Matthews couldn't manage it.

The Collymore factor wasn't enough to avoid an expected 2-0 defeat at Upton Park/the Boleyn Ground in December 1992, the first time that Southend had ever played a league match against West Ham. On the day, we were stuck rock bottom at the foot of the table, while West Ham found themselves in third place. The return at Roots Hall, scheduled for early April 1993, was likely to take on a significance above and beyond a simple clash between the two local Uniteds.

While we waited for the return of the Hammers, United enjoyed a rare decent run in the FA Cup. Another advantage of residence in the second tier was a free pass to the third round, with no first- or second-round banana skins. Wednesday, 13 January 1993 and First Division contemporaries Millwall are at Roots Hall under the lights, with their usual vociferous but generally well-behaved following behind the South Bank fence. The crowd of 8,028 is not a sell-out by any means, but it is the biggest attendance of the season so far and the atmosphere reminds me of big Roots Hall nights of the past. With roars of encouragement from the United supporters mingling with healthy doses of invective from the Millwall contingent, Collymore produces another *tour de force* to score the winner with the surging run and emphatic finish we've come to expect and creates bedlam in the Millwall defence from start to finish.

Jubilation is only slightly tempered by the fourth-round draw away to third-tier Huddersfield Town at their crumbling Leeds Road ground. It's all the same to Stan. His two goals secure a 2-1 win and we are into the last 16 for only the second time in my life. Inevitably, our 'reward' is an away tie at Premier League Sheffield Wednesday. Inevitably, Kim and

I are on holiday in Australia, otherwise we would have made the trip to Hillsborough. Inevitably, our run ends with a 2-0 defeat by a Wednesday team on their way to the final, where they inevitably lose to the Arsenal after a replay.

Back home, I'm at Roots Hall on Sunday, 20 March 1993. We are still in the relegation zone but another lung-bursting sprint and forensic finish from Stan opens the scoring against Millwall and he puts himself about in no uncertain terms to help Steve Tilson and United pull back a two-goal deficit for a scintillating 3-3 draw and another vital point on the quest for recovery. This match, memorable for its hectic back-and-forth rhythm, is also memorable for being shown live on television. I am shouting my lungs out in the West Stand, but I appreciated the novelty of re-watching it on *The London Match*, courtesy of my NICAM video recorder. Fronted by Ian St John (who didn't end up sweeping the streets after all), with commentary from the venerable Brian Moore and punditry from one-time goal machine Clive Allen, that's what playing in the second tier earned you.

By the time of the West Ham return match, Colin Murphy had, slightly unfairly in my view, walked the plank to continue his literary discombobulations elsewhere in places as diverse as Shelbourne in Ireland, Notts County, and the Vietnam and Myanmar national football teams. His successor Barry Fry had escaped from his own dirty rag experience at Barnet and was appointed on April Fools' Day 1993. Brett Angell had finally recovered from his injury and Fry inherited a team with at least some stuttering momentum with Angell and Collymore up front, a partnership of short but momentous duration.

Wednesday, 7 April 1993 under the Roots Hall lights has seen both Uniteds improve by one position since December: highly promising for West Ham who find themselves in the automatic promotion places; highly dangerous for us, still marooned in the drop zone. A crowd of 12,812 Southend, West Ham and, I dare say, turncoat supporters are inside

Roots Hall for our largest attendance since, well, the last time West Ham visited Roots Hall in 1979. With one empty seat – mine. Work has called me to Manchester, but that's no problem: with my background in logistics and the help of British Rail timetables I have worked out a foolproof way to get back home just in time for kick-off. Unfortunately, the vicissitudes of Inter City Rail, the London Underground and Network SouthEast see me kicking my heels in Fenchurch Street station at 7.15pm, just too late: match ticket in pocket, frustrated and crestfallen, 30 minutes from kick-off and more than an hour from the distant floodlights.

By the time my train finally approaches the outer suburbs of Southend, Stan Collymore is hurtling down the left wing, then spearing a driven low cross into the middle for Brett Angell to leather the ball into the roof of the net from five yards out in front of the West Ham supporters on the remains of the South Bank. A neighbour tells me later that she could hear the Roots Hall celebration from her kitchen, but I am still too far away to hear it. I learn about United's improbable 1-0 victory from the Ceefax pixels when I finally arrive home.

United's one and only win against West Ham in my lifetime and I wasn't there to see it. What kind of supporter am I? The kind of supporter who still, when I feel like a laugh, occasionally puts on my old 1992/93 season video to relish, once again, the Collymore run and cross, the Angell finish, the silenced West Ham supporters on the South Bank. That's who.[37]

Another feature of being in the second tier was that the burgeoning Collymore reputation attracted attention well beyond Southend. Much of it was positive, judging by the line of big clubs starting to queue up at the Roots Hall door.

---

37 The Collymore cross and Angell's finish appeared in the *Southend United Official Video 1992/93 Season Highlights*, and does still (for as long as my old VHS video player holds out). But the video of the goal is also accessible on YouTube. Seventeen seconds of bliss.

Some of it negative, judging by the strident hostility directed his way from opposing supporters. West Ham and Millwall predictably, but Newcastle United – how the hell did they ever find out about him?

Despite the Collymore-Angell transformation, by the last game of the season against Luton on Saturday, 8 May 1993, we still need a win to stay up, and so do Luton. In one of the noisier matches I remember at Roots Hall, 11,042 supporters have packed inside and are enjoying the warm sunshine. Today, every single seat in the West Stand has been taken, so I am paying a rare and, as it turns out, final visit to the terraced steps of the old North Bank. Early on, Stan is storming down the right wing towards me, ball at feet. A searching low cross, partially cleared by a Luton defender, and here comes Andy Sussex, 25 yards out. A first-time volley of stunning power and direction flies high into the net, right in front of me. It's a goal from the instant Sussex strikes and may well be the best Southend goal I have ever seen. The North Bank goes nuts, just the way it used to. Now a free kick from the right, swung in by Tilson. A header into the middle by Spencer Prior and Angell dives to head in at the far post. More nuttiness from the North Bank, moderated by a Luton reply before half-time in front of their own vociferous fans on the South Bank.

In our hearts, we all know that this will be Collymore's last game for United and Stan must score. Into the second half, he's on the left, collecting a through ball from Sussex and arrowing a low drive into the Luton net: no fuss, no nonsense and the cue for an eruption of raucous rapture. Incredibly, the linesman flags for offside; why I don't know, but I am not in the best position to tell. Stan turns away, disappointed, the jeers and boos of the Luton fans following ringing in his ears; they know who he is as well.

One last effort. A late free kick, 30 yards out and of course Stan will take it. His kitchen sink thump screams just over the bar. So be it. At the end, United have won 2-1 to save their bacon and defy the clean slate rule. Poetic justice means that Luton have stayed up as well, because Brentford's last-day aberration in a 4-1 defeat at Bristol City has sent them down instead. Rejoicing all round. The pitch invasion is massive and enthusiastic but I'm not an immediate part of it, because I'm in the North Bank behind that nasty fence and, at the age of 37, there's no way I'm climbing over the damn thing.

***

Could Stan Collymore be the greatest player in Southend United's history? OK, he spent less than one full season at Roots Hall. But 18 goals in 33 games (including all the goals in our brief sortie to the fifth round of the FA Cup) and Stan's rescue mission to lift United out of the relegation mire weighs heavily in the balance. As did his inevitable big-money transfer to Nottingham Forest: some reports had it as £2m, others at £2.2m, but that was pretty impressive, given what we had paid for him. And, in the brave new world of sell-on clauses, where the original selling club picked up an agreed percentage of onward transfer deals, his subsequent moves to Liverpool and Aston Villa resulted in a reported all-up contribution of £3.57m to United's ever-hungry coffers. Or £4.6m, according to the *Southend Evening Echo*.[38] That was A LOT of money in the 1990s. Whatever else people said about Colin Murphy (and they said plenty), that's good business in anybody's book. And the answer to the question at the start of this paragraph is – a definite maybe.

***

Collymore's reputation as a goalscorer blossomed at Forest, where he lifted them back into the Premier League and then to a top-three position the following season. His reputation was further burnished when he joined the mighty Liverpool

---

38 The total payout mentioned by Barry Fry was reported in the *Echo* of 3 May 2020. The £3.57m payout came from *A Century United*.

for a shedload of money and scored lots of goals very quickly. Nostalgic Southend fans could call up memories of his lurk with intent on the left wing, the power and precision of his finish, the cheeky gallop and grin of celebration after his last-minute winner for Liverpool against Newcastle United at Anfield in April 1996. The 4-3 result broke the hearts of Newcastle United and their manager Kevin Keegan in a season when they really should have won the Premier League but let it slip to Manchester United at the death. Another reason to remember Stan Collymore with affection, if you're a Southend and Manchester United fan.

The trouble with Stan, however, was that his legend seemed to be one step ahead of him at times. After just one more year at Anfield, he was on his way to Aston Villa for another mighty fee, but he didn't really work either on the pitch or off it, according to stories which do not interest me in the slightest. Fleeting appearances at Fulham, Leicester City, Bradford City, a spell at Spanish club Real Oviedo of history-making brevity and Stan Collymore hung up his magic boots prematurely at the age of 30.

Did he really turn down the opportunity to return to United as a player in 2001, as reported by BBC Sport Online? Did Stan really make his own bid to return as player-manager in 2003? So reported the *Southend Evening Echo*.[39] My friends in England used to hear the dulcet tones of Stan's mid-Staffordshire accent delivering his own brand of punditry on BBC Radio 5 Live – until they didn't any more. He moved on to talkSPORT, but news from the Collymore-Southend front went relatively quiet for a few years.

And then, in April 2021, back came Stan with an offer to buy the club. Or he may have been a part of a takeover consortium. Or he may have been looking to install an acolyte

---

39 The Collymore-go-round. Sources: bbc.co.uk 5 January 2001, www.gazette-news.co.uk 19 November 2003, www.echo-news.co.uk 22 April 2021.

as chief executive. So reported the *Echo* (again). Whatever, it didn't seem to get very far, but it also seemed that the narrative had some way to go. If he could host a football show on Russia Today, if he could get himself into the cast list of *Basic Instinct 2* – and he did both of these things – anything was possible. The abundantly cautious side of me murmured 'ooh-err' when I contemplated the prospect, but the rebel side shouted 'Yes! Yes! Bring it on!'

Stan the Man (that's what we called him, before a Swiss tennis player named Wawrinka took on the mantle), an enduring Southend United legend. Greatest United player or not, life is certainly more interesting when he's around.

Chapter 18

A Rung Too Far

PLAYING THE lower-division rivals of my childhood and early adulthood week in, week out, year in, year out could not quite compete with Southend United's new rivals in the second tier. Hartlepool United or Sunderland? Exeter City or Bristol City? Mansfield Town or Leicester City? Walsall or West Bromwich Albion? Leyton Orient or Crystal Palace? Even Colchester United or Norwich City? The teams we used to look up to with wishful thinking were now the weekly opponents we could almost, but never quite take for granted.

Long-time United supporters were living in a time of challenge and hope, anticipation and apprehension. In other words, it was great fun. On Saturday, 22 August 1993, I am one of the lucky 10,273 to experience the first league game in Millwall's brand new all-covered, all-seated New Den stadium. United thump Millwall 4-1 to spoil their big day, with goals from new boys Jason Lee, Ricky Otto and Tommy Mooney with another from old boy Andy Ansah. The result is a hoot, but my favourite memory is sitting in the shiny new concession area under the stand, where I watch *Football Focus* on what then passes for a widescreen TV, with a pint of lager in one hand and a Big Mac in the other. Not one of Roy Keane's prawn sandwiches in an Old Trafford corporate box, but not an anaemic Maxwell House in a plastic cup and a soggy gristle and kidney pie either. There weren't many football grounds where you could do that in 1993, trust me. All this, and a 4-1 second tier away win in London too. That didn't happen very often, either.

It was just a shame that the general public of Southend-on-Sea did not feel the same way. Allowing for the odd sell-out, average attendances remained stuck around five to six thousand; better than the years of struggle in the 80s, but nowhere near the crowds Roots Hall used to see. Apart from the vacant seats, Southend were gradually evolving into what a second-tier club looked like in the last decade of the 20th century. Bit by bit, the remaining standing areas in Roots Hall, with their nasty fences, were replaced by seats on all four sides. Roofs were extended and quadrants filled in to make Roots Hall the all-seated and all-covered ground we know today. The sad remnant of the South Bank made way for a little two-tiered stand named after Frank Walton, the only club chairman who was universally liked and respected in all my years of watching the Blues.

***

When I arrived on the Roots Hall scene in 1964, United's manager was Ted Fenton, who was gone at the end of that season. Long-serving managers have not been a way of my life at Roots Hall. From serene pipe smokers to manic gum chewers, from suits and ties to designer tracksuits, 11 aspirants to immortality had joined the manager-go-round and two of those, Arthur Rowley and Dave Smith, had registered 13 years between them. The 1990s saw a swirl of managerial comings and goings unique in the club's history. David Webb's five (staggered) years at the helm should have qualified him for a long service award.

Barry Fry stayed but a short while, to depart with indecent haste for the attractions of Birmingham City, a time when we were again in fleeting danger of climbing that final rung of the ladder. The anointed saviour of Southend United from May

1993 revealed himself to be Judas Iscariot just seven months later. This infuriated United fans which is why the password for the first laptop computer I ever possessed summarised bitterly – JudasFRY93!.

Less than one month after Fry's treacherous departure, Vickie, daughter from my first marriage, paid a very rare trip to the Hall. She still retains memories from New Year's Day 1994. It was freezing cold (no surprise there) and the crowd of 10,731 was bigger, louder and angrier than she'd expected. Unaware of the politics behind the return of Fry with Birmingham City, she found the stick he received from United fans something to behold. 'Are you watching, are you watching, are you watching, Barry Fry? Are you watching, Barry Fry?' crowed the Roots Hall faithful as each goal crowned a 3-1 win for United. Despite this, the mystique of Southend United didn't take for my 13-year-old daughter. And it still hasn't, but there's no escape; her partner James is a devout Southampton supporter and he's at least as bad as me.

The victorious new boy in the home dugout was Peter 'Spud' Taylor, just arrived from little Enfield with no previous league management experience, but known to Roots Hall as the rising star and occasional goalkeeper from the early 70s. Sadly, New Year's Day 1994 was as good as it got for Taylor, who rode the managerial rollercoaster for a couple of years before a near-terminal slump in form heralded his demise. United's feet were pulled out of the fire by the short but fondly remembered reign of Steve Thompson, who then allowed himself to join Colin Murphy at Notts County.

***

Southend, as befits their history in the lower reaches of the Football League, have always been a selling rather than a buying club. From Chico Hamilton in the 60s to Bill Garner, Peter Taylor and Chris Guthrie in the 70s; to Colin Morris, Richard Cadette, Shane Westley and Glenn Pennyfather in the 80s, we became accustomed to seeing our best players climb their personal ladders away from Roots Hall. Stan Collymore was simply the latest and most lucrative. One by one, the heroes of 1991 moved on. Peter Butler moved on to West Ham quite quickly, as did Dean Austin to Tottenham, both for significant transfer fees. We waved goodbye to Brett Angell, Spencer Prior and Chris Powell, off to Everton, Norwich City and Derby County respectively for even more significant fees. Others left for more modest locations for more modest sums. By the start of the 1996/97 season, faithful servant Steve Tilson was the only one left – and that was a pity. Thanks to the big-money goodbyes and the Collymore millions, however, some of the players United brought in were a distinct cut above what we were used to. Gary Poole, a classy wing-back arrived from Plymouth Argyle for the head-spinning sum of £400,000. We enjoyed, for a couple of years, the antics of Ricky Otto, a real crackerjack of pace, power and showmanship, snaffled from the Orient. Andy Thomson, a skinny but deceptively tricky striker from Queen of the South in Scotland, didn't score many, but often seemed to pop up just at the right place at the right time. Keith Dublin, veteran warhorse and defensive Colossus – ex-Chelsea, ex-Brighton, ex-Watford – was another.

Remarkably, United managed to entice Ronnie Whelan from a long and outrageously successful career at Liverpool: 362 league games, six First Division championships, three FA Cups, three League Cups, one European Cup – Ronnie had won everything there was to win on Merseyside, apart from the Grand National. Oh, and 53 caps for the Republic of Ireland in his spare time. The most decorated footballer in Southend's history – and there's no maybe about that. Not surprisingly, I make sure I'm at Roots Hall on a sunny Saturday afternoon, 17 September 1994 for Whelan's first home match, even though United have started the season poorly (as usual) and there are only 3,662 others sharing the experience. Ronnie doesn't let us down. In the second half, United win a free kick 25 yards out. A swerving, dipping masterpiece of power and placement flies over the Bristol City defensive wall, past the floundering keeper and high into the top corner of the net, right in front of the newly completed Frank Walton Stand. It is just as well I'm there, for that proves to be the only goal scored by Whelan for Southend. It's a sublime memory all the same.

The Whelan and Collymore effect worked in other ways as well, as a clutch of significant football names started to arrive. Steady and classy midfielder Mike Marsh from Galatasaray in Turkey, a regular starter in recent memory for Liverpool and West Ham. Mercurial but inconsistent Paul Byrne, an attacking midfielder-cum-winger from Celtic. Mike Lapper, an American international defender from German Bundesliga club VfL Wolfsburg (now *that* was exotic). And, characteristic of the period for clubs with upwardly mobile aspirations, a sprinkling of Europe was added to the squad, with mixed success: Dutch striker Jeroen Boere, Denmark's John Nielsen, the briefest of brief cameos from Norwegian Petter Belsvik.

The departure of Steve Thompson had left us with Ronnie Whelan to see if he could translate his vast experience as a top-level player into tracksuited heroics in his first ever coaching role. Nothing to worry about there, eh?

* * *

The tidal system of the River Thames at Southend is not unique, but it is distinctive. The sea water slowly retreats deep into the bowels of the Estuary at low tide, exposing the dun-coloured mudflats for which Southend is famous. Over the next few hours, water creeps back over the mud to break against the pebbles of the Southend seashore at high tide, followed by another slow retreat and return towards the shore a few hours later.

Extrapolate 24 hours or so into nine months and United's seasons in the second tier started to take on a tidal pattern.

A routinely poor and muddy start, followed by a creep up the table with the tantalising lights of the Premier League flickering into view in December and January, like the distant lights of the Kent coast on a clear night. The lights then fade and finally disappear into the chilly mists of February and March as the latest slew of draws and defeats edges us towards the turmoil of a relegation struggle. Inexorably, late ripples of improved results turn up in the nick of time during April, culminating in a triumphant finale against opposition unfortunate enough to face us at Roots Hall in May. Derby County, Barnsley and Ipswich Town were all submerged by the waves of United's redemption as we ended up in mid-table comfort to wonder what all the fuss had been about and look forward with naïve confidence towards the next season.

***

FootballSpeak is my name for a *patois* owned by the community of football tragics. One example is the Monday morning question from one tragic to another, 'Did you go to Birmingham?' Now this doesn't mean that I jumped on a train at London Euston bound for Birmingham New Street. Nor does it mean that I chucked my *AA Road Atlas* into the car and sped to one of the M6 turn-offs in Brummieland. All it means is, 'Yes; I went to Roots Hall to watch Southend United play Birmingham City.'

Which is where I go on Saturday, 2 December 1995, a dry, cool afternoon; an afternoon when it seems like the metaphorical tide may be on its way in. Dad is paying what is now an infrequent visit to Roots Hall and his arthritis is playing up, so we take our seats in the East Stand, almost precisely where we used to stand in the old South Paddock. City can see the flickering lights of the Premier League more clearly than we can as they sit just outside the promotion places, while we are secure in mid-table, but with upward aspirations.

It is one of Roots Hall's biggest matches of the season because Birmingham are still managed by Barry Fry. A respectably large and vocal crowd of 7,770 take their seats around us. Southend supporters have a long memory, so Fry can expect another barrage of abuse. Not only did he leave us in the lurch without prior notice, the cheeky bugger then poached some of our best players. Today, ex-Southend favourites Gary Poole, Andy 'Eagle' Edwards and Jonathan Hunt are turning out for the Brummies. At least Ricky Otto is missing from their line-up for reasons unknown, otherwise there would be more of our last Fry-era team playing for Birmingham than we have starting for United. At least we turned a decent profit out of it.

A cacophony of boos, cat-calls, whistles and descants of 'Judas', 'wanker' and 'you fat bastard' accompanies Fry's self-conscious emergence from the players' tunnel and his short passage to the away manager's dugout – the same welcome as he received two years previously. A creditable tribal roar at kick-off as United attack the North Bank in the first half. Thankfully, there are no crowd renditions of 'Yellows, Yellows' any more, because the garish shorts have been consigned to unlamented history. We are the better side by some distance, until the 30th minute. A long ball finds City breaking down the right, our goalkeeper Simon Royce embarks on a kamikaze charge to Nowhereland, undone by a routine low cross into the middle, and Steve Claridge steers the ball into the empty net. Deflating, but not disastrous. Two minutes before half-time, Byrne fires in a free kick from the left and Mick Bodley, a no-nonsense and highly vocal central defender, crashes an angled header past the Birmingham goalkeeper. There's just enough time for Byrne to fire in a low dipper which seems to catch the goalie in the face, allowing Dave Regis, an escapee from Fry's Birmingham regime and our latest 'big 'un up front', to prod in the rebound, to the huge delight of Regis and the United fans. Half-time and 2-1 to Southend, as Fry runs the gauntlet on his way back to the dressing room. Cue the return of 'Are you watching, are you watching, are you watching, Barry Fry?' One of our favourite songs directed at our favourite pantomime villain, with pantomime season just around the corner.

More of the same in the second half. Gary Jones is in the middle of his latest goal famine and misses a sitter so we have to wait until 70 minutes for Byrne to pick up the ball on the right once again, mesmerise the ex-Blues in the City defence with a swerve to the right, then to the left, then to the right to drill a low shot off the far post and into the net. Byrne sprints directly towards Dad and me, with his shirt manically pulled over his head. Fortunately for him and us, he wheels away before he collides with the East Stand. 'That lad needs to calm down a bit,' remarks Dad. Some cheeky and optimistic United fans in the West Stand point derisively and sing 'We're going up, we're going up, you're not, you're not' to the despondent City fans; how they must hate Roots Hall. A comfortable 3-1 win at the final whistle – the same result as two years ago. United move into the top half of the First Division table in front of our biggest crowd of the season. Byrne has played a blinder and Barry Fry is confounded. As good as it gets.

It got even better, too; for a little while. At the beginning of February, United were in fourth place and beating Millwall at Roots Hall after a run of seven wins in ten. On our way to the Premier League to join Manchester United, who are sweeping all before them, maybe. No such luck. A major nosebleed set in and we finished the season with three wins in our final 18 matches. In the end, our December win against Birmingham had given us the three points we needed to finish above them in the final league table – and Barry Fry ended up getting the sack. A tumultuous 2-1 win against promotion-chasing Ipswich Town at Roots Hall and our final position of 14th disguised a hulking elephant in the room.

The elephant was the clean slate rule, where our decline in the latter end of the 1995/96 season ran the risk of continuing into the next. Ronnie Whelan was optimistic for 1996/97. I don't recall much agonising about impending disaster from the stands either, but sometimes one just experiences a vague disquiet.

By August 1996, Kim and I had rented a place in west London, so that we could both commute to work without having to cross multiple time zones. Our nearest Football League clubs were now Brentford and Queens Park Rangers and indeed we did pay visits to Griffin Park and Loftus Road – but only when United played there. Although we kept our place in Westcliff vacant except for occasional visits at weekends and bank holidays, the frequency of my visits to Roots Hall declined significantly, so I suppose it was all my fault.

Yet another slow start, but we were used to that. A stuttering recovery of sorts in October as expected, but then the tide turned long before reaching the seashore and stubbornly refused to return – which was not expected. On a wintry Saturday afternoon, 14 December 1996, Kim and I make the short trip to Queens Park Rangers' Loftus Road ground. The cold wind of relegation is already blowing around us. Shivering in the upper tier of the stunted School End stand, the Southend travelling support wince and groan as the Rangers hammer us 4-0. United are so bad that we console ourselves with mordant gallows humour, adapting the Crystal Palace taunt with several choruses of 'WE'RE not very good, WE'RE not very good, we're not very, we're not very, WE'RE not very good'. Happy to twist the knife in The Loft, the home choir teases us with choruses of 'Going down, going down, going down'. In response, we fatalistically but quite wittily respond with 'So are we, so are we, so are we'. It wasn't just the result; a Rangers-supporting work colleague was in The Loft that day, and I was already anticipating the stick I would get on Monday morning. I was right on that score.

Now planted in the relegation zone, United needed their best players to step up. Unfortunately, the simultaneous loss of Marsh and Byrne to injury didn't help. Curiously, QPR aside, United still tended to perform moderately well when I turned up. Wins at Roots Hall against Reading, Stoke City, Portsmouth and even a rare win against the Palace briefly kept the hope alive; the trouble was that it always seemed to be one step forward and two steps back. One win came in our final 14 matches and, fittingly, Grimsby Town were on hand to wallow in our grief and dispatch us 4-0 in United's final match after six glorious seasons in the second tier.

***

Just when you think it couldn't get any worse, it got worse. Ronnie Whelan got the order of the boot. The last remaining hero of 91, Steve Tilson, left for non-league Canvey Island. A demoralised team and a dwindling band of disillusioned supporters presented themselves to new manager Alvin Martin, another with no previous managerial experience. Why we kept doing this to ourselves was beyond me. Early in the new season, Marsh succumbed to a career-ending injury, to be followed by the departure of Byrne, who proved to be too mercurial once too often for Chairman Vic's liking. Slumping into the relegation zone at Christmas, United ended up rock-bottom of a division for the second season in a row.

We were back where we started ten years earlier, back in the fourth tier, now called the Third Division. The change of name didn't make it feel any better. Yet more drama off the pitch didn't make things any better either.

Vic Jobson finally handed over Southend United to an outfit called South Eastern Leisure, a joint venture between property development companies Martin Dawn plc and Delancey Estates for £4m. In 15 tumultuous years strapped to the mast at Roots Hall, Chairman Vic had pulled United out of a near-terminal financial catastrophe, steered us to the second tier for the first time in our history and put up the money to buy Stan Collymore, for much of which he was only faintly praised. On the other hand, he was pilloried mercilessly for proposing the move to a new stadium in Basildon (which was NOT going to happen), the absence of the new stadium in Southend, the demise of the South Bank, the to-ing and fro-ing with David Webb, the appointments of Bobby Moore, Dick Bate, Colin Murphy, Peter Taylor, Ronnie Whelan and Alvin Martin, relegation from the second tier and – why not – the Southend Pier fire of 1995.

New chairman John Main was, within two years, succeeded by Ron Martin (who immediately became Ron Chairman to me) with United languishing in obscurity. The extrovert that was Ken Bates, long-term chairman of Chelsea, once commented, 'I'm doing what all the bloody moaners would like to do – I'm the chairman. A supporter's dream is to own a football club.' The more restrained long-term Crystal Palace chairman, Ron Noades, offered a different perspective, 'Everyone thinks he can run a football club, but it's the most difficult business in the world.' I'm sure Chairman Vic could have testified to both sentiments.[40] In my opinion, his legacy was secured by saving Southend in the mid-80s, but not every United supporter over 30 will agree with me, and for supporters under 30 it will be a question of 'Vic who?'[41] Being the owner of a football club is a thankless task, if you ask me.

On the pitch, in a season so nondescript that I can hardly bear to mention it, we shuffled around the lower reaches of the division. I finally succeeded in having a beer or two in each of the pubs which used to stand on each corner at Brentford's old Griffin Park when I completed the set in November 1998. And then Brentford demolished us 4-1. United spent the season just too good for relegation but nowhere near good enough for promotion. The last six weeks at Roots Hall summed it

40 The Ken Bates and Ron Noades quotes are sourced from *Broken Dreams*. Written by Tom Bower. Pocket Books, 2007.

41 'Chairman Vic' Jobson sadly passed away in September 1999 at the age of 62.

up perfectly. Hull City at home – lost 1-0. Scunthorpe United at home – lost 1-0. Cardiff City at home – lost 1-0. Brentford at home – lost 4-1. A guard of dishonour from two, arguably three of our more painful bogey teams.

The final match is against Hartlepool United at Roots Hall on the dullish Saturday afternoon of 8 May 1999. I take a few photographs of the relentlessly grinning Sammy Bloody Shrimper, currently in his pink period. From our seats in the East Stand, Kim spots Hartlepool's Peter Beardsley, snaggle-toothed England star and veteran of two World Cups, ex-Newcastle, ex-Liverpool, ex-Everton and still playing at the age of 150. 'Peter,' Kim calls out. 'Peter!' Beardsley interrupts his slow jog around the pitch, turns and trots over towards us. 'Will you marry me, Peter?' 'Fancy a beer, Peter?' 'Got a spare cup final ticket, Peter?' may be going through his mind as he peers in our direction. I'm sure he's heard it all. As he draws to a stop, Kim stands up, waves and yells 'Hello Peter!!' – and 'click' goes my camera. Beardsley smiles indulgently, briefly waves back and turns away, back to his jogging routine in what turns out to be the final Football League appearance of his career. The match is a turgidly meaningless 1-1 draw watched by 4,865 hardcore and only brightened by a smartly taken goal by one of our new kids on the block, Kevin Maher. At least Southend didn't lose.

* * *

Manchester City fans still sing 'We're not really here' to commemorate their anomalous solitary season in the third tier, which climaxed in a penalty shoot-out win against Gillingham in the play-off final at Wembley. By the bye, Kim and I were walking along the banks of the River Brent, a few miles away from the old stadium that day. We didn't know the score until later, but the 50,000-strong vocal sonic boom we heard in the distance when City's goalkeeper, Nicky Weaver, made the match-winning penalty save left us in no doubt that City were on the long, sometimes tortuous, ladder to fame, fortune, Sheikh Mansour and Pep Guardiola.

In another galaxy far, far away (otherwise known as the Camp Nou, Barcelona), my other United defeated Bayern Munich 2-1 in the Champions League Final to complete the treble of Premier League, FA Cup and Champions League in one season. Never done before. That was momentous.[42]

***

Talking of momentous, we moved to Australia a few weeks later.

---

42 No English team won the treble in the years of the old First Division, FA Cup and the old European Cup. Liverpool came closest in 1976/77, only to be thwarted by Manchester United in the FA Cup Final.

Chapter 19

Seven Point Seven Seconds

FOOTBALL HEROES are such a schoolboy thing but, unlike pimples and punk rock, they are something some people never really grow out of. On Saturday, 30 April 2005, Southend United have languished in the fourth tier of the Football League for six years. But this season there is real cause for optimism, because we are pushing for promotion. With two games to go, United are in second place in what is now called League Two. We're behind Yeovil Town on goal difference and they just happen to be playing at Roots Hall today, in one of those beguiling coincidences that the fixture list periodically conjures up. We are one point ahead of Scunthorpe United and three ahead of Swansea City – and we have a better goal difference than Swansea. Four teams are chasing three automatic promotion places.

After the usual indifferent start, United have managed to stitch together a 14-game unbeaten run from January to April. Even though we have recently contrived to lose at home to Leyton Orient to absolutely no one's surprise and then lose at Oxford United, we are so close that a short, firm push will get us over the line. If we can win today, it will take an improbable combination of results on the final day to deny us a long-awaited return to the third tier, now called League One.

It is the match of the season and has caught the imagination of the town, judging by the difficulty I've had in getting tickets. Even the weather tips its hat to the importance of the occasion with a beautifully warm, sunny spring afternoon. I make my hopeful and expectant way towards the looming floodlight pylons of Roots Hall as a building throng, many in their blue replica shirts, feeds in from the side streets of Southchurch and Prittlewell. Hopeful because we could be promoted today if results go our way; expectant because we have Freddy Eastwood.

Phenomenal Freddy has appeared from nowhere this season and is now a first-choice striker, although he wears the number 23 shirt, like Michael Jordan (basketball), Shane Warne (cricket) and David Beckham (Real Madrid). Pure coincidence of course. He is 5ft 11in (my height), fair-haired (as I used to be), slim but not skinny (as I still am, I think); and there the similarity ends. Unlike the player I was, he is good with both feet, more than useful in the air and comfortable with dropping back into midfield to win the ball and use it to good effect. In other words, he is the footballer I wish I'd been.

Freddy has other assets. He's a local, signed from Grays Athletic, a non-league club 20 miles up London Road; he even shares his surname with one of the original parishes of Southend; all the allotropes of a local hero.[43] In his first league appearance the previous October, he took the ball from the kick-off, promptly passed it out wide and then sprinted forwards to meet a cross from the left and laser a header into the Swansea net: all in precisely 7.7 seconds, an all-time Football League record for a debutant and unlikely to ever be beaten. Then he scored another two goals for a debut hat-trick. Thirty games later, he has weighed in with 18 goals – not bad for a player released from the West Ham academy. Freddy is already a proven match-winner, waiting for his chance to dot the i's and cross the t's of Southend's elevation. I've seen him live twice this season and he's scored both times.

43 Freddy was not born in Essex (as I wasn't), hailing from Epsom in Surrey. But he grew up in Essex (as I did) so he is local enough for me.

There is a fly in the ointment, however. The fly is Kim. In 2005, we have been together for 14 years and married for five of them. In all this time, the number of times Kim has seen United win is dwarfed by the number of times she has seen them lose or draw. She is the Mark of Cain on Southend; it's a standing family joke. But there was no way Kim was going to miss this match and she is wearing one of my United replica shirts for the first time. It's the red away shirt, but Yeovil don't play in red, so no harm, no foul. Maybe it's a good omen, and any good omen is useful. Joining us is brother-in-law Nacer, no stranger to the Southend madness.

Dad passed away two weeks earlier after a short but distressing illness. That is why we are in England. We push our way into the crowded Railway Tavern and raise a toast to him. Dad would have hugely enjoyed this occasion. We are surrounded by Yeovil supporters in their retro green-and-white-hooped replica shirts; something you would perhaps expect to see on a rugby union team from the West Country or Glasgow Celtic circa 1960. Fair enough; Yeovil are from the West Country and the club has only been in the Football League for two seasons, so they do have some excuse. Their fans are a boisterous, friendly crew and seem pleasantly surprised at their own success. The Southend supporters, in traditional blue and white, are also boisterous and friendly, but with more of a sense of entitlement. Nevertheless, the banter is good-natured, typical lower-division self-deprecating camaraderie.

***

Although I secured our tickets a week earlier, my usual vantage points are booked out. So we take our seats in the second row from the front of the North Bank – the first seat I have ever bought for the North Bank and, indeed, the first time in 12 years I have watched a match from there. That is what happens with a full house at Roots Hall. Our eye-line is roughly at pitch level and puts me in mind of gazing across no man's land from a first world war trench parapet. It's a good job the seats in the front row have been deliberately left unsold.

Another era. 'Welcome to Roots Hall; the home of SOUTHEND UNITEDDD!!' yells the current, more youthful version of Roots Hall Ron. Sammy Bloody Shrimper, in one of his white periods, parades on the pitch with his relentless grin, although he now appears to be known as Sammy the Shrimp. The 21st century has also seen the emergence of another mascot, a prodigiously ugly offsider with an authentic Southend ancestry: one Elvis J. Eel (J for jellied – get it?). This strange creature, as thin as Sammy is fat, has a Mod hairstyle and his own manic grin is also a matchday fixture at Roots Hall. Dance music booms out to all corners as an accompaniment to the Blue Belles, a dancing troupe of wholesome young ladies who adorn matchdays in outfits of variable brevity, depending on the weather. Today, the outfits are as brief as good taste allows. The attendance is 11,735, the biggest crowd in 12 years and the biggest ever all-seated crowd at Roots Hall.[44] Where else would any local football fan want to be on the penultimate day of a long season with honours at stake?

One more ear-splitting blast from Roots Hall Ron and the teams emerge together into the bright sunshine, trotting past a guard of honour comprising Sammy, Elvis and a delegation of Blue Belles. The welcoming roar is as loud as 12,000 people can muster. The Yeovil players, in their green and white hoops, wheel away to accept and return the rapturous applause of their supporters.

Another era. In the reconfigured Roots Hall of 2005, the old North Bank is officially the 'away end' although 1,000 or so Southend supporters, including Kim and me, occupy

---

44 The official capacity of Roots Hall is currently 12,392, but we're unlikely to see that many in the old ground any time soon. Source: *Sky Football Yearbook*.

one third of it. Five yards to our left are a few columns of empty seats covered in tarpaulin, a line of fluorescent-jacketed stewards, and beyond them roughly 1,500 green and white hoops. The diminutive two-deck Frank Walton South Stand opposite is now officially the 'home end', complete with a small group of musicians in the upper tier rhythmically thumping large kettledrums to keep the punters on message.

In the old days, we wanted United to win the toss and kick towards the South Bank in the first half and the North Bank in the second, to capitalise upon the ramped-up noise after half-time. But for Southend supporters in 2005, the preference is to play north towards the away end in the first half and towards the home fans in the Frank Walton Stand for the second. Unless, that is, we have a bright sunny day like today, because an additional benefit of our traditional preference was the position of the sun in the first half as it slowly moved westwards directly into the eyes of the opposing goalkeeper. Many things have changed at Roots Hall, but the sun hasn't.

The coin is tossed, but the United goalkeeper Daryl Flahavan trots towards us. Kicking the wrong way is a notoriously bad omen. On the other hand, the Yeovil custodian has to contend with the sun for 45 minutes. He's sporting a cap with a seriously large sun visor. Did we win or lose the toss? This conundrum makes me ponder permutations while the teams prepare for kick-off. Pathetic in a way, but most football stalwarts are either born superstitious or have superstition thrust upon them. It's also plain common sense. How often do you see Liverpool kicking towards the Kop in the first half?

A rising crescendo climaxes as the match kicks off. As expected, the sun is playing a part. Every time the ball is moved into the Yeovil half, 3,000 hands in the East Stand are simultaneously raised to shade eyes, rather like the choreographed mass salute in a North Korean military parade. Unfortunately, the Yeovil keeper is not as challenged as he might be, as the teams feel each other out, reluctant to take risks. As for the crowd, the current songs of choice have evolved to a succession of 'duh, duh, duhs' and 'nah, nah, nahs' to the beat of the drums, concluding with a bellowed 'SOUTHEND'. Elmer Bernstein's theme tune to 'The Great Escape' meets 'Vindaloo' by Fat Les. But 'Sea-Sea-Seasiders' and 'Come on Southend' are still part of the repertoire, and the refrains are now regularly taken up by all sides of Roots Hall, even in the East Stand.

With 7.7 seconds passed Freddy hasn't scored, but that only happens once in a lifetime. Another ten minutes pass and not much has happened. To our right, a Blues supporter, eyes locked on to his mobile phone, mutters '1-0 to Swansea'. Groans break out as other eyes divert to their screens. My mobile is turned off. Back in the days of the Sony Walkman, I inadvertently picked up a progress score I profoundly didn't want to know, so I'm superstitious that way; '1-0 Scunthorpe' follows almost immediately. In the old days, we had to wait for score updates (if we were lucky) from whoever had a transistor radio or the good offices of Roots Hall Ron at half-time, but now we know in real time and neither of these scores are good news. Fifteen minutes gone, '2-0 Scunthorpe' announces the mobile man. 'Oh, shit – COME ON SOUTHEND!' screams out a voice as the percussion section and 'Vindaloo' starts up again with more urgency.

I don't know if anyone on the pitch knows the scores from elsewhere (fans usually find a way of letting them know), but the match sparks into life. The ball is driven into the Yeovil penalty area and a United head guides the ball to Freddy, 12 yards out. A swing on the volley, a miskick and the ball bounces harmlessly away for a goal kick. A few minutes later, United win a free kick and Mark Gower's screamer looks in all the way from our position, then the ball hits a defender and deflects past the far post. Roars of triumph are cut off in midstream and some occupants of the South Stand have their heads in their hands. Then it's half-time; we haven't done much, but Yeovil have done less.

During the interval, seats around us empty for a few minutes while people do their half-time things, with many eyes fixed on mobile screens. I have a pen and the matchday programme open to the league table. As it stands, Scunthorpe go top, one point ahead of Yeovil and us, with Swansea just one point behind. We are still in a good position – even better if we win. Championships, trophies, I don't care. Let Scunthorpe have the trophy, as long as we get the three points. If we can score a couple of goals in the process, that will give Yeovil the panics and almost certainly take Swansea out of the equation.

But now we are kicking towards the 'wrong end'. The heat of the day starts to take effect and the importance of the win is now apparent to both sides. From the voice to our right comes '3-0 Scunthorpe'. To hell with Scunthorpe: the world has now collapsed into Southend, Yeovil and Swansea, playing Shrewsbury Town 200 miles away. 'Come on Southend' rings around Roots Hall as it always used to, now more pleading than uplifting.

Freddy picks up the ball 30 yards out. He bears down on the Yeovil back line at an angle, trying to work a position for a shot at goal or a burst into the penalty area. He takes the ball past a defender and moves laterally across the edge of the area, looking for a space to pull the trigger. Drill it low past the keeper's dive and into the far corner; he's done it more than once this season. The United supporters in the North Bank are rising. Trigger pulled. I can see that the ball will miss the target as soon as Freddy connects. Pulled and slightly scuffed, the shot zips past the goalie and the far post and comes to rest on the running track not five yards from me. The Yeovil fans jeer, arms spread wide. The rest of Roots Hall slump back into our seats; '4-0 Scunthorpe' comes from our right. Oh, shut up!

Seven minutes to go. Scunthorpe out of sight, Swansea still one up, and our match is now end-to-end, as both teams have decided to go for it. Roots Hall is on the edge of its collective seat, almost too tense to shout. An angled United cross is caught cleanly by the keeper, who immediately chucks it to a forward called Phil Jevons, lurking near halfway. A nudge past a United defender, a quick pass inside and Yeovil are away, the home defence backtracking frantically. From my trench parapet view, this doesn't look good. A shot attempted from 25 yards is half-blocked by a defender and the ball deflects back to the feet of Jevons who has galloped down the left wing in anticipation. Without breaking stride, he dinks the ball perfectly over the on-rushing Flahavan and into the net. Southend attack to Yeovil goal in 7.7 seconds or thereabouts. The green and white hoops go barmy, as do the Yeovil manager and coaching staff.

'Bloody hell! Ouch!' I exclaim as I thump the back of the empty seat in front with the palm of my hand – hard. Good job nobody was sitting there. I slump back in my seat and rest my chin in my hand. 'Come on Southend, you can still do it!' shouts Kim, because she's like that. Doomed, that's how I feel – I just sort of know it. As the seconds stream away, the 'Come on Southend' cries from the West Stand take on a frenetic note. A few flurries at each end, a couple of late corners, a bit of added-on time but all to Noah Vale, who pays an unwelcome return visit.

The final whistle. Yeovil have won it 1-0 and are promoted. Players, coaching staff and the Jolly Green Giant, Yeovil's scary-looking mascot, hurtle towards the North Bank. As the gutted home supporters around me wander towards the exits, Kim and I hang around for a few minutes to add our own polite applause to the West Country celebrations because we're like that and then slowly, despondently, we beat our retreat to join the despondent multitudes making their despondent way back to their homes, cars and buses. As we leave, Swansea's 1-0 victory is confirmed. Freddy's had an off day; after the season he's had, he's owed one, just a shame it had to happen today.

'It's not over yet,' offers Kim, gamely trying to cheer me up. And she's right of course. Yeovil are pretty much beyond us now, probably Scunthorpe as well, but all we have to do is better the Swansea result next week and we're up. Swansea's last match is at Bury, United's at Grimsby Town; both opponents have little to play for, but Grimsby have a long history of raining on our parade. In any event, in the space of just 94 minutes, we are now the team behind the eight ball, and long, bitter experience has taught me where that leads. I can guess what Dad would have said about it. 'Typical. Just typical.'

***

Grimsby did rain on our parade; pissed all over it, in fact. Despite being on top for virtually the whole match, we could only manage a single goal – from Freddy – in a 1-1 draw. Yeovil and Scunthorpe did the necessary and Swansea nicked a 1-0 win at Bury. Once again, defeat plucked from the jaws of victory. Swansea were the third team promoted, to their possible surprise but undoubted delight.

United's fate was a two-legged play-off semi-final – against Northampton Town, who were not noted for their generosity when it came to playing the Blues. Despite this, United managed to keep them out in a tight goalless draw at Sixfields. In the second leg, under the Roots Hall lights, it was just as tight, but Freddy scored with a nerveless penalty early in the second half. Flahavan executed an impeccable flying horizontal save to deny a Northampton header in the last minute and we held out for a 1-0 win we barely deserved. Too bad, so sad for Northampton.

And so to the temporary Wembley stand-in, the Millennium Stadium in Cardiff for the play-off final against Lincoln City. United had recent experience of playing at the Millennium. In 2004, we played Blackpool in the final of the Also-Rans Cup (called the LDV Vans Trophy that year) – and lost 2-0. Six weeks before the play-off final, we played in the

LDV final again – and lost 2-0 to Wrexham. Not the best record to take to the Lincoln match.

Kim and I were back at home in Sydney. Our cable service hadn't got around to showing the match live on TV. Tabby cat Rimmer had decided to retire to bed, as usual, while black cat Scamp was vaguely interested from a distance. As usual. Meanwhile, I was stuck with a computer monitor and the BBC Football website for company in the chilly early hours of a New South Wales Sunday morning, 29 May 2005, so I had to rely on my end-of-season DVD to see what happened on the pitch.[45] In old South Wales it was a hot, sunny Saturday afternoon and Lincoln were on top but couldn't find the goal their pressure probably warranted. In New South Wales, I was a nervous wreck, pressing 'refresh' with feverish regularity as the Beeb reported no scoreboard action from either side in the first 90 minutes.

Into the first period of extra time, United finally started to get their act together. In added time, we won a corner. A delivery to the near post, a towering header miraculously bundled off the line by a Lincoln defender, one of the shortest and smartest square passes in United history by substitute Lawrie Dudfield and Freddy rammed the ball into the net from all of six feet.

Five minutes into the second period, Lincoln were pressing again, but the ball broke out of defence and made its way to Freddy near halfway. This time he outdid Phil Jevons: he skinned the marking defender and motored into the Lincoln half, with their defence all over the place. In the meantime, our full-back Duncan Jupp was steaming up the right in an acre of space. Freddy's pass was perfect; one touch and Jupp steered his shot expertly into the far corner of the net for his one and only goal for Southend. Game over: a tiring Lincoln done for and a final score of 2-0.

---

45 Saturday, 28 May 2005 in the UK.

It wouldn't be Southend United if there wasn't a false dawn or two but it turned out OK in the end. Promotion back to the third tier was secured and we ended up with silverware after all: a small angular affair signifying a play-off final win, the second of the four significant trophies United have ever collected. Some say that achieving promotion by winning the play-off final is the best way to do it because of the occasion, the all-or-nothing atmosphere and all that jazz. Fair comment, so long as you can handle three weeks of buttock-clenching tension, the feeling of peering over a cliff edge as an entire season condenses into three games.

How could we have doubted Freddy? Maybe he didn't catch fire against Yeovil. But the icy-calm penalty against Northampton, the crashing finish for the first goal at the Millennium, the craft and vision to set up the second and clinch the game propelled him toward legend territory in his first season. We waited with bated breath for what he might achieve in his second.

Chapter 20

Love in a Warm Climate

AROUND THE corner from our home in the Eastern Suburbs of Sydney stood a pleasant little bungalow painted in royal blue and white. Its immaculately maintained front garden included a garden gnome or two and a cute little stone bridge over a pond nestling in the greenery. Fixed above the garage door was a traditional-looking white metal street sign:

'City of Liverpool

GOODISON ROAD L4'

Proud Everton supporters residing in a Sydney suburban street, just 12,000 miles from their spiritual home. It does happen in Australia: just not very often. I would have loved to attach a Roots Hall sign to my house. Sadly, the word 'Roots' means sexual intercourse in Australia, so that was a non-starter.

***

Football means many things in Australia and association football is among the least of them, despite the perennial efforts of round-ball advocates to claim the name as their own. In New South Wales and Queensland, football generally means rugby league and the National Rugby League (NRL) premier competition. In Victoria, South Australia, Tasmania and Northern Territory, football generally means Australian rules football, which has appropriated the label as the

Australian Football League (AFL). Western Australia is a mixed bag of footballing traditions, but mainly Australian rules. Even 'footy' means something different, depending on where you live. Rugby union – just called rugby in Australia – is the poor relation of Australian football codes, miles behind the other egg-chasers in terms of participation, support base, sponsorship and media exposure. Although union straddles the whole country, to my mind it remains self-consciously uncertain of its place in the sporting hierarchy.

In Australia, as in the United States, association football is generally called soccer. It spans the whole nation, but does not predominate anywhere; jack of all states, master of none. Its broad roots more closely reflect the influx of migrants from central, eastern and southern Europe following the second world war than the influx from Britain which preceded it. The most ethnically diverse terrestrial television station, the Special Broadcasting Service (or SBS) has spent much of its history labouring under the unflattering sobriquet of 'Soccer Bloody Soccer'. Or at least it did until the SBS progressively disengaged itself from the televised football scene, more's the pity.

In my Sydney suburb, rugby league ruled and the green and red horizontal stripes of the South Sydney Rabbitohs, fronted by their ubiquitous little white cartoon bunny, dominated the replica shirts, car stickers and car number plates. My wife Kim traditionally supported the Sydney Roosters, the local rivals from a few miles up the road. Over the years, we have watched the Rabbitohs and Roosters very rarely; we went to the 2000 Grand Final between the Roosters and the Brisbane Broncos with 94,000 fans at the newly built Olympic Stadium – which the Roosters lost, to maintain Kim's reputation as the sporting kiss of death. As a spectacle, it was fine but I was struck by the unfamiliarity of the crowd atmosphere, because Australian rugby league crowds don't chant all that much and sing less. If anything, the atmosphere reminded me of English football crowds before the advent of coordinated community noise in the mid-60s. The NRL in general, the Rabbitohs and the Roosters are attractions that have mostly passed me by.

Our local Aussie rules team was the Sydney Swans who played at the famous Sydney Cricket Ground, a short bus ride up the road. Back in England, Channel 4 used to broadcast a one-hour show of highlights on Saturday mornings. I quite enjoyed the TV spectacle and wondered what the real thing would be like. Rules crowds turn up in droves but don't chant and sing very much either and much of my infrequent visits to the SCG has been spent trying to decipher what is going on at the far reaches of the cricket-sized field from the big-screen TV monitors around the stadium. The annual Grand Final at the Melbourne Cricket Ground is a stellar event, played in front of 100,000 enthusiasts and a good watch on television, but AFL doesn't float my boat either, I'm afraid.

Professional soccer (sorry, football) is manifested in the A-League, introduced as recently as 2005 after a century of short-lived attempts to create a proper national competition. Our local team was Sydney FC, whose 15,000 fanbase shared, with the Rabbitohs and Roosters, the concrete monstrosity of the old Sydney Football Stadium next door to the SCG. Identical in basic structure to the original English Football League from 1888 to 1892, the A-League has only 12 teams (now 13) with no underlying league pyramid, so these teams and their supporters don't get to experience the exhilaration of a promotion challenge or the frisson of a relegation battle. At the end of the regular season, the top six teams embark on a set of play-off matches for the right to take part in the season-ending pinnacle of the Grand Final; if you win that, you've won the equivalent of the English Premier League.

Sydney FC have won four Grand Finals and we haven't been to any of them, although we did get to the old Sydney Football Stadium to see Central Coast Mariners beat Newcastle Jets a few years ago and we do watch the occasional match on TV. I suppose we should have tried harder to get into it but, once again, Sydney FC and the A-League in general have not got the juices flowing.

We have made an exception for Australia's World Cup qualifying matches when played at the principal Sydney 2000 Olympics venue once called Stadium Australia, then the Telstra Stadium, then the ANZ Stadium and now the Accor Stadium. Over the years, we've been to most of these matches and, with 80,000-plus in the ground the atmosphere is pretty good, so long as I tune out the repetitive 'Aussie, Aussie, Aussie; oi, oi, oi' emanating from some sections of the stands, a distant relative of the old Cornwall 'Iggy-Oggy' and a more recent descendant of the 'Oggy, oggy, oggy, oi, oi, oi' used by Welsh comedian Max Boyce to open his shows.

Here lies the paradox of Australian soccer/football. Although men's A-League average crowds are lower than the NRL or AFL (and seem to be in decline), soccer has the highest public participation rate of any football code.[46] And, judging by the success of the 2023 Women's World Cup hosted by Australia and New Zealand, we should expect a future surge in interest, partly depending on whether the women's game develops in concert with, or in place of, the men's.

In 24 years of living in Australia I have acquired an Australian passport in addition to my British version but when it comes to sport I have never 'gone native'. Perhaps it's because I made the big move in my 40s, and my sporting allegiances have remained as unswerving as my accent, which remains stubbornly English. I suspect, however, that the main reason has been the ultimate panacea for football-loving expatriates: pay TV.

---

46 The word 'football' instead of 'soccer' seems to be adopted more and more in Australia, but very slowly. In an August 2023 poll, 44 per cent of those surveyed nominated soccer as 'top of mind' when associated with football, followed by 39 per cent for AFL. Source: *Sydney Morning Herald*.

Prior to the 1990s, Kim tells me, exposure of English football in Australia was limited to insomniacs hunched over a crackling BBC World Service broadcast on the radio, Monday night's *Match of the Week*, a made-for-Australia version of *Match of the Day* shown on the ABC, pre-season forays down under by one of the leading lights and the FA Cup Final, resolutely broadcast live on the TV and the focal point of nationwide midnight booze-ups. If, like Southend United, the team you supported was not famous enough to justify this exposure, it was the tiny print in the back end of the sports pages in Monday's *Sydney Morning Herald* for you.

Pay TV was entrenched when we set up in Sydney and the Foxtel Sports service had it all. We could watch more Premier League matches than even we could handle. A weekly live Championship match and an hour-long weekend wrap showed all the goals from the rest of the Football League – even Southend United goals. The FA Cup, the Champions League, the UEFA Cup and its successor, the Europa League – you name it, we had it. Even the Soccer Bloody Soccer terrestrial channel weighed in with a live Premier League match every week and the latter stages of the FA Cup. Our set-top box worked overtime managing all this traffic, and we ended up watching more English football than we ever had in England. Over time, commercial renegotiations and the advent of pay-per-view streaming services have significantly changed the landscape for English football lovers down under. Today, we get our Premier League from Optus Sports and another overworked set-top box. Our Foxtel service retained the Championship, supplemented by the occasional offering from League One and League Two until last year when beIN Sports decamped to the Optus portfolio but we have to pay our subscription to a streaming app curiously called Stan for the Champions League and Europa League. Our FA Cup fix was delivered via another app called Paramount+ until Optus Sport did the decent thing and acquired the rights this season. The extensive and diverse offerings from YouTube pick up the slack for the rest. Terrestrial TV (known in Australia as 'free-to-air') is now out of the picture completely as far as English club football is concerned and is restricted to the attractions of the A-League. Thankfully, Soccer Bloody Soccer lived up to its name by securing the rights for the 2022 World Cup in Qatar.

In the ever-changing world of today's football media, it's pure guesswork who'll be showing what in two years' time, but the new era of subscription-based streaming services looks to be irreversible.

***

They are easy to spot as their owners stroll along the suburban streets and shopping malls of Eastern Sydney. Replica shirts, the sporting fashion accessory of the 21st century. The red and green of the Rabbitohs predominate, closely followed by the red, white and blue of the Roosters.[47] The white shirts with the red 'V' worn by Swans fans also feature strongly. From the A-League perspective, we see the sky-blue Sydney FC shirts and the odd red and black striped number denoting supporters of Western Sydney Wanderers, Sydney FC's noisy neighbours.

But we can also spot the replica shirts of Manchester United, Liverpool, Arsenal, Chelsea, Tottenham and Leeds United. A more careful look distinguishes the Manchester City replicas from their Sydney FC lookalikes. Some of them will be expats like me: others are true-blue Aussies with cable TV and a handful of sports apps, or an English football-supporting family heritage, or an allegiance picked up in an extended rite of passage trip to the UK. In the case of Leeds United, allegiance may have been driven by notable Australian football legends Harry Kewell and Mark Viduka from the Leeds side which enjoyed a spell at the top table of English and

47 Traditionally known as Souths and Easts, reflecting their common Sydney heritage.

European football in the early 2000s and part of the Aussie golden generation that nearly turned over Italy in the 2006 World Cup.

It's a fact that the most replica shirts I have ever seen worn in one venue anywhere was in Sydney on 20 July 2013 at the Olympic Stadium (or the ANZ Stadium as it was that year). Manchester United, reigning Premier League champions, played a pre-season friendly against A-League All Stars and, in a crowd of 83,127, I reckon at least 70,000 were wearing red shirts adorned with over 30 years' worth of sponsored logos. Kim wore the current AON shirt and I squeezed into her old AIG United shirt, so I was only a couple of years out of date. The Reds won 5-1 to all-round satisfaction.

Kim's collection of Manchester United regalia attracts the occasional comment but Southend shirts are rather thin on the ground in Australia. Let the record show that I possess eight, going back to 2003, and four polo shirts, all adorned with the club crest. Let the record also show that my collection of United gear has rarely aroused more than mild curiosity and generally nothing more than a studied indifference.

There must be other English lower-division enthusiasts like me in Australia and indeed there are, as I could clearly see at Sydney Cricket Ground when England played Australia in an Ashes Test. Yes, I've got my England's Barmy Army jersey all right, but the replica United shirt tended to get more of an airing on Ashes days. And there were the others, thousands of them emerging out of the woodwork: Bristol City, Sheffield Wednesday, Crewe Alexandra, Swindon Town, Gillingham. I broke my own rule to secure a selfie with Spencer Prior, the Spenno who slipped in the mud of Roots Hall on Boxing Day 1990 and a Fox Sports Premier League pundit in Australia for a couple of years – neither of us had a pen handy. The SCG is a lower-league football melting pot. Communication in the queue for the bars and the food concessions largely comes in the form of a brief nod of recognition or a perceptive passing comment such as, 'You lot are in trouble this year.' I don't know where they hide the rest of the time.

In all my 18 years of living in Sydney, I only ever saw two cars with a Southend rear window sticker and both of them were mine. Two Honda Civics: the older one prominently displayed 'Southend United Football Club' while the newer one boasts a slightly smaller 'Southend United on Tour' label, supplemented by the good old club crest.

**

English football fans were also scattered about my office. Fellow expatriates were self-confessed supporters of Tottenham, Arsenal, Nottingham Forest and Aston Villa, with accents to match. We even had a temp for a few months who was related to the great John McKinven, scorer of the first Southend United goal I ever saw. Staunch Australian-accented fans of Manchester United, Manchester City, Liverpool, West Ham and Leeds also took more than a passing interest in sporting events 12,000 miles away.

As a Southend lifer, I was an ugly duckling when it came to setting out my stall but, on my first day at work, I unpacked a United computer mouse mat, adorned with the trusty three scimitars, the football, the waves and the shrimp. The shrimp attracted particular interest but was quickly dismissed as a prawn, because shrimps don't really happen in Australia. So United were christened 'The Prawns' by my working colleagues from day one. Hence the perennial Monday morning question, 'How'd the Prawns go on the weekend?' At least the fair city of Southend was not a complete unknown. One Australian colleague had spent a few months working behind the bar at the Ship on Marine Parade. A few had even sampled the delights of ToTS as part of their English rite of passage.

Football enthusiasts or not, the banal eccentricities of English FootballSpeak excited great amusement from fellow wage slaves. They had such a giggle hearing about David

Webb being 'treated like a dirty rag' that it entered the office vernacular for a range of injustices, real or imagined. Ian Holloway, a peripatetic manager across England, from Plymouth Argyle to Grimsby Town, from Crystal Palace to Blackpool, is a FootballSpeak laureate. His quotes could fill a library, but I recall with pleasure a TV interview when he described the possibility of being sacked as 'getting a tap on the shoulder and given the old hello'. My circle of work colleagues was incredulous, 'But that's gibberish! It means the exact opposite of what it's supposed to mean!' Not quite: the clue is in the way you say 'hello'. No matter; this deathless phrase was quickly adopted as a euphemism for disciplinary action.

For sheer delirium it would be difficult to beat another peripatetic football character: ex-Bristol City, ex-Newcastle United, ex-Manchester United, ex-Manchester City, ex-everywhere, Andrew Cole, the footballing artiste formerly known as Andy Cole. At half-time in the semi-final of the 2016 European Championship, beIN Sports guest pundit Andy (sorry) Andrew bemused football enthusiasts in North Africa and the Middle East who thought they knew a bit of English, plus Australians and New Zealanders who most certainly did, by solemnly declaring that Pepe, the Portuguese central defender, 'had a rick in the bag'. Back to my work colleagues, 'What the? It doesn't mean anything. What does it even mean??' Patiently, I explained that 'rick' is an abbreviation of 'ricket', which is Cockney for 'mistake' – nobody quite seems to know why. Therefore, according to Andrew Cole, Pepe was prone to make unexpected mistakes and, indeed, he often was – but not during this semi-final, which Portugal won. Another entry in the ledger of English verbal lunacy which confers undeserved kudos on those in the know and totally baffles those who aren't. And another addition to the office vocabulary to qualify errors major and minor.

***

Absence makes the heart grow fonder and I'm living proof because my devotion to the Blues seems to have grown over the last 20 years. Not that I was completely cut off from the English Football League vibe. Wall-to-wall Premier League on the TV helped, as did the weekly wrap show for the lower divisions. So did the internet, prompting my extensive Sunday morning perusal of the BBC Football and Southend United websites. And, for one reason or another, I was able to make my way back to Roots Hall five times in the first five years following our departure from England. That United failed to win any of the five matches I attended, culminating in the Yeovil Town ricket of April 2005, was disappointing but I bore it steadfastly. As previously recorded, I was back in Sydney for the play-off final against Lincoln City which was just as well.

Our rise from the depths was all the more remarkable because Ron Chairman had decided to emulate Chairman Vic and taken a punt on another manager with no Football League management experience. Ah, but it was different this time, because Steve Tilson was already part of United's coaching staff and, importantly, he was one of our playing heroes of 91. Cut him and he'd bleed blue and white. Within a year of his appointment, two other heroes of 91, Spencer 'Spenno' Prior and Andy 'Eagle' Edwards returned to Roots Hall. Adam Barrett, a balding goalscoring centre-back and another stalwart with blue and white blood in his veins, arrived to join the latest United project. Darryl Flahavan was short in stature for a goalkeeper but huge in agility between the sticks. Duncan Jupp, Che Wilson and Lewis Hunt completed the defending unit, none of them strangers to the finer and the darker arts of the game. Kevin Maher had matured into an inspirational captain and serene midfield general. Mark Gower, Luke Guttridge and Mark Bentley were midfielders of a feistier stamp. A well-rounded squad, underpinned by a nucleus of locals ready, willing and able to die for the shirt. All without our customary 'big 'un up front', although bustling Wayne Gray could do a decent impression on his day. Tilson added a living legend from another football universe: the veteran Shaun Goater, one-time nemesis of Manchester United, whose two goals in a 3-1 victory had earned undying love from City fans in the last derby at Maine Road and turned Alex Ferguson's nose a deeper shade of purple. 'Feed the Goat and he will score.' And we still had Freddy Eastwood.

***

After that brief flurry of visits back to England, finances and a shrunken annual leave balance precluded a return trip in the 2005/06 season and – wouldn't you know it? – that season promised to be consequential. Unfortunately for me, all I saw of it were the results from the BBC and United websites and the goals shown on Setanta's weekly Football League wrap – but there were plenty of them to see.

Following our usual sluggish start, Colchester United did us a favour by capitulating 3-1 on a high summer Roots Hall Saturday, sent packing with two goals from the Goat. A flawless run of eight successive wins took United to the top of the League One table by November. Even the usual dip in form before Christmas was not enough to derail our promotion challenge, which saw us back in top spot by the new year. Holy smoke, it was 1991 again! Despite my absence, attendances at Roots Hall were back up to a level not seen since the 70s. And the Monday morning question and answer session became routine. 'How'd the Prawns go? Won again, did they?' It was only the dreaded Colchester who were challenging us, not just for top team in Essex, but also for promotion and championship honours themselves. Saturday, 4 March 2006 saw the United of Southend demolish the United of Colchester 3-0, with first-half goals from Freddy (as ever), Maher and Wilson (first of the season for each of them), a performance that my spy at tumbledown Layer Road told me was a masterclass in ruthless footballing domination.

The run-in was made more traumatic by successive 1-0 home defeats at the hands of Gillingham and Doncaster Rovers, but promotion was safely secured on 29 April at Swansea City's brand-new Liberty Stadium. Freddy drilled in two goals of supreme opportunism to steer us to a 2-2 draw, to the ecstasy of 2,000 Blues fans in Swansea and at least two more 12,000 miles away.

There was no way that United's final match, against Bristol City at Roots Hall on Saturday, 6 May 2006, was going to be shown on any Australian television service, cable or otherwise. I know, I tried.

Frantic searching for options other than more nervous prods of the 'refresh' key unearthed an online audio broadcast, thanks to the miracle of digital radio. I don't remember which radio station it was but, judging by the stridently partisan commentary, it may have been BBC Radio Essex. Or Essex Radio, the Beeb's commercial counterpart. Or a radio service conjured up by Southend United. Anyway, with the match goalless and three minutes to go, Kevin Maher nicked the ball in midfield and passed it to substitute Wayne Gray, on the left and in oceans of space. Just like Yeovil's Phil Jevons against United the year before, Gray bore down on goal, checked for an instant and then steered a shot sweet, true and very slightly deflected past the City goalkeeper to hit the net in front of the Frank Walton Stand. At least that's what I saw later on the Football League wrap show and on the season's DVD a little later still. Like live radio broadcasts since the beginning of recorded time, the details were lost in the rapid-fire garbled semi-hysteria: the building roar, the distorted explosion as ball hit net and the commentator's barely coherent 'WAYNE GRAY!!' bawled across the airwaves. Not to mention the distorted explosion, 12,000 miles away, in our third bedroom doubling as a home office. Amid the madness on air, it took me a moment to take it in. Then I heard the celebratory anthem, DJ Ötzi's version of 'Hey Baby' booming out from the PA and 11,397 spectators around Roots Hall. 'Heyyyy, Wayne Gray, OOHH-AAHH, I wanna know-oh-oh-oh-oh-oh, how you scored that goal?'[48] That's when I knew for certain that United had secured the most important trophy in our history and laid the ghost of that final trophy-denying defeat by Brentford back in 1991.

By the winning score of 1-0. Of course. The March humbling of Colchester at Layer Road provided the points cushion needed to see us top the table and push them down to second. 'Champeones, Champeones, olé, olé olé' sang the Roots Hall crowd for the first time ever, as the silverware was presented to Kevin Maher on the pitch.[49] All on the 100th anniversary of the club's foundation: 'A Century United 1906–2006', as emblazoned on my favourite replica shirt.

***

Euphoric Ron Chairman announced progress on Fossetts Farm, a project already several years old. Located on the edge of town, not too far from Roots Hall and the old Grainger Road ground, our new stadium would deliver 22,000 seats, a flash hotel and the adjoining retail park which would underpin Southend United as a rising star in the new firmament that was English football in the 2000s. I watched the virtual reality video and it was magnificent, while Roots Hall was mooted as the site for a new Sainsbury's superstore.

United returned to what was now called the Championship a bigger club than on their first appearance. The trouble was that one could also say that for most of the other Championship clubs, a testimony to the recovery of English league football from the 1980s. Our average attendance of 10,000 would be easily eclipsed by rivals pulling in 25, 30, 35,000; the Norwich

---

48 The original version was written and recorded by Bruce Channel in 1961, without the 'OOHH-AAHHs'.

49 The 'Champeones' song, appropriated from the Spanish word *campeones*, is now an English football staple, but it wasn't around in 1981.

Cities, the Derby Counties, the Sunderlands and the rest. We had a challenge in front of us.

A new division brought another pre-season transfer kerfuffle. We already knew that the Goat was a one-season wonder and he retired on cue. Part of the 2006 heroes ensemble was dismantled, prematurely in my view. Goodbye to Jupp, Bentley, Edwards, Cole. But their replacements Simon Francis, Peter Clarke, Steven Hammell and Jamal Campbell-Ryce looked sound enough. We even managed to retain the highly marketable Freddy Eastwood with his 23 league goals from the previous campaign. But could I believe that Wayne Gray, scorer of the historic winner against Bristol City, would leave for Yeovil Town? Look, don't get me started.

***

Sydney is world-renowned for its achingly picturesque harbour, the towering Harbour Bridge and the unorthodox Opera House. For a few years, I could see them all from my office window. Casual holidaymakers may not be aware that, three miles west of these icons, a suburban hinterland rolls out, stretching westward beyond the horizon, a sprawl of houses, offices, factories and shopping centres all the way to the foothills of the Blue Mountains 35 miles distant. Snaking through all this brick and concrete are ribbons of major roads, beset by innumerable sets of traffic lights. For ten years, I unwillingly traded the harbour view for these suburban roads every weekday from home in the south-east of town to my new office campus in the north-west suburbs, partaking in the ritual of pulling up every 100 yards or so, waiting for yet another red traffic light to turn green. I would glance in the rear-view mirror and see legions of tradespeople (known as 'tradies' in Australia) waiting behind me in their pick-up trucks (known as 'Utes') peering down at my rear window stickers and saying to themselves 'What the bloody hell is THAT?' I could see some of them rapidly poking the keys on their mobiles trying to find out who or what Southend United was. Some of them laughed or rolled their eyes or shook their heads in disbelief; a few even beeped their horns in sympathy or derision. Maybe some of them would start tracking the Blues on the internet.

I was delighted to project Southend United deep into the western Sydney suburbs of Wiley Park, Greenacre, Homebush and Concord. But it would take more than window stickers to address the perpetual question: Southend United. Who are we?

Chapter 21

Who Are You? Who Are We?

ONE SATURDAY lunchtime in October 1986, I was at
a loose end in central London. Southend United were at
home, but I had spent too long at the office, putting in the
weekend hours that the marketing consultancy I worked for
too often required. Instead, I made a last-minute decision to
hop northwards on the Victoria line for Tottenham Hotspur
against Sheffield Wednesday at White Hart Lane.

Both teams were doing quite well in the old First Division,
but I knew I would have no trouble getting in, because full
houses were rare events in 1986. I was right: I easily bought
my ticket to luxuriate in the newish West Stand and took my
seat in a crowd of less than 27,000. It was a good game; two
well-matched teams played out a creditable 1-1 draw. As a
self-evidently neutral spectator, I struck up a conversation with
the friendly Tottenham supporter next to me, something I do
at matches when I don't really care who wins. After a while
came the obvious question.

'Who's your team, then?'

'I'm a Southend supporter, I'm afraid.'

'Hard luck,' he remarked with a non-malicious grin. 'How
are they doing this year?'

'All right, thanks.' And we were doing all right, albeit
light years away from Tottenham and Sheffield Wednesday.
So, after a short, sympathetic chat on what life was like down

in the bottom division of the Football League, conversation reverted to the merits of Glenn Hoddle, the most super of Tottenham's superstars and the likelihood of him still being at the Lane next season (the subsequently revealed answer was no). I figured it was unlikely that the Tottenham supporter knew much about Roy McDonough, Glenn Pennyfather and other United leading lights, so a conversation on their merits would have been rather one-sided.

Move forward to March 1991 and Southend's season of the realised dream. Birmingham City under the lights at Roots Hall and both crowd 'choirs' are in full voice, singing with gusto their versions of the classic William Williams (no relation, no relation) hymn, 'Guide Me, O thou great Jehovah'. In the West Stand, we are impertinently singing, 'You're not famous, you're not famous, you're not famous any more; you're not famous any more.' After a pause, back comes the refrain from the few hundred travelling Brummies, 'Who the fuck, who the fuck, who the fucking hell are you? Who the fucking hell are you?'

The West Stand responds with a sarcastic round of applause, followed by a few choruses of something more modern, adapting the Gap Band R&B incantation 'Oops Upside Your Head'. 'We are top of the league; I say, we are top of the league' we chant back, because we are top of the league and I am only 35 years old going on 15.

But it did make me think later on. Birmingham City, *née* Small Heath Alliance FC, poor relations of Aston Villa in England's second city, bouncing between top tier and second tier since 1892: they were not all that good and not all that famous but they were still much better known than Southend. Exactly 20 years later, Premier League Birmingham City beat Arsenal 2-1 in the Carling Cup Final (that year's name for the League Cup) in front of 89,000 at Wembley, and United were languishing in the fourth tier and not vying for any trophy. So: who are we?

Move forward again to September 1995 and I was sitting high in the towering East Stand (now the Jack Charlton Stand) at Elland Road, courtesy of a free ticket from a corporate partner of my employer. The match was a first round second leg UEFA Cup tie between Leeds United and AS Monaco.

With Leeds already three up from the first leg, there wasn't much at stake as a quite ordinary game played out. Monaco scored in the first half, and that was about it. To pass the time, I got talking to an old guy in a cloth cap and the white scarf of his home club. He quickly took me for a neutral, helped no doubt by my distinctly un-Yorkshire-like accent.

'And what team do you support?'

'Umm – Southend United, actually,'

'Oh.'

After a pause, the old guy spent some time reminiscing about the English south coast, where he had spent some time during the war. Gradually it dawned on me that he was reminiscing about a town called Southsea. Now, Southsea is a seaside resort, but it's also part of the city of Portsmouth, Hampshire, 116 miles away from my hometown. It doesn't have a Football League club either: never has, almost certainly never will. In 1995, Southend had never played Leeds, so I could understand his confusion and was too polite to put him right, so I let it pass. I was used to it by then.

Commiseration. Ridicule. Misunderstanding. Welcome to the world of those who support lower-division teams in England.

One of the views from down here is learning to deal with your anonymity in the football world. All fans in England and most across the world probably know that Manchester United and Manchester City play in a northern English city called Manchester; that Liverpool and Everton play in another northern English city called Liverpool; that Arsenal, Chelsea, West Ham and Tottenham play in a big southern English city called London. Perhaps if Southend were major players in the

Premier League, more people would know where Southend is – but we're not, and never have been.

The lower divisions of the Football League have quite a few Southend Uniteds. A friend of mine supports Gillingham, whose history parallels Southend's in many ways. Entered the Football League in 1920. Never played in the old First Division or Premier League, a lifetime shuttling between the third and fourth tiers of the Football League, a few precious years in the second tier. My friend has also seen the Saturday morning exodus of London club-supporting turncoats from his local railway station. And I'm guessing that a fair number of people outside the south-east of England don't know exactly where Gillingham is either unless, as a rival supporter from another lower division club, you have taken the car or the train or the supporters' club coach to Priestfield.

A combination of work and desire has given me the chance to see big clubs play big matches and has taken me to most of the large towns and cities in England. But it's debatable whether I would have visited places like Scunthorpe, Bury, Hartlepool, Newport, Grimsby, Walsall or Mansfield unless there was a football ground with Southend playing in it. It's a taste of the real England (or Wales in the case of Newport), it's eye-opening and it's what you get when you support a lower division club. Obscurity sometimes brings its rewards.

***

To Cambridge, a suburb of Boston, Massachusetts, in February 1997. Kim was on a work trip, I was on holiday, but I'd been to Boston a few times and knew my way around. I decided to walk into the city centre the long way, along the bank of the Charles River on a frigidly cold, clear winter's day.

I was also on a mission. If it's 1997 and it's the United States and you don't have a radio that gets BBC World Service and the *Boston Globe* only prints the Premier League results and the internet hasn't (quite) been rolled out everywhere and you can't be bothered to buy international roaming for your mobile, how do you find a Southend result? Well done the *International Express*, a weekly condensed version of the *Daily Express*, which I eagerly picked up from a news stand near the city's North Station and immediately tucked into my daypack, resisting the temptation for a sneaky peek inside.

It was about noon. I had warmed up from my walk, I was thirsty and I needed to be sitting down for the news, good or bad, preferably with drink in hand. A bar appeared before me. As I turned towards it, I registered an expansive Irish tricolour flag in the window and wondered if I was wise, given that I was wearing a padded Kangol jacket with a Union Jack brand motif on the back. As I pushed open the door and felt the comforting rush of the heating, I observed a mere handful of people in the place, so I concluded all would be well. Not that the welcome was overwhelming. Maybe the large, heavy, tough-looking barman was having a bad day, maybe he didn't like the look of me, but he turned from the beer keg he was wrestling and gave me a 'Who the hell are you?' glare.

'Help you?' he challenged, brusquely. I did my best to act as local as possible and asked for a 20oz draft Guinness (that is to say, an imperial pint of draught Guinness), which the barman slowly, wordlessly and very properly delivered, complete with shamrock stencilled in the off-white creamy head. As he returned to his keg, I settled myself on a stool, took a sip and opened my paper to the football pages.

It was not a disastrous result, but United were deep in relegation trouble and badly needed a win. I let out an involuntary groan.

Another hostile glare. 'You got a problem, pal?'

'No, sorry, it's just that my soccer team got a bad result.'

A flicker of interest as he started to move along the bar towards me. 'You English? Thought so. Who do you follow?'

Rather than explain, I passed the *Express* to the barman and pointed out the score. After sniffily handling the journal as if I'd wiped my nose on it, he rested his elbows on the bar and stared down at the results page. 'South-End United one, Norr-Which City one,' he read slowly. 'So that's a tie, right? Is your team South-End or Norr-Which?'

'It's Southend, but the trouble is we're near the bottom of the league and we really needed to win this one.'

The barman settled on the Premier League results. 'Man-Chester United, yeah, know them. Liverpool, know them. Noo-Castle, yeah. OK, Arsenal, Tot-Ten-Ham, Chelsea, they're London teams. I know that.' He looked at me dubiously. 'South-End: never heard of them. They in London?'

'No.' I started to outline where Southend was, but I could tell I had lost him at 'no'. He returned to the results page and his gaze drifted through the four league divisions. 'How many soccer league teams in England?' In response to my answer, he did a mock double-take. 'Ninety-two? In England?' I started to explain the structure of the English Football League, but I'd lost him at '92'. His eyes continued to wander down the page to the more tightly packed non-league scores and stopped at the Northern Premier League. 'Hey Al, there's a soccer team in England called Boston United!'

Another large, heavy and tough-looking gent ambled up and peered past the barman's pointed finger. 'Interesting,' said Al, making it sound like the most uninteresting thing in world history. 'Looks like they got a way to go.'

'And this guy supports South-End United.' 'Wow,' murmured Al before ambling back to his seat.

'You know, we got English soccer on TV at the weekend. You live round here?' The barman nodded towards a rather splendid-looking widescreen television; or at least rather splendid for the time. 'Just visiting,' I replied.

'OK. I'll keep my eyes open for South-End United.' 'Don't hold your breath,' I nearly responded, but decided not to. I was on a roll. So, I did my bit for Anglo-American relations, as well as enlightening one, maybe two Americans that there is an English 'soccer' team called Southend United from a town called Southend, which is not in London. And, as it worked out, heralding an English 'soccer' team from Lincolnshire called Boston United who, within five years, made their triumphant entrance into the Football League. Unfortunately for them, Boston spent a few short years periodically doing Southend harm before the club subsided back into another era of non-league obscurity. Spreading the word, people. Just spreading the word.

***

Fortunately, it doesn't always depend on me. On the late autumn evening of Tuesday, 7 November 2006, Manchester United, serial Premier League champions, holders of the League Cup and my forever second team, are at Roots Hall for a Carling Cup (as the League Cup is known this year) fourth round tie. The ground is sold out with 11,532 inside and a full contingent of visiting fans gathered on the North Bank – presumably by the Essex and London chapters of the Manchester United Supporters' Club. In another life, I might have been there myself.

'Man U', a sobriquet disliked by real Manchester United supporters, have spent a few seasons letting Arsenal and Chelsea try on the Premier League crown, but this season they are top of the table and on the charge toward another title; and then another, and then another. Meanwhile, Southend are resident in the unfamiliar heights of the Championship, which is what the second tier has now become, but are currently bottom of the table, which is not so unfamiliar. Nevertheless, we have earned our passage to a night out against Manchester United. By a quirk of fate, which seems even more quirky in retrospect, we have progressed through the early rounds by beating Bournemouth and Brighton at a time when both of them are looking up at us. We have made our own bit of history by beating fallen giants Leeds 3-1 at Elland Road in the third round, a result which would have generated shock waves in the football world three years previously.

It is not quite Manchester United's first 11 out there. No Rio Ferdinand, no Nemanja Vidić, no Michael Carrick, no Ryan Giggs, no Paul Scholes. But Wes Brown, Gabriel Heinze and Mikaël Silvestre are semi-regulars. John O'Shea and Darren Fletcher are up and coming. Up front, the Reds have Wayne Rooney and Cristiano Ronaldo so they are quite enough of a challenge for a struggling Championship club. But we have an ace up our sleeve and its name is Freddy Eastwood.

The Blues win the toss and are kicking towards the North Bank, with its shabby, semi-moribund scoreboard perched on the roof. In a previous existence, it had advertised the delights of central Southend's retail options from the top of High Street. Now it is just about able to display the score. From the start, the match hurtles at a crackling, jumping-jack pace: loud bangers of near misses, whirling Catherine wheels of high-speed interpassing, a red-hot bonfire of an atmosphere, as if Guy Fawkes Night has been postponed for 48 hours.

The great Ronaldo is booed every time he touches the ball, probably due in part to his antics in getting Rooney sent off during the recent World Cup quarter-final between Portugal and England. And the cheeky grin and wink to his bench after he'd done it, of course. Ironic choruses of 'Who are you?' accompany the boos. Ronaldo looks somewhat bemused and put out but, come on, he must have expected it. Droning around the stadium is 'Sea-Sea-Seasiders', the only chant that we can justifiably call our own, although Blackpool supporters might have something to say about that.

The mighty Manchester United against lowly Southend United. But if the Reds of Manchester think that the Blues of Southend are lambs to the slaughter, they are getting a rude awakening. Strange things can happen in a cup tie. Rooney is a bag of querulous grumpiness – he gets it, no question. Ronaldo's body language betrays head-shaking frustration.

He probably gets it. The Argentinian defender Heinze looks perplexed as Southend's right-winger Jamal Campbell-Ryce takes him to the cleaners. Maybe he doesn't get it.

With 26 minutes gone, Campbell-Ryce is fouled, not for the first time, 30 yards out. Captain Kevin Maher and left wing-back Steve Hammell stand over the ball. Eastwood stands back a few paces; nobody seriously doubts that he'll take it on. 'Come on Southend,' bellows the crowd. Hammell steps over the ball as Eastwood trots forward, swings his right foot and connects perfectly. From the Frank Walton Stand, it will look as if his drive is missing the right-hand post, then the ball swerves leftwards at pace and buries itself in the top corner. Manchester's goalkeeper, Tomasz Kuszczak, must have seen the ball a bit late and he's still in mid-air diving across as it passes him by, but realistically no goalie in the world could have stopped it.

Freddy sprints towards the West Stand and performs a long and elegant slide, arms outstretched. Three sides of Roots Hall explode in roman candles of delight. The public address system strikes up Freddy's goal celebration, an electro dance-punk rhythm of 'Papa's Got a Brand New Pigbag' (Middlesbrough fans know: I had to look it up) and the crowd responds with 'Duh Duh duh-duh-duh, FREDDY EASTWOOD!' 'Southend 1 Man Utd 0' announces the shabby old scoreboard, pixels askew.

As the pace of the game increases from hectic to manic, Jones hits the post, Eastwood is in a race for the ball with Kuszczak, which the keeper just wins. Then Ronaldo executes a swerving drive and Flahavan dives to turn aside – and it's not even half-time yet.

The second half starts as the first half ended. As the United of Manchester begin to turn the screw, the match becomes the Ronaldo and Flahavan show. Ronaldo drives, Flahavan flings himself to turn aside – and then again. Ronaldo pings a trademark free kick known as a knuckle ball, swerving and dipping towards the top of the net but Flahavan leaps to touch over. Prior and Flahavan are sharing exhilarated laughter at the sheer effrontery of it all. And the Southend crowd, just as it did in the Watford and Tottenham matches of years ago, is playing its part. The pleading 'Come on Southend' booms out from the West Stand for the millionth time in United's history. Songs and chants are ringing out from all corners. Some seat-warmers in the East Stand are standing, waving their arms and singing, and I can tell you that doesn't happen very often. 'We love you Southend, we do, ohh Southend we love you.' More head-shaking from Ronaldo, more grumpiness from Rooney.

As the game moves towards added time, it's the Blues who are channelling the crowd and asking the questions. Eastwood stings Kuszczak's palms with a fierce shot. From the ensuing corner, Southend's central defender Efe Sodje heads just over. At the death, an unmarked Maher collects a pass on the edge of the penalty area: he spots his chance to lob an out-of-position Kuszczak, but glory doesn't beckon as his mishit becomes a backpass. In the background, the Southend supporters are raising their voices for the final crescendo. The final whistle is unheard, a barrage of metaphorical rockets launches into the dark night air and some young fans manage to nip around the cops and stewards in a joyous pitch invasion.

A massive result in Southend United's history: 1-0 against Manchester United. The first time we have ever progressed to the quarter-final of a major cup competition. Cold reality returned when our reward was Tottenham away, where we were beaten by a clearly offside 'goal' deep into extra time at White Hart Lane – at least according to an old friend who witnessed it from an executive box.

Nevertheless, Southend's defeat of Manchester United settled two questions in my mind. Firstly: people had asked who would I support, how would I feel if my favourite team ever played my second favourite team. I suspected that I already knew the answer, but could now confirm it: the answer was I would support Southend and it felt great – absolutely bloody great! Tilson's Southend United against Ferguson's Manchester United. Played one: won one. Winning record: 100 per cent. No other English football club can boast that. There's one for trivia night.

Secondly: could Southend escape a lifetime of commiseration, ridicule and misunderstanding just for one day? For 24 hours at least, the name of Southend United and the video of Freddy Eastwood's swerving 30-yard thunderbolt reverberated around the world.

***

Time to reveal a guilty secret. Throughout this book, I've used the present tense when chronicling noteworthy United matches I have attended in the flesh (apart from West Ham, April 1993, and that wasn't my fault). But I wasn't at Roots Hall on that magical night in October 2006. Nor was I in England, nor Europe, nor the Northern Hemisphere. I didn't even watch the match live on television, because Setanta shamefully failed to broadcast it. My detailed account was informed by the DVD I purchased online from the club's merchandise store. *Giant Killers – United we Conquer* covers the occasion, from the teams in the claustrophobic players' tunnel to the earth-moving roar at the final whistle. From Ronaldo's gloomy shaking head to Rooney's simmering fury. From Flahavan and Prior's laughter to the constipated look on Alex Ferguson's face. All narrated by the reassuring voice of Alan Parry.[50]

This is what I actually did on that famous day. With an 11-hour time difference between Southend and Sydney, kick-off at Roots Hall was 6.45am for me. I dressed rapidly, fed the cats and positioned myself in front of the laptop and the BBC website, coffee cup in hand. I was just in time to 'refresh' myself with Freddy's first-half goal before I was off to work on

---

50 Originally broadcast by Sky Sports in the UK.

bus and train, eyes glued to the mobile screen – something I used to swear I'd never do. By the time I turned on the office computer, the match was approaching its close. When the letter 'R' gloriously attached itself to the 'Southend United 1 Manchester United 0' score on the BBC website, I let out an unconstrained whoop of joy and embarked on a short lap of honour around the office to the amusement of my colleagues. 'Prawns won then, did they?' enquired one, eyes rolling.

By the time I returned home that evening, the news was out. I'd had the foresight to record two hours' worth of the Sky News UK channel, which I immediately turned on to see Eastwood's free kick for the first time. More entertainment was provided by the spectacle of harassed Sky News anchor Eamonn Holmes, evidently a Reds supporter, being mercilessly tormented by his on-air colleagues. It wasn't just Sky News UK though. Freddy's goal and Alex's face predictably featured on the evening news edition of Soccer Bloody Soccer, but they also made the sport segments of Channel Seven and Channel Nine news – the two most popular terrestrial TV channels in Australia. That's a lot of Australian media exposure for a small football club in Essex.

Southend United have had their 24 hours of worldwide fame, and that is a fact. And for a few days afterwards, my car was the happy recipient of the occasional toot from the citizens of Sydney. Still spreading the word, people; just spreading the word.

***

Back in the Football League Championship, United tried but never quite rose above the trauma of a relegation battle. Our return to the second tier had seen, for the first time, the occasional live match from Roots Hall finding its way on to Australian TV screens. One was a stunning 5-0 slaughter of QPR in February 2007, when United supporters briefly dared to dream of salvation. Our next TV outing was a miserable

Good Friday against the vengeful Colchester United when, to my coffee-spilling horror, we conceded a soft goal after 40 seconds and ended up subsiding to a 3-0 defeat, hammering one more nail into our Championship coffin. Even from this distance, it is painful to recall that United couldn't pull enough results together, and six defeats in the final eight games meant that all our efforts were to Noah-sodding-Vale.

Kim and I didn't get back to England until the autumn of 2007. I had managed to get hold of tickets for Manchester United against Wigan Athletic in the Premier League. On the day, Southend, seventh-placed in League One, lost 2-1 in front of 7,819 spectators at Roots Hall. United were minus one Freddy Eastwood who had made his expected move following our relegation, but unexpectedly to Championship Wolverhampton Wanderers for a scandalously underpriced £1.5m.

Meanwhile, we were sitting in the top row of the top tier of the huge East Stand at Old Trafford, occupying what had been an open terrace called the Scoreboard End on my earlier visits. Next to us were an enthusiastic group of youthful visiting Norwegians – as you do at Old Trafford – in a crowd of 75,300, nearly ten times larger than the Roots Hall turnout. Manchester United, top of the Premier League, won 4-0: scorers, Cristiano Ronaldo (two), Carlos Tevez and Wayne Rooney. After my shameless delight in the demise of the Reds of Manchester at the hands of the Blues of Southend one year previously, I felt I owed them some small recompense. Call me a traitor if you like, I don't care. If you've paid £160 for a pair of tickets to see the current Premier League champions and league leaders, that's where you're going to be. There was always going to be a next time for Roots Hall.

Back in the third tier of the Football League, United teased and tantalised their fans to another play-off semi-final, but this time we fell apart against Doncaster Rovers. The next season we were close, but not quite close enough, to earn another shot at the play-offs. Also in the mix was a surprising 1-1 draw at Stamford Bridge against Premier League aristocrats Chelsea in the third round of the FA Cup. Peter Clarke's screaming header from a last-minute 'everybody up' corner was great fun to see in Australia thanks to a TV highlight reel. United's 4-1 defeat in the Roots Hall replay, not so much fun. Never mind, let Chelsea have the cup (and they did). We were knocking on the door of the second tier, we were competitive and we could hold our own with the best. Only a matter of time, it seemed – and it was.

In season 2009/10 United were in mid-table by November, just off the pacesetters, as we often were when girding our loins for another dash at the promotion places. The next 29 games delivered four wins and down went Southend, back to the Football League basement, where they had been when Kim and I left the old country ten years before. Where they were ten years before that. And ten years before that. And ten years before that. 'Plus ça change, plus c'est la même chose.' The more things change, the more they stay the same.[51]

---

51 An epigram from French journalist Jean-Baptiste Alphonse Karr (1849). Original author identified by www.en.wiktionary.org.

Chapter 22

Welcome Back, My Friends …

IT WAS Sir Richard Gordon Turnbull, a senior diplomat from the British colonial sunset years of the 1950s and 60s, who once observed to Denis Healey, one-time British Secretary of State for Defence and Chancellor of the Exchequer, 'When the British Empire finally sinks beneath the waves of history, it will leave behind it only two memorials: one is the game of association football and the other is the expression "fuck off".'[52] Given the historical linkage between the two, this is not totally surprising. You don't have to be a lip reader to get the drift when a footballer misses a sitter or messes up a pass or stuffs up a tackle or lets a soft one in or has a go at the referee; even players who don't have English as their first language. You would have to be hard of hearing not to hear the expression bandied about in the stands, short-sighted not to see the wave of the reverse 'V' sign, the expression's visual counterpart, at football stadia the length and breadth of England.

Which brings me to the subject of homesickness after nearly 25 years as an Australian resident. I still get asked about it now and then. Although I obviously miss family and friends, my frequent return trips (12 in total before COVID-19) have helped to relieve the separation. WhatsApp and FaceTime help as well. England has changed, but to me the changes are

---

52 *The Time of My Life*, written by Denis Healey. Penguin Books 1990.

barely perceptible between one visit and the next. I arrive at Heathrow Airport, pick up the hire car, turn on the radio and join the M25 motorway. By South Mimms services, it feels as if I've never been away.

The same goes for Southend-on-Sea. The dodgy rides, the waterchute, the Cyclone and the draughty arcades of the Kursaal closed down years ago. The most time I ever spent there was in the slightly faded Ballroom, which hosted a succession of iconic rock bands in the 70s: from Deep Purple to Black Sabbath, from 10cc to AC/DC. The site once occupied by the biggest amusement park in the south of England and United's second stadium is now a housing estate and, at the time of writing, the elegant domed entrance pavilion accommodates a lonely Tesco Express.

As for the Southend/Grainger Road Stadium, I paid a visit once just to say I had been there. I sank a beer or two in the reasonable comfort of the old West Stand and threw some money away on a succession of dishlickers I liked the look of, but whose good looks disguised the fact that they couldn't run very fast. I gazed out over the twilit vista to where a football pitch was just discernible inside the dog track but I couldn't get a feel for what the place might have been as a football ground. Even the canine-punting fraternity eventually gave up and the stadium met the bulldozers 40 years ago. Today, the Greyhound Retail Park occupies the space where my football club spent 20 years of its life. Not even a mention of Southend United. What a blooming cheek.

As for the climate, winters scraping ice off the car windscreen and summers dodging the showers do not inspire much wistful nostalgia, frankly. Football and Southend United is something else.

Most of our return trips have been during the English summer – it's just worked out that way – when Roots Hall is an empty stadium, a quiet merchandise store and the Thursday open-air market in the car park behind the East Stand. As a result, Roots Hall has only seen the colour of my money seven times since I left, and some of those have not been memorable. But I still get the feeling. Take a Boxing Day or New Year's Day or a Good Friday or Easter Monday and I don't have a match to go to. Even after all these years, it gives me a vague feeling of disconnection, as if there's somewhere I should be. The third round of the FA Cup produces a similar effect, at least when United actually grace the day with their presence although, God knows, it doesn't happen as often as it should.

On Saturday, 4 January 2014, I am where my alter ego thinks I should be. I'm back in Southend-on-Sea but it's a long time since my home was 15 minutes' walk from Roots Hall. For old times' sake, I drop into the Melrose, my local pub for 15 years. The first Saturday in January is traditionally third round day and this season Southend are rubbing shoulders with the big clubs. Although United have been stuck in the fourth tier for nearly four years, away wins against Morecambe and Chesterfield have earned us a home tie against Millwall. The downside is that Millwall are two divisions above us. The upside is that we have beaten them in the FA Cup before and it's a local derby where strange things can and do happen.

It's the type of cold, damp and murky January day I'd almost forgotten. The floodlights are already beaming out at two o'clock, illuminating my path towards the ground. I am nice and early, I have secured a ticket for my traditional seated position in the centre of the West Stand and the draughty old place feels familiar and homely as I take my seat. The Millwall supporters, noisy but well-behaved as usual at Roots Hall, are already occupying the North Bank. United supporters are slower to take their places, but eventually the ground fills up around me. No clouds of cigarette smoke eddy above the terraces, because smoking isn't allowed any more and the terraces at Roots Hall are now a distant memory.

At 58, I am fully qualified to be a 'moaning old git', but that was never my style and the West Stand lost that reputation some years ago. The Blue Voice starts up its limited repertoire of songs and chants – more Great Escapes and Vindaloos – but is struggling to compete with the elongated incantation of 'Miiilllwaaallll' and the defiant anthem of 'No one likes us, we don't care', adapted from Rod Stewart's 'Sailing', bouncing off the roof of the packed North Bank designated for away supporters. Sammy Bloody Shrimper and Elvis J. Eel, the Blue Belles, the latest hyperventilating Roots Hall Ron, all the usual suspects are here in a slightly disappointing crowd of 7,923, emblematic of the sad decline of the FA Cup in recent years as well as Southend's currently straitened condition, but the noise is impressive enough.

United are kicking an orange ball towards the updated, advertisement-strewn, digital scoreboard above the North Bank, anticipating the sleet and snow we are led to expect. And the crowd can soon see that we are up for this: Millwall have recently sacked their manager and look distinctly half-baked, but United are pressing, moving the ball around with pace and purpose. A cross from the right: a towering leap and clever glancing header into the net from the giant Barry Corr, our current 'big 'un up front'. Alf Smirk would have loved him. The rain and sleet begin to drift in, transported by razor-sharp blasts of bitingly cold wind, just as it always did. A few minutes later, to ironic cheers from all sides, the floodlights start to flicker, blink and then die. The crowd is savouring the moment, helpfully waving the torches on their mobiles around the gloom, but I'm not. I'm thinking, 'Oh crap! I've come 12,000 miles, we're one up and now we're not even under the lights any more. Just my luck if it's called off.' Fortunately for my mental wellbeing, the floodlights flicker on after 20 minutes of mounting concern and off we go again.

Half-time approaches and United are comfortable at 1-0. Now there's a bit of rough stuff in front of the East Stand, a United body on the ground, the seats rising in unison, bellowing in fury, accusatory fingers pointing. Neither I nor the vast majority of Southend fans saw what happened but, as the referee runs over to the scene of the alleged misdemeanour, we adopt the instinctive response of English football fans since Adam was a lad. 'Off, off, off' bawl three sides of Roots Hall, followed by derisive jeers and dismissive waves as the red card is lifted to the sky and the Millwall players surround the referee in futile protest. It's all going on here. Within the blink of an eye, United break in midfield, a through ball puts midfielder Will Atkinson in the clear, a 20 yard sprint and a lovely little chip over the goalkeeper for our second goal – right in front of the glum south Londoners, some of whom are already on their way round the back for a coffee, a Coke, a pee or a smoke. It's 2-0 at half-time and most of Roots Hall is buzzing with excitement. Something to talk about over the interval: where do you start?

Into the second half, and the United fans are already starting the 'olés', dangerously early in my experience. Sleet and rain persist, as standing water starts to glisten in the goalmouths. Some Millwall supporters in the unsheltered front rows of the North Bank edge towards drier vantage points. Welcome to my world of 45 years ago, guys. Nightmares of waterlogged pitches and abandonment now circulate in my febrile brain. But no: the well-drained Roots Hall pitch is up to the task and midfielder Michael Timlin dances through the puddles to put us 3-0 up. Done and dusted – except the done is rarely dusted for Southend.

Millwall get one back, to a subdued response from the North Bank; sometimes opposition supporters get it before we do. And United play on as if nothing has happened: a long-distance lob desperately tipped over by the Millwall goalie, Corr rises once again to head against the woodwork as gaps of empty seats start to yawn where Millwall fans were sitting earlier. After 84 minutes, another reason why I am sitting in the West Stand runs on to the pitch. Freddy Eastwood returned to the Roots Hall fold in 2012 after years of trial and tribulation at Wolverhampton Wanderers and Coventry City. Playing in a deeper role than in his United heyday, the instinctive smarts are still there, with a bit of added guile but a slightly slower, slightly heavier Freddy is no longer the goalscoring machine that I remember. But he is on for Timlin, allowing me to pay my own final respects to a United legend in what proves to be his last season.

Into added on time, midfielder Ryan Leonard streaks through a crumbling defence and drives emphatically into the roof of the net. 'Heyyy, hey baby, OOHH-AHH' rings around the ground for the fourth time and it's 4-1 to Southend at the final whistle. A brilliant performance, the best I have seen in the flesh for years. I stay in my seat for a few minutes and watch the crowd leave Roots Hall. I'm in no hurry; maybe this will be my last adventure inside the old ground, but I've said that at least three times since 1999. I barely notice the rain as I return to the hire car parked just round the corner from my home of 15 years. 'Flick-flack' go the windscreen wipers as I drive back to Thorpe Bay and relay the good news to Mum, who is suitably surprised and impressed.

Into the fourth round of the FA Cup we go, but we're never going to win it, so it's down to the best draw we can get. Home tie – tick. Premier League team – tick. Hull City – bugger, bugger and thrice bugger. Back at home in Sydney and the Hull love affair with football on again for the year, I don't see them gently nudge us aside 2-0 on their way to the final, where they contrive to lose to the Arsenal after going two up in the first ten minutes. As for United, we are left with another abortive play-off venture. Thank you and goodnight.

***

The Millwall cup tie was a rare moment of satisfaction as United laboured under a spell in League Two which could justifiably be summed up by the British Empire's most memorable expression. After our relegation back to the basement in 2010 and the departure of Steve Tilson, stoic United fans endured two demoralising play-off semi-final defeats in three seasons when, against Crewe Alexandra and Burton Albion, we were unable to turn around a first-leg single-goal deficit in the second leg at Roots Hall. That I was able to watch these calamities live on cable TV was little consolation as the alarm clock rudely awoke me in the dark of an early midweek morning in Sydney, followed by a couple of hours of teeth-grinding, followed by a miserable day of grumping and grouching at my desk.

Another season and another welcome return for Southend. The talismanic Adam Barrett, combative defensive giant from the class of 2006 was sprung from the clutches of Gillingham and made the journey back across the Thames Estuary to Roots Hall (which made a nice change): bigger, broader, balder than ever and part of the Roots Hall continuum encompassing our greatest moments, from Paul Clark in 1976 to Paul Clark and Spencer Prior in 1991, to Spencer Prior and Adam Barrett in 2006 and back to Adam Barrett again in 2015.

Armed with Barrett, most of the line-up from our Millwall success, and Phil Brown, the man who had managed Hull to the Premier League for the first time in their history, United assaulted the League Two play-offs again and, with 30 minutes left in the first leg at Stevenage's miniscule Lamex Stadium, United were one down and my furrowed brow contemplated the latest Groundhog Day. But not this time: Corr got his head on to a cross to equalise and we held on for a 1-1 draw, with the second leg at home to come. Another bleeping of the alarm clock, another dark Sydney morning parked in front of the TV, another second leg under the lights and the driving rain of Roots Hall – the usual routine.

True to form, Stevenage score early in the second half to go in front and my chin drops deeper into hand as I feel another tilt at the promotion windmill slipping away. But on 67 minutes Leonard drills a firm shot into the net to equalise.

Chances come and go, but we can't get the decisive goal. We miss a penalty in the very last minute, when Corr belts the spot-kick against the bar and over, so 90 minutes become an additional 30 minutes. Chin meets hand once again, but justice is finally served with two goals in the second period of extra time to secure a 3-1 win. As most of Roots Hall happily spills on to the pitch, I am hopping into the car for the journey through the traffic-light jungle to the office. I'll be a bit late, but I don't care. Congratulations to 'The Prawns' are graciously received. No grumping or grouching today.

***

It is not United's first time at the new Wembley. In 2013, we fought once again for the Also-Rans Cup (known as the Johnstone's Paint Trophy that year). United supporters filled half of the stadium to see us lose 2-0 to Crewe Alexandra. In the alternative vocabulary of FootballSpeak, I can say that United lost in the final of the Paints and every supporter of a lower-division club will know what I mean. Silverware: how I dislike that word.

Another year, another final. For the Southend United and Wycombe Wanderers exiles in Australia, kick-off time is 2.30am on Sunday, 24 May 2015. Kim has suggested, quite reasonably, that we could record the match and watch it later. Reasonable, yes, but I generally prefer my suffering in real time. So here we are again in front of the TV, the lights of our house the only ones shining in our sleeping Sydney neighbourhood. The beIN Sports broadcast doesn't mess about with preamble: the start of transmission sees the teams marching on to the pristine green turf of the new Wembley, United decked out in what is an unfamiliar all mustard-yellow away strip. It is gratifying to see Blues supporters filling the bottom two tiers on the west side of the stadium; more than 25,000 strong, double the Wycombe contingent in a crowd of 38,252. 'God save our gracious Queen,' and down we settle for the kick-off:

no banal routines, no bizarre totems conferring good luck on the Blues, no lucky pants – I'm superstitious that way.

The match is a slow burner, with United and Wanderers sparring warily at each other. Fifteen minutes in and a free kick to Southend on the left. The ball is driven in hard, a beauty, right on to the head of the leaping Barry Corr and he plants the ball in the net. To my initial mystification and then spluttering dismay, the 'goal' is disallowed for the alleged manhandling of a Wanderers defender by one of our defenders nowhere near Corr's sledgehammer. I have seen that incident many times on DVD and I can tell you that 'alleged' says the least of it. The rest of the 90 minutes is watchable, if not classic, full of honest endeavour, chances at a premium but no goals. Time for the Wembley crowd to draw breath and for me to put the kettle on.

The first period of extra time passes nervously. One mistake, one piece of bad luck can settle the game and both sides know it. Goalless into the second period. At 108 minutes, there's a free kick to Wycombe just outside the United penalty area. A cheeky, chirpy Wycombe tyke named Joe Jacobson cracks a dipping swerver over the defensive wall, over the diving keeper Daniel Bentley and on to the underside of the bar. Then the ball drops on to Bentley's back, bouncing slowly and excruciatingly into the net. 'That's it,' I flatly announce, despite Kim's continued optimism. I just know it's not going to happen; I've seen it so many times before.

All too quickly, we are in added time at the end of extra time. At the United end, I can see a few red seats exposed by early departures. I can see lines of hunched shoulders threading their despondent way up the gangways towards the exits.

A once well-known but now slightly *passé* bit of FootballSpeak talks about a 'Fourth Division ball', a long punt into the opposition penalty area from anywhere on the pitch in the hope that someone gets on the end of it. And United are a fourth-tier team, so why aren't we doing it? Because we don't play like that, never have done in my totally unbiased opinion – but what a time to rediscover our footballing cultural heritage. United win a succession of throw-ins in the Wycombe half. 'Come on, just hoof that bloody ball into the box, will you?' comes my strangled cry and the pleadings of the 25,000.

But that bloody ball will not get hoofed in as the clock approaches 122 minutes. Myles Weston, an authentic winger brought on as a substitute, receives the ball near the halfway line. Why doesn't he give it the hoof? Instead, he canters down the left wing towards the massed ranks of United fans, drifting past tiring defenders, picking up speed. A short check as a Wycombe defender closes in, then off down the wing he goes again. Now Weston is level with the penalty area and a roar is building from the United end. A few of the early leavers stop and turn back towards the play. Weston fires the ball into the middle, the best cross of the match by a country mile. Positioned near the penalty spot, striker Stephen McLaughlin connects, nodding the ball downwards and sideways. Joe Pigott, another substitute, brings it under instant control and from 15 yards out drives the ball straight and true across the Wycombe keeper and into the far corner of the net.

It's as if the whole West Stand of Wembley has drawn a momentary breath and then exhaled in a blasting explosion. Kim jumps up and shrieks. As for me – I'm literally dumbstruck. After a few seconds, I can bring myself to mutter 'I don't believe it' more than once, as I watch the manic scenes of celebration and barely register the final whistle.

Southend United 1 Wycombe Wanderers 1. Promotion will be decided by a penalty shoot-out. When previous shoot-outs have occurred in United's history, our success rate has been patchy, to say the best of it. I can't see some of the faithless early departures scrambling back to their seats, though the gaps seem to be filled in quite quickly: nobody sits down for a penalty shoot-out anyway.

As I compose myself with a very late or a very early glass of white, beIN Sports runs Phil Brown's touchline reaction to United's last-ditch equaliser.

He trots a few yards towards the appalled Wycombe end and roars out the expression for which the British Empire will always be remembered, accompanied by a defiant fist thrust to the sky.

United must have lost the toss, because the penalties will be taken in front of the baying Wycombe supporters. The upside is that United have the first spot-kick. In my experience, this confers a slight advantage. Playing catch-up often works on the nerves of the other team, especially at the sharp end when penalties become a sudden death affair. Not so good if it doesn't get that far, however, so time to perch on the edge of the settee and grit the teeth. To the credit of both, Brown and his opposite number Gareth Ainsworth choose to watch the *dénouement* together on the touchline. Whatever will be, will be at Wemberley.

Pigott, still on a high from his last-minute goal and with his right foot this time, slots into the corner; 1-0 to Southend.

Murphy scores confidently for Wycombe, sending Bentley the wrong way; 1-1.

United's captain, Coker, whacks one down the middle. The keeper blocks with his legs. Coker buries his head in his hands. Cue deep groan from the other side of the world; 1-1.

Mawson scores for Wycombe, into the corner. Bentley nearly gets a hand on it, but not quite; 1-2.

For Southend, Leonard buries his penalty high into the net with minimal fuss and celebration; 2-2.

For Wycombe, Hayes sends Bentley the wrong way again and the ball rolls comfortably into the net; 2-3.

Payne drills his spot-kick low into the corner past the Wycombe keeper's despairing dive; 3-3.

Bloomfield of Wycombe directs his kick toward Bentley's right-hand post but it's a bit too close, as Bentley dives horizontally to save. The West Stand of Wembley is ecstatic and so are we; 3-3 and 'back on serve'.

Timlin's eyes are barely visible under his padded head protector, the consequence of a nasty injury against Stevenage. But he sends the Wycombe keeper the wrong way, and glares under his helmet at the Wycombe fans, waving his fist; 4-3 to Southend.

Bean, calm and collected, sends Bentley the wrong way – again – and rolls the ball in for Wycombe; 4-4, and we are now in sudden death territory.

'Mr Southend United', Adam Barrett, paces nonchalantly up to the spot. Three steps and an unstoppable piledriver screams high into the net. Barrett turns towards the United fans and spreads his raised arms, both fists clenched, his singular way of celebrating; 5-4 to Southend.

Joe Jacobsen, the scorer of Wycombe's goal, dribbles the ball down the middle, but Bentley has already chosen his dive and is nowhere near it. Jacobsen takes the opportunity to have a quick grinning chirp at the Southend custodian. At 21 years old, Bentley is young to be a goalkeeper in the Football League but he's possessed of a steely eyed stare and an outwardly inscrutable demeanour, so his reaction is hard to decipher; 5-5.

Weston, the creator of United's equaliser and seemingly nerveless, slides a perfect penalty into the corner as the Wycombe keeper chooses the wrong side; 6-5 to Southend.

Wycombe's Amadi-Holloway looks as if he would rather be somewhere else and scuffs his spot-kick. Bentley is almost there, but the ball hits the inside of the post and trickles in. 'How's your luck?' remarks the TV commentator; 6-6.

Bolger, not renowned for goalscoring finesse, drives the ball high into the top corner beyond the acrobatic leap of the Wycombe keeper, the best penalty so far. On the touchline, Ainsworth nods his acknowledgement of a job well done and Brown registers mild surprise; 7-6 to Southend.

Wood, the Wycombe captain, looks in imminent danger of vomiting as he makes his way to the penalty spot. Bentley looks icy calm and spits into his gloves. Wood's shot is well hit and aiming towards the corner, but Bentley's picked this one. He dives full length to his left and his telescopic arms deflect the ball on to the left-hand post and out. Game, set and match to Southend United.

***

The delirious celebrations, the endless delay before the 107-step climb to the Royal Box, the handing out of medals to the heroes in mustard yellow: players, substitutes, coaching staff, old Uncle Tom Cobley and all, the final presentation of the fourth significant trophy in our history, the benign smile from Ron Chairman as if it had all been planned in advance and the jubilant lap of honour, all laid out for the delight of the 25,000 Blues fans in Wembley and supporters worldwide.

So much joy, even for the Blues faint-hearts who had already left or were climbing the gangways to the exit in the 122nd minute. Today, I watch gobsmacked as the seats start to empty in the Alex Ferguson Stand at Old Trafford, the Kenny Dalglish Stand at Anfield and the East Stand at the Etihad with four or five minutes still to play, irrespective of the score. Quite apart from the cost of a match ticket in the Premier League, I just can't believe that beating the traffic is really worth it. If there is a moral to this little tale, it is: take my lead from Newport County at Roots Hall back in December 1977 and don't leave before the final whistle.

Football and popular music have shared a cultural heritage throughout my years of football fandom, but I've sometimes wondered why English football enthusiasts have such a passionate affection for cheesy pop songs on big occasions. Actually, I don't, because I'm as susceptible as the rest. Back in May 1968, Cliff Richard's 'Congratulations' blasted out of the old Wembley PA system after West Bromwich's defeat of Everton in the FA Cup

Final and the exhilarating night 11 days later when Manchester United steamrollered Benfica 4-1 in the final of the European Cup at the same venue; a song so cheesy that it nearly won the Eurovision Song Contest. The quintessential rock anthem 'We Are the Champions' by Queen was immediately taken up by football supporters and did the job in the 80s and 90s, though there was nothing remotely cheesy about it. 'No time for losers, 'cos we are the champions – of the world.'

The new century heralded the return of the cheese. When Southend won the League Two play-off final at the Millennium in 2005, '(Is This the Way to) Amarillo', a wedge of vintage cheddar by 70s warbler Tony Christie resounded around the stadium, with 'Sha-la-la-la-la-la-la-la, OOH OOH, Sha-la-la-la-la-la-la-la, OOH OOH', merrily belted out by the victorious United supporters. In the euphoria of our penalties win in 2015, the United faithful serenades half of Wembley and the deserted East End recently vacated by the hapless Wycombe supporters with the strains of 'Sweet Caroline', a classic from the Big Cheese himself, 60s groaner Neil Diamond. 'Sweet Caroline, DUH-DUH-DUH, good times never seemed so good (so good, so good, so good).' It's a bit nuts, it's fun and it's English football folklore. And every time I hear the latest musical silliness echoing around an English football stadium, a pang of the old homesickness kicks in. For a little while.

Back into the third tier after a five-year absence, we waved a fond farewell to Adam Barrett on his well-deserved retirement, a regretful farewell to Phil Brown and his short-lived managerial successor Chris Powell, our very last representative from the heroes of 1991. On the pitch, United flirted with promotion and relegation, just managing to avoid both. The show that never ends.[53]

---

53 *Welcome Back My Friends to the Show That Never Ends.* A shameless appropriation of a 1974 live album title by progressive rock band Emerson, Lake and Palmer. Couldn't resist it.

Chapter 23

The View From the Coast

KIM AND I moved to the Australian Sunshine Coast of Queensland in 2018. I quite like the symmetry of it. After all, Southend-on-Sea is on the coast, there are a few skinny palm trees on the seafront and it's always sunny, as we know. Therefore, my football club inhabits England's Sunshine Coast, no matter what they think in Clacton. When it comes to interest in English football, however, there is literally a world of difference.

Compared to south-east Queensland, the Eastern Suburbs of Sydney are a hotbed of English Football League passion. In our new locale, 'footy' usually means rugby league, the Brisbane Broncos and now the Dolphins. Less frequently, it means Australian rules and the Brisbane Lions. The Brisbane Roar, our 'local' round-ball team 70 miles distant, rates barely a mention, and we haven't yet made the pilgrimage down the Bruce Highway (surely the best name ever for an Australian road).

It's not that our part of the world is an expatriate Brit-free zone, far from it, but maybe they lost the love somewhere or, more likely, never had it in the first place. We do have a local friend originating from south London who is a staunch follower of Charlton Athletic and we can occasionally shoot the breeze about the latest problems afflicting our teams. A few months ago, I spotted a shiny new expensive four-wheel drive at our local shopping centre, complete with an expensive Queensland number plate adorned with a royal blue background and the word 'Pompey' picked out prominently in white. You can do this with number plates in Queensland if you're prepared to pay enough. Portsmouth supporter; good for him – or her. More recently, in the car park of a local golf club, my attention was captured by a silver X-type Jaguar. This sleek, classic motor also sported an expensive Queensland number plate, this time with a scarlet background and the number '42 LFC' in bold white. My polite enquiry confirmed it. Liverpool supporter – there's always one. Proud English football supporters waving their flags on the other side of the world. Just like waiting for a bus; you wait ages for one to turn up and then two arrive in quick succession.

And we have Kim's Anglo/Aussie family living nearby. Manchester United (mother-in-law), Arsenal (father-in-law), Tottenham (brother-in-law), Don't Care (sister-in-law). Otherwise, it's Kim and I, subscription television, the bookcase accommodating books, videos and DVDs, the collection of replica shirts, the mouse mat, the car key ring and the sun-faded Southend United stickers on the rear window of the Honda Civic.

***

The balcony of our Queensland home has a view of the deep-blue Pacific Ocean to the east. From where we sit, no matter how hard we look, the nearest land mass is way, way beyond the horizon, all the way to South America. Somewhere even further east sit Southend-on-Sea and Roots Hall: a mere 36 hours away door to door, if we're lucky with the connection at Los Angeles International.[54] It is a journey we will continue to make. And when Southend United get to the Champions

---

54 Thirty-six hours from my front door to the West Stand turnstiles following the Pacific route. The Asian route takes around 30 hours, depending on the stopover.

League Final, the FA Cup Final, or even the Championship play-off final, I expect we will move heaven and earth to get hold of the tickets and the short-notice flights, so long as we're not completely decrepit by then. Back in England, daughter Vickie is an avid tournament fan (as in World Cups and European Championships), but the Blues are not prominent on her personal radar. Holly the granddaughter looks destined to become a Southampton supporter like her dad, so the family connection with Southend probably ends with Kim and I (although Vickie is showing more interest recently).

David Goldblatt is a prolific and perceptive football historian. According to his wiki and to his eternal credit, he is a supporter of both Tottenham Hotspur and Bristol Rovers. I wonder who he'll support when the Spurs next play the Gas. To Goldblatt, football 'is a game that thrives upon chaos and uncertainty ... yet retains the notion that anything is possible'.[55]

The United and City of Manchester, Liverpool, the Chelsea, Arsenal and Tottenham of London, the so-called current 'big six' in England, seem to be immune from the chaos and uncertainty which afflict the other 86 professional clubs – for now. But, no matter what proponents of the European Super League may like to think, English football has always been subject to seismic shifts which have overturned assumptions in the past and may challenge today's status quo in the near future. A few disastrous forays into the transfer market, a peed-off superstar or two, a blizzard of key injuries, a manager gone feral, owners and directors gone feral, breaches of Profit and Sustainability rules, disaster may happen for one or more of these teams sometime soon. Nobody saw Leicester City's 2016 Premier League win coming. It's all possible.

55 *The Age of Football*, written by David Goldblatt. Macmillan, 2019.

And in my view Goldblatt's assertion is even more relevant for those of us who are manacled to undying support for our lower-division clubs. Chaos and uncertainty have been central to my Southend United story for 60 years. Snakes and ladders are our destiny. What we experience may shred the nerves and test our patience to the limits of endurance, may build us up sky-high or reduce us to the depths of despair, but the next big change is just around the corner.

***

It is painful but true to observe that three of United's closest rivals from the days when I first became a supporter, Brentford, Brighton and Bournemouth, have enjoyed time in the top division. Brentford spent a few years in the First Division just before and just after the second world war. In 2021, they made their triumphant return to the top tier after an interval of 74 years. The old Griffin Park ground with the pub on each corner is no more, replaced by the new Brentford Community Stadium with its strange Scrabble board seat design greeting the great and the good of the Premier League.

Brighton & Hove Albion made it to the First Division in the 80s, including an FA Cup Final in 1983 against Manchester United. I managed to secure a Wembley ticket for the 2-2 draw, a match Brighton should have won. Then I queued for an aeon to get a ticket for the replay, which the Reds emphatically won 4-0. No prizes for guessing who I supported; sympathy for the underdog has its limits. The Albion were within one goal of falling out of the Football League altogether in 1997. They also managed to lose their elderly but quite respectable Goldstone Ground and spent a significant time as Poverty Row nomads: a couple of years as tenants of Gillingham's Priestfield and ten years' residence at a converted athletics track in Withdean on the outskirts of town. Now Brighton & Hove Albion are among the Premier League's elite, with the large, spanking new stadium we should have which holds nearly 32,000 and is packed to the rafters on matchday.

As for AFC Bournemouth, we seemed to have played them for ever. Until a few years ago, Bournemouth were notable for three years in the second tier and bugger all for the rest of their history. They, too, pulled themselves clear of an even closer flirtation with non-league in 2009 and then went nuts ending up, almost by accident, in the Premier League. Their boxy, old-fashioned little ground once known as Dean Court is now a boxy, modern little ground called the Vitality Stadium; it has an even smaller capacity than Roots Hall. How is AFC Bournemouth possible?

Over 100 years in the lower divisions, United have played the three Bs a total of 311 times in Football League, FA Cup and League Cup (Also-Rans Cup encounters excluded). We have won 38 per cent and lost 38 per cent of these games. First Divisions, Premier Leagues, FA Cup finals (even if you lose, at least you can say you got there) and Southend have not experienced any of them. Always under the lights of the big league. And am I a wee bit envious? Ahem; ah, good luck to them.

What I can do is delve into the scrapbook of my mind for a lifetime of United memories and daydream about what was, what wasn't and what might have been. The top tier of the Football League has always been Never Never Land. Silverware has proved to be Southend kryptonite. And Europe, for Southend supporters, is a holiday destination.[56]

Still, I will always have Colchester United 1964, Workington 1968, Mansfield Town 1969, Watford (times three) 1978, Lincoln City 1981, Wolverhampton Wanderers and Derby County 1987, Tottenham Hotspur

---

56 Apart from the Anglo-Italian Cup, a second-tier anomaly of the 1990s where a select few English teams played their Italian counterparts. United didn't trouble the honours board in any of their three visits. I found the attractions of Brescia, Foggia, Pescara and Padova too elusive and didn't turn up at Roots Hall for any of these matches.

1989, Peterborough United 1990, Bury 1991, Yeovil Town 2005, Manchester United 2006, Millwall 2014, Wycombe Wanderers 2015, Newport County for ever.

And an unforgettable night at Roots Hall in January 1979.

Chapter 24

Frozen in Time

ON TWELFTH Night, Saturday, 6 January 1979, Southend United, seventh in the Third Division, should have claimed their reward for beating Watford 1-0 in the second round of the FA Cup: a home draw against Liverpool, holders of the European Cup and runaway leaders of the First Division. Except it didn't happen. From memory, it was *Grandstand* on BBC TV bringing the news that the match was postponed due to snow on the pitch and ice on the terraces, or both, or vice versa – and I was relieved, to be honest.

I was standing in front of the television set in a heavy polo-neck jumper, swathed in my old parka with the faux fur-lined hood from uni, United scarf over my shoulders, car keys and gloves in one hand, a pair of Wellington boots in the other. Outside, snow was cascading down, adding to the deepening expanse of white that had been accumulating all morning and the day before – and on and off since Christmas. Well, it would all have to wait another five days, kick-off at 7.30pm under the lights.

At the time, my home and my job were in Basildon, a challenging 15-mile drive from Roots Hall in the teeth of the most severe English winter I can recall.[57] To complicate

---

57 The British winter of 1962/63 was notorious for its longevity. But, as I remember it, the English winter of 1978/79 was shorter, albeit more severe.

things further, I was the not-so-proud owner of a 1969 Singer Gazelle, a piece of metal that was old-fashioned on the day it was built. Grey in colour with maroon 'racing' flashes, the Gazelle was not a sewing machine but a sturdy saloon motor car boasting a dead classy walnut dashboard and a dead funky gear lever mounted on the steering column. It also leaked oil like a busted sieve and possessed the road-holding ability of a cow on an ice rink, which is why I'd bought it so cheaply. Not the ideal conveyance for an icy January day in England.

At least I had the precious match tickets. Earlier generations of United directors were not slow to rake in an extra few quid when the opportunity arose, the decision to play home games on Friday nights being the most brilliant. For the Liverpool tie, the biggest game in Southend's history, a voucher, redeemable for a real match ticket, is on offer. All you have to do is turn up for United versus Brentford at Roots Hall on the Saturday before Christmas, pay at the gate and the turnstile guy hands you the slip of paper with your change. As a result, 13,552, a crowd three times as big as would have otherwise been expected, turn up on the day renowned as the graveyard for football attendances in the era before mass season tickets and Sunday shop opening. The atmosphere is strangely muted; 5,000 regulars are volubly disenchanted with the 1-1 result, but the 9,000 day-trippers don't seem to mind very much. What would the Roots Hall atmosphere be like on the big night?

***

At four in the afternoon of Wednesday, 10 January, I slip on the polo-neck jumper, scarf, jeans, football socks, trainers and trusty old parka. Suit and tie are consigned to the boot of the Gazelle where the wellington boots are ready (just in case) and I embark on the journey from Basildon, nice and early as planned. As I pick up Hilary from her office, it is seasonally dark already but, instead of inky blackness, the sky is a forbidding battleship grey.

The roads are glistening with stubborn dustings of snow from the weekend and a coating of slowly solidifying ice underneath. There are only two roads from Basildon to Southend in January 1979: still are. On London Road, the approach includes Bread and Cheese Hill, a fairly steep, winding climb which I don't fancy one bit. The Southend Arterial Road also has a curving uphill stretch but it's not as steep or winding as Bread and Cheese, so I decide to play safe. Eventually, the bonnet-to-boot line of crawling traffic on the Arterial gets us to the bottom of the slope, just as snow starts to fall again: not a blizzard, but a mass of large, drifting flakes confounding the windscreen wipers and plopping on the road around us. I manage to tease my leaky old tank of a vehicle eastwards by performing a laboured uphill slalom in third gear as the inadequate radial tyres strive to bite on the rapidly settling snow. As we approach the outskirts of Southend-on-Sea, at five o'clock, kick-off is two and a half hours away.

Another 45 minutes pass by the time we battle through the thickening snow to Thorpe Bay, where we have planned to pick up Dad and join a small convoy of family friends who had joined us in the Brentford experience. True to form, Mum has steadfastly refused to join us at Roots Hall tonight, but she laughingly wishes us luck and repairs to the warmth of the lounge with Estelle the sister and Tilly the bitza-spitza dog. Opposite my parents' house is a road with a short, shallow uphill slope, looming tonight as a pristine expanse of whiteness. And, despite my efforts, I can't massage the old tub up the slope, even after turfing my protesting passengers out into the snow. It doesn't take long to conclude that the car is too hard, so I carefully guide the ill-named Gazelle into the snowdrift on the side of the road, fish out the wellies and lock up. Thorpe Bay at six o'clock, the kick-off now 90 minutes away.

Time for a council of war with the now-defunct convoy. Given the weather, do we think the match is still on? BBC

Radio 4 reports nothing to the contrary. OK: as it's miles too far to walk and getting hold of a taxi cab in Thorpe Bay is a fraught endeavour at the best of times, we are left with a choice between bus and train. I contribute the mournful insight that I have seen far fewer buses than would normally be expected in the evening rush hour. So off we trudge towards Thorpe Bay station a mile away, more in hope than expectation. But glory be, British Rail Eastern Region (predecessor of the infamous Network SouthEast) steps up to the plate on this night of all nights and we can see the lights of the 1822 to Fenchurch Street, bang on time, emerging though the driving snow. Trundling into Southend Central reveals no forlorn folk in blue and white favours waiting for a train home, so it looks like the match is still on. It's 6.30pm and kick-off is an hour away.

Now for the big question. 'Come on Dad, who are you supporting tonight?' 'Not telling you,' is his teasing reply as we start our trek up the dirty-white High Street pavement and join a river of people trudging along with us. Good job I'd decided on the wellingtons. As the river absorbs more streams from right and left and our marching feet crunch through the snow into Victoria Avenue, we can pick out our first sight of the Roots Hall floodlights blinking through the snowfall which has now returned to large, drifting flakes. The horde ahead of us is cast into a silhouette of bobbing heads and swaying shoulders, crowned by the steam of condensed breath and the ubiquitous cigarette smoke: an undulating, amorphous mass of anticipation. On the roadway, we are almost reluctantly passed by occasional blue and white Corporation buses and their green Eastern National counterparts, their slowly revolving wheels whispering to us through the slush. Eventually, we see another large human tributary lumbering past St Mary's Church as we reach the Prittlewell traffic lights and turn left into West Street.

And the start of the queue is right here, across the road from the Blue Boar, where it all began for Southend United 73 years ago. We have tickets for the West Stand but, as a police presence is nowhere in sight, we have no way of knowing if we are in the right queue. Never mind. We're English, aren't we? We see a queue and we join it. New arrivals take their place behind us and our crocodile of weather-ravaged optimists shuffles forward at a glacial pace, eventually rounding the corner into Shakespeare Drive, a formidable 60 yards from the turnstiles. The time is seven o'clock and kick-off is 30 minutes away.

Talking of glacial, the brisk walk through the snow from Southend Central has kept us reasonably warm up to now. Inching forward in the restless queue, we can now feel the chill penetrating to the bone. In the meantime, the word goes around that kick-off has been delayed because of the crowds stuck outside. The word was correct but where it came from, I'll never know. It makes us feel a bit better. Logic suggests that we are bound for either the South Bank or the West Stand entrances, but at which turnstile we'll end up is uncertain. 'Dunno, mate' is the shrugging consensus around us, a confused combination of South Bankers and West Standers.

In the continued absence of the boys in blue, I negotiate a temporary release from the crocodile and stroll down Shakespeare Drive. Finally, at the small concourse shared by West Stand and South Bank entrances which is literally groaning with people, I spot a contingent of the local constabulary doing their best to organise an orderly passage towards the turnstiles, even a copper on a horse, something I have never seen before at Roots Hall. What concerns me more is another crocodile as long as ours, weaving out of the concourse and down the lower end of Shakespeare Drive as far as the eye can see. My polite enquiry confirms that this is in fact the crocodile for the West Stand with a few bemused South Bank ticket holders mixed in and we have been shivering in the wrong queue for more than half an hour. In the meantime, the crocodile containing my little group has continued to shuffle its way forward and is now inching into the concourse.

Time for more negotiation, because I have a plan. I made a mental note of the bemused South Bank ticket holders I spoke to who now realise that they, too, are in the wrong place. I can see a few now turning into the concourse, ten yards away. Behind the backs of the thin blue line, I call out, 'You're in the wrong queue, so are we. Want to swap?' Hearing a relieved answer of 'Yes', I appeal to the other people I'd spoken to, 'Is that OK?' There are a few grumbles but no loud objections, so two small groups rapidly switch crocodiles. A few swaps take place after ours with no active opposition from the police, to their credit. We probably did them a favour.

With the entrance to the ground looming closer, I can hear the hum of the crowd inside Roots Hall – much more humming than usual – and a few disembodied drones from Roots Hall Ron, but can't pick up what he's saying. Chants from the Liverpool supporters filter through but I don't remember hearing any live pre-match entertainment, the old supporters' club band having disbanded several years ago. At 7.45pm, 15 minutes after the originally scheduled kick-off and well over three hours since the quest began, the 'click-clack' of the turnstile finally disgorges us into the West Stand.

***

It was the first sight and sound of the mountainous Spion Kop terrace, choc-a-bloc with heaving, swaying Liverpool supporters, that remains my salient memory from Anfield in April 1962, the first real football match I ever attended. There was always something awe-inspiring about towering old-style packed-out terraces at old-style football grounds that I never really grew out of – still haven't, as you might have noticed. But back in January 1979, after 15 years of supporting Southend, Roots Hall and I have never seen a full house because we'd never climbed higher than the Third Division and never hosted an FA Cup match against an elite outfit like Liverpool. As we nudge and ease our way down the steps of the West Stand to my usual first-half position, I delay the tantalising moment until I take my place and then look to the right.

Ever had the feeling when you think you know what to expect but the reality knocks you for six anyway? My jaw drops and my eyes widen. 'Oh my God!' I gasp. And before me is a sight I have never witnessed before and will never witness again: the 72 steps of the South Bank engulfed in a mass of heaving, swaying spectators under the lights, some holding banners too far away to read, capped by the densest clouds of steam and smoke I have ever seen at Roots Hall.

The North and South Paddocks are already fit to burst, and all the seats in the East Stand are occupied, including the couple of blocks allocated to Liverpool supporters for the huge sum of £1.50 per ticket. The North Bank is filling up quickly: the half allocated to the travelling Scousers already bears more than a passing resemblance to the Kop, a heroic gathering considering the journey they must have endured to get here. They are separated from the United North Bankers by a lightly policed gap in the middle of the terrace which is immaculately respected by both sets of supporters. In the West Stand a few, a very few spaces await the hordes still emerging from the concourse and are disappearing as the rhythmic 'click-clack-click-clack' of the overworked turnstiles behind me testify.

The pitch itself is a winter wonderland of virgin white, geometrically dissected by brown/green lines where the ground staff have diligently swept the snow away from the touchlines, centre line and around the penalty areas. I am so enthralled by the scene that I barely register the entrance of the Liverpool team to lusty cheers from their fans and scattered boos from ours; just for form – nothing personal.

The Southend players canter purposefully on to the pitch surrounded by a rolling roar of welcome and perform a brisk wave of appreciation before quickly getting down to their warm-up routine. And you can't blame them. The snow is still falling as is the mercury in the thermometer and these guys are kitted out with those short shorts that were *de rigueur* in the late 70s: apart from Ray Clemence, Liverpool's and England's goalkeeper, who has decided to be a man in tights tonight.

Liverpool:	**Southend United:**
1. Ray Clemence	1. Mervyn Cawston
2. Phil Neal	2. Mike Stead
3. Emlyn Hughes	3. Steve Yates
4. Phil Thompson	4. Mick Laverick
5. Ray Kennedy	5. Tony Hadley
6. Alan Hansen	6. Alan Moody
7. Kenny Daglish	7. Colin Morris
8. Jimmy Case	8. Ron Pountney
9. David Fairclough	9. Derrick Parker
10. Terry McDermott	10. Phil Dudley
11. Graeme Souness	11. Gerry Fell
12. Steve Heighway (sub)	12. John Walker (sub)

Liverpool are showing respect for the occasion by putting out a full-strength side. Ten out of the 12 on their team list are full internationals – ten more than the United line-up can boast – because the third round of the FA Cup is a big deal in 1979.[58] The BBC TV cameras have also turned up to capture the action for the broadcast highlights on *Sportsnight* later in the evening and lead commentator John Motson is freezing his proverbials off on the exposed gantry reserved for TV commentators and camera crew on the West Stand roof. The man in the middle is tall, burly and stern Keith Hackett, the apex of the refereeing A-list and definitely not one to be messed with. A big deal indeed.

---

58 The two uncapped Liverpool players were Jimmy Case and David Fairclough.

***

An ear-battering roar greets the kick-off. United are kicking towards the South Bank in the first half but, with the massed ranks there and the Liverpool supporters in the North Bank, who knows if we won the toss? Weather conditions dictate the use of an orange ball, so that referee, players (and the crowd) can actually see it, but the pitch provides another challenge all its own. The snow often holds up the ball part-way towards its intended destination and is even prone to gathering small gouts of white as it rolls along the pitch. Nevertheless, the early pace is frantic enough and Liverpool start as if in 'let's get this over with' mode. Near misses from Dalglish and Fairclough as the Scousers in the North Bank surge and sway like they do at Anfield. 'Oohh,' intones Dad with a chuckle as 'Liv-er-pool, Liv-er-pool' rings out from the north-east side of the ground. A couple of young kids in front of us are piping out 'Come on Liverpool!' in irritating falsetto tones bearing not the faintest hint of a Merseyside accent. Unnatural little brats!

Fortunately, the home supporters are not to be outdone. As in the Watford match, the rhythmic chants of 'Southend [clap-clap-clap], Southend [clap-clap-clap]' arising from the kids in the East Stand are picked up around the ground by young and old, including the supporters for the day who have filled the South Bank and West Stand but this time the chanting starts up from the kick-off. Loud choruses of 'Come on you Blues' reverberate around Roots Hall and, to my relief, the atmosphere is as supercharged, partisan and loud as I'd hoped. To complete the picture, snow is now falling quite heavily, bathing the whole floodlit scene with a soft, milky aura. Nothing soft and milky about the contest, mind you. Souness and McDermott are midfielders endowed with great skill, but neither are shrinking violets. Nevertheless, Pountney and Laverick (they're not shrinking violets either) have managed to keep them in check. The battle for midfield is robust and uncompromising but it's also an honest battle, with remarkably few bad tackles or clumsy fouls despite the conditions, under the gimlet glare of the ever-vigilant Hackett.

Not just in check either, as United start to take control. Their elegant footballing defenders Hadley and Moody are handling Dalglish and Fairclough comfortably and our forays up the pitch are increasing pressure on the Liverpool defence. Twenty-five minutes in, Dudley attempts a lob which clears Clemence but also clears the crossbar, inspiring agonised 'oohhs' and raising the noise level even higher. Gerry Fell, replacing Andy Polycarpou, the hero of the Watford replay, is capable of occasional moments of genius. It's his quite brilliant reverse pass from central midfield that releases Derrick Parker in the clear with the Liverpool defence rent asunder. He gallops head down on goal, ball at feet, only for Clemence, using his experience accumulated from keeping goal behind a decade of leaky England defenders, to charge out of his penalty area, slide in and block with his feet. Fine margins, as they say. The Blues are on a roll, buzzing menacingly around the Liverpool box for the next 15 minutes without creating another clear chance.

Keith Hackett blows for half-time and it feels as if the whole of Roots Hall has exhaled simultaneously, followed by a stirring ovation for the United lads. There's plenty to discuss. Supposing Parker had been a bit quicker and/or Clemence a bit slower? The great Dalglish: hardly had a kick, has he? When's this bloody snow going to stop? On the running track, we have stewards in fluorescent yellow with old-fashioned loudhailers directing spectators towards the slivers of remaining space, as I sometimes used to see at big-ticket First Division matches back in the 60s. Nobody's changing ends tonight.

The teams retake the pitch, now scarred with ugly gashes of brown and green criss-crossing the remaining patches of white, recording the exertions of the first half. From the West Stand, this makes the orange ball more difficult to track, but it doesn't seem to bother the players. And, as the snow continues to fall, it gets perceptibly colder. If the first half was a winter wonderland, the second is *Ice Station Zebra*.[59] In the middle of the West Stand and securely under the roof, I am barely aware of the snow-laden blasts of air driving in from the north; unlike the unfortunate masses on the South Bank who cop them full in the face.

'We all agree, Southend United are magic' echoes around the ground as both teams fight the elements and each other to a standstill. It now looks as if every square inch of Roots Hall is filled to the brim. Some brave spectators have climbed on to the roof of the tea kiosk in the south-east corner. Above the kiosk, others can be seen catching a precarious and slippery view from the grassy bit forever, and inexplicably, left untouched by concrete. Even the most reticent day-trippers are getting sucked into the vibe as the chants and songs increase in frequency and volume. The snow eases up and we only have the grinding ambient chill to contend with. The expression 'Too cold to snow' is the subject of some amusement in warmer parts of the world but, if you're English, you know what it means all right.

Despite the crush, the icy wind is now seeping into the depths of the West Stand and I realise that my numbed feet no longer belong to me despite the wellies, the thick football socks and regular stamping on the frozen terrace steps. But, 'We shall not, we shall not be moved; we shall not, we shall not be moved; it's like a team that's gonna win the FA Cup; we shall not be moved' is now the cheeky refrain from the West Stand Blues. As if reminded of what's at stake, Liverpool have their own spell of pressure. Maybe they'll pull something out of the hat, as they often do.

Fairclough is almost through, ploughing through the slush in front of the South Bank, but Cawston risks terminal frostbite by diving at his feet to snatch the ball. Some not-so-

---

59 *Ice Station Zebra* was the classic 1963 Alistair MacLean novel set in the Arctic and the 1968 Hollywood movie based on the novel.

bright Scouse scallywag in the North Bank chucks a flare on to the pitch, which belches out waves of red smoke to strident boos from the United fans. Thankfully, the smoke disperses quickly. Then United win a free kick on the left, 30 yards out. The first cross is feeble and easily blocked; the second effort is driven hard into the penalty area. Out goes Thompson's leg and the ball ricochets off his boot on to Hansen's outstretched arm. Roots Hall leaps in the air, hands aloft. 'Handball! Oi!! Oi!! Ref!! Ref!!!!' we shriek en masse. 'That's handball!' shouts Dad. In the ensuing chaos, the ball breaks to United's Parker who ends up spreadeagled on the deck ten yards out with Thompson in suspiciously close attendance. More shrieks. Both claims for a penalty are summarily rejected by referee Hackett to the wrath of the Southend supporters who can't clearly see what was going on. These incidents create enough pandemonium as it is but, if they hadn't taken place in front of the quadrant occupied by Liverpool supporters, I'll bet the roar of protest would have brought the house down and maybe given Hackett more pause for thought. But it didn't, and he didn't, and we'll never know.

Roots Hall is in ferment for the dying moments as United throw the kitchen sink at Liverpool. Right at the end, Morris gets the ball on to his left foot and drills a decent shot at goal, but Clemence dives smartly to save. All too soon, Hackett finds the whistle he omitted to blow during the penalty incident(s) and ends the game, drowned out by a tumult of appreciation from the massed ranks of Southend, all true-blue for tonight. Dave Smith emerges from the dugout, as he did against Watford, and waves his appreciation to all and sundry. Another pitch invasion by the kiddies because they can. The players, red and blue, look physically spent as they shake hands and trudge off the pitch, a rousing standing ovation ringing in their years. And well-deserved it is too.

Over the public address system rises the voice of Roots Hall Ron, a tad more excited than usual, and we have been waiting all evening for it. 'Tonight's official attendance [long pause] 31,000'; the 'and 33' is submerged by another mighty roar. A new club attendance record: some sources quote a crowd of 31,090 – 57 people perched on the tea kiosk perhaps. Either way, it easily surpasses the previous record of 28,059 for the visit of the omnipresent Birmingham City back in 1957 (*Southend United: The Official History of the Blues* records it as 28,964) and the unofficial record, reputed to be 29,500, when Manchester City came to town the year before that.

It takes an age to get out of the ground, but the place is abuzz with backslapping, hand-shaking, exhilarated laughter, animated debate. All this for a goalless draw. And Dad reveals with a twinkle in his eye that he'd decided to support United all along but had amused himself by keeping us guessing. As the circulation painfully returns to my feet and I leave the shelter of the West Stand on to the Shakespeare Drive concourse, I can finally give a coherent voice to my immediate feelings. 'Shit! It's absolutely freezing out here!' Colder than the Colchester match ten years earlier? Not quite; nothing could beat the experience of 45 minutes spent on the exposed South Bank for the Saint Valentine's Day massacre in 1969. The difference was that in a crowd of 13,000, I could get the circulation going a bit by moving around but in a crowd of 31,000 I am rooted to the spot for two hours. So not quite as cold – but not far off it.

The import of the evening takes rather longer to sink in but, like an unexpected power outage, my memory of Southend's biggest night so far, so vivid in my mind for 45 years ends at this point. Maybe it was the cold. How did Hilary and I get home that night? (Car, train, bus?) Did we get home that night? (Could have stayed with parents.) What did we do next morning? Try as I might, my after-the-event memory banks fail me completely.

And where's the Video Assistant Referee when you need him? This innovation wasn't even a gleam in a techie's eye back in January 1979. With the passage of years and a medium serving of sour grapes, I can reflect on Alan Hansen's raised arm being in an 'unnatural position' when the ball ricocheted off Thompson's boot, to use today's VAR-inspired parlance. On the Parker penalty area tumble, I must have replayed the incident dozens of times, firstly in my mind and more recently through courtesy of YouTube. I can only console myself with the time-honoured lament for penalty non-decisions on a football pitch, 'Seen 'em given.' Perhaps a word in Hackett's ear from the 'Buffoon in the Box at Stockley Park' (my unflattering moniker for the remote official who reviews the video footage and advises the on-pitch official). But perhaps not – I wouldn't have fancied contradicting Keith Hackett. We are left with Plucky Little Southend United 0, Lucky Big Liverpool 0. A carnival of experiences under the lights. You can watch the highlights on YouTube. But you weren't there.

***

I still had a few ageing relatives alive and kicking in Liverpool in January 1979. I could, probably should, have made the journey up to Anfield for the replay one week later. But I didn't – and barely thought about doing so. Apart from the weather, which had not significantly improved, I felt that I would be spoiling the memory of the Roots Hall night by subjecting myself to the reality check that I fully expected. And my expectation was correct.

On the night, 37,797 spectators, including nearly 4,000 United travellers massed in the Anfield Road End, saw Liverpool ease to a comfortable 3-0 victory with goals from Jimmy Case, Kenny Dalglish and Ray Kennedy. Also present was the friend studying Veterinary Science at the University of Liverpool. He reported that the Scousers gave our team a polite ovation at the end, which was nice, but his most vivid recollection was of a lone United-supporting nutcase in the Kemlyn Road Stand occupied by Liverpool regulars loudly and (we presume) drunkenly volunteering to take them all on in a bout of fisticuffs. Fortunately, nobody was prepared to take up his generous offer and the impeccable crowd behaviour at Roots Hall (flare-chucking prat aside) was maintained for the replay. Despite my absence, I wasn't quite finished with Merseyside for that season: three months later, I was enjoying my evening out at Tranmere Rovers – which is where this story began.

History records that Liverpool went on to claim the First Division by eight points, a wide margin in the days of two points for a win. Their attempt at a third successive European Cup had already been foiled by Nottingham Forest and they had to wait another two seasons to regain it. Instead, it was the Forest who went on to win it that year, and then won it again. Britannia ruled the European Cup waves for a few years in the late 70s and early 80s and Liverpool, Nottingham Forest, and Aston Villa were the Dreadnoughts. It was such a long time ago. In the FA Cup, Liverpool navigated their way through Blackburn Rovers, Burnley and Ipswich Town to earn that 2-2 draw with Manchester United at Maine Road in the semi-final. Liverpool finally met their own reality check in the replay at Goodison Park where Manchester United prevailed 1-0, thereby proving that there is justice in this world. It was a shame they had to lose the final 3-2 to the Arsenal.

As for Southend, we returned to the Third Division dogfight and our mild flirtation with the promotion places lasted until the beginning of April, when we, unbelievably, beat Watford 1-0 again. Then that run of seven defeats in the last nine games reduced us to unfulfilled mid-table mediocrity. Move forward four years and United are struggling in the Third Division while the First Division sees yet another championship triumph for Liverpool, with Watford, of all teams, runners-up. You couldn't make it up if you tried.

***

Every family has a story or two. Over time, sharp edges are honed down and mundane elements embellished to build an idealised version of what actually happened. Here's a story from mine.

On Saturday, 5 January 1957, my father was an English teacher at St George's High School, Bootle, deep in the northern suburbs of Liverpool. Yes! THAT Bootle. He was also an elected member of the old Litherland Urban District Council. It was in this capacity that Dad, together with a few other council colleagues, scored a weekend junket to a town in Essex called Southend-on-Sea. It was the third round of the FA Cup: Liverpool, then of the Second Division, were playing Southend, then of the Third Division (South) at Roots Hall. A London Midland steam train from Liverpool Lime Street to London Euston; a short trip across town on the electric Circle line; an Eastern Region steam train from Fenchurch Street to Southend Central and the six-hour railway odyssey ended with a seat in the East Stand.

On a mudheap of a pitch, for which Roots Hall was notorious in its early years and an early 2.15pm kick-off in those pre-floodlight days, a small gathering of Litherland councillors among 18,253 spectators saw United tear up the form book and defeat Liverpool 2-1, one of several notable FA Cup tussles against higher-division teams in the 1950s.[60] Mildly but not desperately disappointed at the result in the other-worldly atmosphere of a seaside resort out of season, Dad spent part of his Saturday evening strolling along the winter-quiet Marine Parade with the high tide lapping gently against the night time seashore. In wandering around the scenic cliff paths below the late Georgian house fronts on Royal Terrace he would have passed Never Never Land, darkened and closed until the summer. He braved a bracing hike along the pier in

60 Ronnie Moran and Jimmy Melia played in the Liverpool side beaten by United in 1957. They also scored the goals when Liverpool beat Stoke City in April 1962, the occasion of my first Football League match.

the invigorating chill of an early January Sunday morning before catching the trains home.

Dad must have been impressed by what he saw because he made a serious sales pitch to Mum, extolling the virtues of the seaside town 250 miles away. In all her life, Mum never liked Liverpool much so his pitch fell on fertile ground: less than a year later, the family was on its own railway odyssey to Southend-on-Sea, just ahead of the removal van.

Before I could barely walk or talk my life was destined to change for ever, thanks to Southend United. My club does not define me as a human being, of course it doesn't, otherwise I wouldn't be living as far away from Roots Hall as is humanly possible. But the degree to which things United have woven their way into the patterns of my life is undeniable. Stuck with it doesn't even begin to tell the tale. In another world, my destiny could have been determined by 60 years standing, then sitting, then standing again on the Spion Kop. All that lovely silverware along the way. Why not? I'm an officially documented Scouser; my birth certificate and both my passports say so. But it didn't turn out that way, as we have seen.

And you know what? I wouldn't exchange my Southend United memories for the world. 'If you can meet with triumph and disaster and treat those two imposters just the same.' Triumph, disaster, imposters, all that Kipling stuff. That's what this book's been about. All I needed was a spark to set it in motion.[61]

---

61 Rudyard Kipling's famous poem *If*, written around 1896, contained 'all that Kipling stuff'.

Chapter 25

The Meltdown

IT'S GONE half past four on Sunday morning, 5 May 2019, when I finally turn the TV off. I stand up and gaze out of the front window. A few pinpricks gleam out from the street lamps, but there are no lights showing in any of the houses around us. Evidently, we are the only people in this part of the Sunshine Coast who have just watched the live beIN Sports broadcast of Southend United against Sunderland in our final League One match of the 2018/19 season.

After Sunderland's equaliser, we are 13 minutes away from relegation to the fourth tier. With three minutes of normal time to go, the score is 1-1. Then United striker Stephen Humphrys, disguised by a plastic mask to protect a facial injury, pounces on a loose ball in the opposition penalty area. A quick drag of the ball to one side bypasses a flailing defender, a low shot nutmegs the Sunderland keeper and the ball rolls deliciously into the net. Humphrys pulls off his blue shirt, revealing the strange push-up bra otherwise known as a chest support vest worn by today's professional footballers, and performs a manic sprint and slide in front of the rejoicing Frank Walton Stand and 80 per cent of the season's best crowd of 10,779.

An incomprehensible and nerve-tingling six minutes of added-on time follows but eventually the referee's whistle matches the 9,000 whistles shrilling from the stands and it

297

ends 2-1 to United. The crowd floods on to the Roots Hall pitch in jubilation. Another disaster averted at the last minute, providing the inspiration for me to write this story.

***

Remember the elephant in the room? Remember the clean slate and the rarity thereof? Two wins in the last 18 matches, obscured by the rollicking victory against Sunderland, should have put us on notice. For in 2019/20 the slate well and truly hit the fan. The second-worst team in Southend's history made an indifferent start and that was the best of it. After our first match, which we lost away to Coventry City, we were 19th in the League One table. It was the season's pinnacle. After the second match, which we also lost, we sank to 22nd. And stayed there.

In an early season turn of management merry-go-round, Kevin Bond received a panic-induced and possibly premature tap on the shoulder, to be replaced by ex-Tottenham and ex-Arsenal defensive talisman Sol Campbell. Unfortunately, Sol couldn't turn things around either, as United plumbed depths rarely seen before. I wish I could say there were two teams worse than us in League One, but that wasn't the case. Poor old Bury were a no show, having gone bust before the season's start. Bolton Wanderers were lumbered with a 12-point penalty for going into administration the previous season, but they were showing belated signs of life and were almost certain to overhaul our inadequate points total well before the end of the season.

On Saturday, 7 March 2020, United beat Bristol Rovers 3-1 in front of an eternally optimistic or wearily resigned gathering of 5,806 at Roots Hall. It was our fourth win in 35 games and it was too late, much too late. It was also United's last 'normal' match with a 'normal' crowd in those far-off-seeming days before COVID-19 turned the world upside down. Six days later, COVID-19 suspended the football season and the formal closure was confirmed three weeks after that.[62] For League One, shutdown meant the table would be finalised on points per game; the top two teams at the second week in March gained automatic promotion, the four teams below them contested the play-offs and the bottom three clubs were relegated there and then. United were firmly in the drop zone, 16 points away from AFC Wimbledon and safety, 13 away from Tranmere Rovers in the third relegation place, with the goal difference from Hell and Bolton hot on our heels. So: we were down, nice and early, to the fourth tier yet again. In one way, it was monstrously unfair. In another, it was a merciful release.

***

Take a look at Edvard Munch's painting, *The Scream*. In the 1895 pastel on cardboard version, a skinny bald-headed character dressed in blue and white stands on a jetty, a grey-blue sea and florid red sunset in the background with hands clasped to the side of the head and mouth open in a wordless oval of horror. It could be me, although I'm not that skinny any more, but it is a clear metaphor for a Southend United supporter on the pier looking onshore towards Roots Hall, absorbing the events of the 2020/21 season.

Firstly, Ron Chairman must have been hoping for a repeat of his Steve Tilson coup when he appointed Mark Molesley, a manager from non-league Weymouth with absolutely no Football League management experience whatsoever. Secondly, our first match of the new season was at a deserted Roots Hall against Harrogate Town in their first ever Football League match, and they trounced us 4-0. Thirdly, our tilt at the League Cup (now called the Carabao Cup) ended at the

---

62 The Premier League restarted in June 2020, and Liverpool won it. The Championship also played to a conclusion. Leagues One and Two went into shutdown mode, although teams in third to sixth place (fourth to seventh place for League Two) on points per game at the time of shutdown contested the promotion play-offs.

first hurdle with a 1-0 defeat at Gillingham. Fourthly, our brief campaign in the Also-Rans Cup (now called the Papa John's Trophy) ended with three defeats out of three, culminating in a 6-1 thrashing by Colchester United. Fifthly, an FA Cup first round defeat at the hands of non-league Boreham Wood. Lastly, everything else.

It was just as well that United's trials and tribulations were witnessed by a total home attendance of just 4,000 for that entire COVID-afflicted campaign, spread thinly across Roots Hall in December 2020 for the visits of Scunthorpe United and Grimsby Town. Surprisingly, given the opposition, we managed to win both games, but they were brief highlights punctuating the gloom of another relegation battle. How we might have fared in a season of normal crowds is probably best left unthought.

Mum passed away in October 2020 at the age of 93. The depth of her affection for Southend United was always open to question, but I'm sure she would have cast her critical eye over the latest crisis and been less than impressed. Dad would have been appalled and would not have been reluctant to say so.

So it was that, in late April 2021, the worst Southend team in history confronted the trapdoor and teetered on the edge of the plunge into non-league. Even the return of Phil Brown, architect of our last triumph in 2015 and the late flurry of draws interspersed with the occasional win he inspired were not enough to pull us clear. A cruel 2-0 defeat inflicted by the pitiless Colchester United nudged us closer and dragged them away from the trapdoor.

Twelve thousand miles is a long way from a fight for football survival. In United's season of deepest jeopardy, television coverage on my side of the world was non-existent – understandable, given our plight – and I was too disheartened to track our minute-by-minute decline on the internet. Instead, I consoled myself with the BBC Sport website the morning after. After the Colchester calamity, United were all but mathematically down, a lamentable goal difference compounding our shortfall in points. With three matches to go, it was a choice between two of Colchester United, Barrow, Scunthorpe, Grimsby and us for the drop – and we were clear favourites. An unexpected home victory against the Orient prolonged the torment for at least one more game.

On the Sunday morning of 2 May 2021, I fed our ancient cat Rimmer, poured the orange juice, made the tea and settled down to the laptop and BBC Sport. 'Hello! Barrow 1 Southend United 2; mmm, that's interesting,' I murmured because I was acutely aware that Scunthorpe were on a terrible run of five defeats in a row. All they had to do was to lose and lose big, then the final reckoning would be postponed until the final day. Then I navigated to 'Bradford City 0 Scunthorpe United 0'. No favours from Scunthorpe, as usual. 'Forget it: we're gone anyway,' I wearily reported to Kim, peering at the screen beside me.

In the end, it's the hope that kills you. After 101 years as a Football League club, 57 years of my support, 30 years after United's first promotion to the second tier and 15 years after their second, the final and irrevocable disaster serenely played out for me on a warm, sunny Sunday morning in Queensland between cups of tea. United's swansong was a 1-1 draw with Newport County, but I was over it. Ironically, given their past outrages, Grimsby saved us the humiliation of finishing 92nd out of 92 by graciously accepting the wooden spoon.

In the days before automatic demotion from fourth tier to non-league, failing re-election to the Football League was the ultimate calamity. That's why the 1984/85 season, horrible for many reasons, was so traumatic. In my lifetime, only Accrington Stanley and Barrow had managed to navigate a return path and it took each of them nearly 50 years to do it. Modern-day demotion is not the one-way highway to hell it used to be but losing the TV money, the sponsorships and the players on big contracts can have lasting effects. The trapdoor has been an existential threat for supporters of Southend and other lower-division clubs since 1987. There it is, over there in the shadows and, if we're honest, we all know it's there.

***

Southend's first post-apocalyptic season was a story soon told as English football reopened its doors to welcome back the post-COVID multitudes. The new stadium continued to be the expanse of waste ground on the edge of town and the virtual reality video, the grand retail complex now replaced with plans for a house-building project incorporating Fossetts Farm and Roots Hall. In the cold reality of the National League, Phil Brown lasted just ten matches before his own tap on the shoulder in October 2021. United had just been slaughtered 4-0 at Roots Hall by Chesterfield to underline yet another appalling start and we were, once again, at the wrong end of the table in 21st place. Visions of a third successive relegation and what it might mean for United's future started to rattle around my fevered imagination.

Brown's departure coincided with the death of our dear old Rimmer, who passed away at the grand old age of 21. As old as the century, he'd experienced the whole gamut of United's ups and downs. Promotions, relegations, famous cup victories, calamitous cup defeats, a spell in the second tier, the descent into non-league, all overseen with the expression of lofty disdain he was so good at.

From the wings entered Stan Collymore to make flesh and blood of the smoke and mirrors from April. As 'senior football strategist' Stan looked suspiciously like a power behind the throne of Ron Chairman, but – surely – someone had to do it. Stan, Tom Lawrence (new chief executive officer), Ron Chairman and Gary Lockett (member of a supporters' group elegantly labelled the Shrimpers Trust) formed the panel that selected Kevin Maher, captain and hero from 2006, as United's new head coach. And the tide turned as the team, calmly and steadily, in true Kevin Maher style, climbed the table to finish in a safe, if anonymous, 13th place.

Buoyed by our recovery on the pitch, I was more hopeful for our chances the next season. United were nowhere near Wrexham and Notts County who were pursuing their own return paths, but we were within striking distance of Chesterfield, Woking, Barnet and the rest for the play-offs – until March 2023. After United lost seven games in a row during that wretched month, it occurred to me that this may not be our year. But it wasn't all over and after four wins out of the next six, there was another headache-inducing scenario for the last play-off spot: we had to beat Wealdstone at Roots Hall and Boreham Wood had to lose at home to Yeovil Town.

On the final day, United beat Wealdstone 2-1 before 8,434 hopeful spectators. Boreham Wood beat Yeovil 1-0 in front of a meagre 1,605. It was enough for them on the day but not enough in the end. Wrexham and Notts County achieved their elevation back to the Football League and the four relegated from the National League were ex-Football League clubs who had themselves suffered United's demotion experience, Yeovil and Scunthorpe among them. Return paths meet snakes and ladders meet bogey teams.

***

Times change. In the 2022/23 season, the average attendance for a top-tier match exceeded 40,000 for the first time in history.[63] Across the Football League as a whole, attendances have more than doubled since the dark days of 1986. The horizontal lines of sturdy metal barriers making their appearance across Premier League stadia herald the partial return of a terrace culture with the introduction of safe standing areas – and rightly so. Whether the serried ranks of new supporters can recreate the look and feel of the old terraces

---

63 Statistics courtesy of www.european-football-statistics.co.uk.

is arguable for traditionalists like me, but the old surge and sway will remain an artefact of history thanks to the tip-up seats discreetly nestled behind the barriers. And, with the opening of the new Anfield Road Stand upper tier for the visit of Manchester United in December 2023, three sides of the stadium now look *down* on the Spion Kop, the terraced mountain that captivated me on my first visit to Anfield so long ago.

My forever second team continued to strive toward the return of past glories. A new manager, Erik Ten Hag and a raft of signings delivered the Carabao Cup, Manchester United's first trophy in six years, and a place in the Champions League. It was a shame that they couldn't win the FA Cup Final, allowing rivals City to emulate the 1999 achievement of Champions League, Premier League and FA Cup. Maybe next season for the Reds.

***

And Southend United? If only it was that simple.

Chapter 26

Nine Months to Midnight

IN MY qualified optimism for Southend United's chances on the pitch, I'd averted my eyes from the crisis developing off it. One drawback of distance is that you concentrate on the latest result on the BBC website, the match report on the United website and a few minutes of highlights on YouTube, largely unaware of the seismic upheavals reported by the *Southend Echo*, formerly the *Evening Echo*. I've put that right now.

I'd picked up news here and there about recurring financial problems over 20 years, mostly associated with late payment of tax bills to Her/His Majesty's Revenue and Customs. Fortunately, they were paid before the High Court justices put on their black caps and invoked the winding-up order which would have sent United to oblivion[64]. The transfer embargoes didn't help, though. The year of 2020 saw the financial issues return with a vengeance, coinciding with United's catastrophic decline on the pitch and the disruption wrought by COVID-19. More outstanding tax debts, non-payment of players and staff and issues with utility bills occupied the next three years, as

---

64 The black caps allude to the archaic practice of judges condemning a guilty defendant to death. In the UK, a winding-up order is an instruction from the High Court to close down a company and liquidate its assets. It follows a winding-up petition made by a creditor or creditors, which typically follows a series of unsuccessful attempts to recover their money. Southend United is a plc and creditors included HMRC (as usual) and assorted utility companies. Source: www.ukliquidators.org.uk.

United endured the submission and dismissal of successive winding-up petitions in the High Court accompanied by a barrage of adjournments, a suspended three-point penalty and the perpetual transfer embargo. It couldn't go on. On 17 March 2023, Ron Chairman finally put the club up for sale.

***

There's nothing like a good consortium. After all, who were the Founding Fathers of 1906 if not a consortium? Charles Albert Stein, Oliver Trigg, Frederick England, Thomas Stuart Tidy and the immortal George Hatton Hogflesh.

Oh, how we were teased and tantalised in May 2023 by news of a possible takeover from a consortium of Kimura Capital, London-based asset management company, sports agency Integral Sports Management and Dwayne 'The Rock' Johnson, authentic Hollywood superstar. We had seen other A-listers Ryan Reynolds and Rob McElhenney buying Wrexham in November 2020 and the transformation their presence inspired as Wrexham climbed back into the Football League after 15 long years in the wilderness. I was agog at the prospects for United, but hopes were dashed as negotiations foundered on the rock that was Ron Chairman according to some reports, but not others. In the meantime, another winding-up petition was adjourned for two months. Anyway (sigh).

I read reports of an idea from some supporters' groups which made my blood run cold. A phoenix club is a new entity rising from the ashes of a club that has gone financially bust and assumes a continuation of sporting activity. A similar (though not identical) club name and logo is allowed, as is a similar (though not identical) playing kit. Therefore, Southend United FC would cease to exist, but instead would we have AFC Southend? Because Southend-on-Sea is now a city, Southend City? The old club crest of scimitars, football, waves and shrimp would be defunct, to be replaced by who knows what?

There are three phoenix clubs in the current Football League. Accrington Stanley (1891) was replaced by Accrington Stanley FC as long ago as 1968. Newport County became Newport County AFC in 1989. Wimbledon FC became AFC Wimbledon in 2002. So far so good – except that the new entity starts its life near the very bottom of the football pyramid, which is not so good. It took Stanley 38 years to get back, County 25 years, and Wimbledon a quick-fire nine years. If the Blues repeated the Stanley or County experience, I'd be getting on a bit by the time of our return.

And what about Roots Hall? Who would own it? United might not even have a ground. The good city of Southend is not exactly well-endowed with alternative sports stadia – as in none – so a groundshare out of town could be necessary. I cast my mind back to the 1980s and the boardroom rumblings around relocating to a new stadium in Basildon. As far as I was concerned, Southend United would have become Basildon United, whatever anyone else wanted to call it and that would have ended my support. The outraged Roots Hall refrain of 'We'll never go to Basildon' showed I wasn't the only one. My feelings about a phoenix club in (say) the Isthmian League Premier Division and local 'derbies' with Billericay Town and Canvey Island revolve around two considerations: would it feel like my team any more? Would I even care? I don't know – don't ever want to know either.

***

In August 2023, an Australian tech wizard and founder of successful boutique IT consultancy Eighty20 Solutions appeared without trace. Justin Rees of Sydney, latterly of the Netherlands and an avowed follower of English football, had a consortium as well: David Kreyling and Tom Arnold of Sport for Social Change, promoting grassroots sport in the Southend area; Jason Brown, hedge fund manager and United supporter; John Watson, owner of packaging and taxi businesses and

United season ticket holder for 40 years; Gary Lockett of the redoubtable Shrimpers Trust, member of the panel that appointed Kevin Maher. In the background, Southend's council and local MPs were now weighing in with their own support: but moral support was unlikely to be enough.

The latest winding-up petition hearing in the High Court was adjourned to 23 August and adjourned again to 4 October. In postponing the hearing one more time, High Court Judge Sebastian Prentis pulled no punches, 'If this was not a football club with the attachment of its fans, I would be winding you up today. You will be wound up on the next date if it's not sorted out.' To reinforce the point, United received a ten-point penalty from the National League for not sorting it out, instantly sending us to the bottom of the table.

Thoughts turned to what I would do if I was back in England. Of course, I would have turned up at Roots Hall with the rest of the suffering faithful. I would be a voracious reader of the *Echo* sports pages. I would join the West Stand commemoration of the points deduction by chucking my own tennis balls, with all the hundreds of others, on to the pitch after ten minutes of the Eastleigh match on 25 August. I would join the matchday march of protest from the pier to Roots Hall, behind the defiant drumbeat. Join in another adaptation of 'Oops Upside Your Head' still frequently chanted in football circles into 'We want Martin out, I say we want Martin out.' In other words, I would personify an anxious and disgruntled Southend United tragic, just as I did in Australia. Ron Chairman's rejection of two bids from the Justin consortium in September didn't make me feel any better.

Named after Manchester United legends (linkage to Southend's most famous victory is pure coincidence of course), Rooney the Japanese spitz and Cristiano the black and white cat are but faintly interested in the travails of Southend. My fretful morning prodding of the laptop keyboard meant nothing to them, although they were sometimes disconcerted by my deep groan at another disappointment on or off the pitch. Kim was optimistic, as always, but even her optimism became more strained after each new setback. And the day of reckoning crept ever closer.

***

Saturday, 30 September: The winding-up petition would be heard in the High Court next Wednesday. Rochdale 2 United 2; 23rd place in the National League.

Tuesday, 3 October: In the afternoon, a statement on the Southend United website, 'We can confirm that an agreement for the sale of the club has been reached with a consortium led by Justin Rees. Everyone is working towards a completion date of 1 November 2023, that is when the consortium will formally take control of the club.' Shortly afterwards, my old friend from the 1979 Anfield replay flashed me an email from Thorpe Bay, 'NEW OWNERS TAKE OVER SUFC ON 1ST NOVEMBER! Yippee!' That evening: United 2 Oxford City 0. Up to 21st.

Wednesday, 4 October: With the sale of the club confirmed and payment of the outstanding tax debt, the High Court dismissed the latest winding-up petition.

Saturday, 7 October: Woking 0 United 2; 19th in the National League and United were out of the relegation zone for the first time since the ten-point penalty kicked in.

***

The Justin Rees consortium agreed to pay £4.5m to acquire Southend United, only a few hundred thousand more than Ron Chairman and co. paid to Chairman Vic back in 1998. Justin and co. would get Ron's 71 per cent shareholding for £1, Roots Hall (which we understood would be 'upgraded', assisted by a sizeable contribution from the Ron ex-Chairman housing fund) and the training ground next to the new stadium we'll no longer see.

If a week is a long time in politics, that week in October 2023 may have been the longest in Southend United's history although, with the time difference, I was asleep for most of the juicy bits. But we are talking about Southend United Time, where it takes 40 years to not quite get a new stadium. Instead of 28 days to settle the whole deal, contracts were exchanged after 81 days, a welcome Christmas present on 23 December. Five days later saw the lifting of the transfer embargo to see in the new year. To fill in the time, the Justin consortium added another four individuals: Paul and Ian Redbourn, big wheels in the financial sector, alumni of my old school and United supporters; George Taylor, Hong Kong-based banker and son of long-term Southend East MP Sir Teddy Taylor – and the ubiquitous Tom Lawrence, United's CEO. This eclectic group was now known as the Custodians of Southend United (or COSU for short).

Justin set out his stall in an interview for BBC Radio Essex on 26 January 2024, 'I didn't want to own a football club for the sake of owning a football club. I wanted something where my energy and drive could maybe make a difference … I think most people, if they had the means to own a football club, would hopefully feel like we all do, that it's a huge privilege and an honour.' All very reassuring; more Ken Bates than Ron Noades[65].

Meanwhile, Southend City Council was laboriously executing due diligence on the latest plans for the development of Fossetts Farm with Citizen Housing, the entity now fronting the development.

Just when it looked like plain sailing for the Southend United ship, inky black clouds appeared on the horizon and rolled up the Thames Estuary. Yet another set of dissatisfied creditors instigated yet another winding-up petition in March, with the hearing date set for 15 May (subsequently adjourned to 26 June) Southend United Time. Then 17 May

---

65 The views of Ken Bates and Ron Noades on owning a football club were referenced in chapter 18.

saw the imposition of yet another transfer embargo. For United diehards, it felt like Groundhog Day, and even COSU were starting to get nervous.

On the pitch, United had pulled together an unexpected 15-match unbeaten run to enter another final day with another conundrum. This time, we had to beat Rochdale at home to edge into the play-off positions: but only if FC Halifax Town lost at Eastleigh AND Aldershot Town lost at Dagenham and Redbridge. At Roots Hall, 7,947 Southend optimists and Noah Vale turned up to see United lose 2-1. Halifax won 3-0 to pinch our play-off spot and even Aldershot's 3-3 draw would have been too much for us but wasn't quite enough for them. That ten-point penalty cost us dear in the end, as I always feared it would.

Southend finished last season in ninth place, a heroic effort in the circumstances. The average attendance at Roots Hall was 6,493, higher than we had enjoyed for five of our seven seasons in the second tier, while the size and passion of United's support away from home was recognised as notable for a non-league outfit. The current Roots Hall anthem of choice, 'Ohhh-ohh-ohh-ohh, everywhere we go, going to see Southend United, putting on a show' reverberated around the unfamiliar and homely locations of Altrincham, Fylde and Woking. Say what you like about United supporters; for sheer resilience, they are hard to beat.

Manchester United redeemed another underwhelming season with a revenge triumph over Manchester City in the FA Cup Final – which means more to my generation than it seems to do for younger folk. FA Cup win or fourth in the Premier League and a place in the Champions League? I'll take the FA Cup, thanks.

***

On Wednesday, 12 June 2024, I turned our hire car into the expansive and deserted car park behind the East Stand.

Carefully skirting a large pothole, I parked next to the merchandise store – which was closed. Kim and I strolled in the chilly, windswept morning air, mobiles in hand, to survey and record the shambles that was Roots Hall.

Nobody was about. I couldn't avoid seeing the rust streaks defacing the back of the old East Stand. The time-honoured sign 'Welcome to Southend United Football Club' above the reception area was missing the final 'L' on the 'Football' logo. The 'C' on the 'Club' was also missing, and the following 'L' was seriously askew. Even more depressing was the old 'SUFC' logo above the entrance to the directors' box, today denuded of its letters except for a prominent white 'F', which somehow seemed to sum it all up. Had it really come to this?

I noticed a parked car containing two elderly gentlemen dressed in what looked to me like the outfit of an old-time trad jazz band. One of them wound down the window.

'Excuse me, are you a supporter?'

'Yes, for 60 years,' I admitted, slightly shamefacedly.

'Do you know where the entrance to the Shrimpers Bar is?'

'Just over there.' I pointed to the steps leading down below the 'F', as best I remembered.

'Thanks. You see, we're performing there this morning, but there's no one around to let us in. Mind you,' he conceded, 'we are a bit early.'

It was all too surreal. Time to go.

Wednesday was rubbish collection day in the narrow, congested streets surrounding Roots Hall, but I didn't know that. We spent the next hour crawling behind a succession of stop/start garbage trucks before our release on to the Arterial Road and the drive to south Cambridgeshire where Vickie, James, Holly and the start of the Euros awaited. I pondered the latest experience in my years of supporting Southend United Footbal Lub. My sentimental attachment to the Hall is boundless, but when I see Brighton's American Express Stadium (the ground we should have had) on TV or reprise the new stadium video on the laptop, I must confess to a sharp twinge of regret. And another day of reckoning crept ever closer, faithfully chronicled by the BBC and Chris Phillips of the *Southend Echo* to give me twinges of a more visceral nature[66].

***

Friday, 14 June: after months of due diligence, Southend City Council rejects the Fossetts Farm housing development plan and mandates a deadline of 21 June for a new proposal from Citizen Housing.

Friday, 21 June: the revised development proposal is rejected by the council, but negotiations continue.

Monday, 24 June: the National League informs Southend United that it must post a bond of one million pounds to prove that the club can fulfil its financial obligations for the new season, with 'further sanctions' under consideration if the bond is not posted (which could include old favourites like points deductions, but could also include expulsion from the National League).

Tuesday, 25 June: the creditors instigating the winding-up petition agree a settlement over unpaid debts and will ask for the case to be dismissed.

Wednesday, 26 June: the latest winding-up petition is dismissed by the High Court. In other news, the council has agreed new heads of terms with Citizen Housing, allowing the revised plan to proceed to another round of due diligence. For how long, nobody knows.

Wednesday, 3 July: the *Southend Echo* reports that COSU and Ron Chairman have finally agreed terms for completing the sale – exactly nine months since it first hit the headlines.

Thursday, 4 July: the National League lifts the transfer embargo.

---

66 www.echo-news.co.uk provides regular United news updates from Chris Phillips.

***

Harry Redknapp knows his stuff. I used to see him galloping down the right wing for West Ham during the golden years of Moore, Peters, Hurst and all. In a Football League management career spanning 35 years, he did great things at AFC Bournemouth, Portsmouth and Queens Park Rangers. He nearly did great things at West Ham and Tottenham. In April 2019, he landed at Roots Hall to help then-manager Kevin Bond keep United in League One by the skin of their teeth and then departed too soon.

'If you want to end up with a small fortune, start with a big one and buy a football club,' Harry drolly observed. Ron Chairman must have thrown millions at Southend over 25 years. 'Oh Christ, absolutely – massively,' as he reported to Tim Burrows of *The Guardian*[67]. So: I still have a great deal of sympathy for him, as I previously had for Chairman Vic. It's taken more than one cook to spoil the United broth over the years; a thankless task for sure. But I hope those houses on Fossetts Farm finally get built. Britain needs all the houses it can get – and Roots Hall needs that cash injection, whenever it arrives.

***

Friday, 19 July 2024 brings forth a statement from the club's website, 'The Consortium is delighted to announce that the purchase of Southend United Football Club has been successfully completed.'[68] On Monday, 12 August, the National League withdraws the £1m bond request. And this is where my story ends. Well, it has to end somewhere. Saved. Saved by Australia, my adopted country. Think of it: if Justin

67 Harry's droll observation was in *Fever Pitch – the Battle for the Premier League*, a documentary shown in Australia on the Stan streaming app (no relation). Ron Chairman's lament courtesy of 'The Long Read' in *The Guardian* of 2 May 2024.

68 I picked up the news first from the BBC, then from the *Southend Echo* and last, but not least, from www.southendunited.co.uk, just to be certain.

Rees and United achieve famous things and the Australian media picks it up, the name of Southend United will find its way into Australia's consciousness; and I won't have to do a thing. The consortium names may not be as exotic as Reynolds, McElhenney and The Rock (or even Hogflesh) but they'll do for me. We'll find out about the money soon enough. In terms of today's United heroes, I have a particular regard for Gus Scott-Morriss: firstly because he's a left wing-back who scores goals and secondly because his name resonates in Australia due to strongly resembling the name of Scott Morrison, our erstwhile prime minister. I'm sure more heroes are around the corner.

It may be a long way back for United, but the recent history of one football club is encouraging. Luton Town dived headlong through the trapdoor in 2009 and returned to the Football League in 2014. It took another four years to climb the ladder to League One, quickly followed by another climb to the Championship. In May 2023, 40,000 Town stalwarts celebrated their victory over Coventry City in the play-off final at Wembley to join the Premier League and the big money, the first club to reach the Premier League from non-league. All right, they only lasted a season, but it was a hell of a ride[69]. Luton's Kenilworth Road ground is a small, atmospheric, ageing venue with a capacity of about 11,000, the same as Roots Hall. If Luton can do it, why can't we?

It's one more example of how the English football landscape changes. By the time you read these words, the landscape will have changed again, and very probably in some unexpected directions. That's why we love it. 'A funny old game,' as Jimmy Greaves used to remind us week after week.

---

69 Luton Town have another claim to fame. Failing re-election to the Football League in 1900, they returned as original members of the Third Division (South) in 1920 and made it to the First Division in 1956 – so they did it twice.

But whatever trials face Southend United in the future, I can look back to that Friday evening under the lights at Roots Hall in May 1968, a time of childhood desolation when United's near-certain promotion to the Third Division had just fallen to pieces. I see my 12-year-old self in bobble hat and scarf, defiantly twirling my rattle and singing along with the rest of the North Bank, 'There's always next year [clap, clap, clap-clap-clap]'. Because, hopefully, there always is.

Appendix

The Journey

'Supporting Southend United may not have always been rewarding, but it has not been dull.' Not for me, anyway. To prove it, here is a summary of United's Football League journey.

1920s–1960s:
1920/21: United's first season in the Third Division
1957/58: United's top-half finish secures a place in the Third Division
1965/66: United relegated to the Fourth Division

1970s:
1971/72: Promoted to the Third Division
1975/76: Relegated to the Fourth Division
1977/78: Promoted to the Third Division
1979/80: Relegated to the Fourth Division

1980s:
1980/81: Promoted to the Third Division
1983/84: Relegated to the Fourth Division
1986/87: Promoted to the Third Division
1988/89: Relegated to the Fourth Division
1989/90: Promoted to the Third Division

1990s:

1990/91: Promoted to the Second Division

1996/97: Relegated to the Second Division (now the third tier)

1997/98: Relegated to the Third Division (now the fourth tier)

2000s:

2004/05: Promoted to League One (now the third tier)

2005/06: Promoted to the Championship (now the second tier)

2006/07: Relegated to League One

2009/10: Relegated to League Two (now the fourth tier)

2010s:

2014/15: Promoted to League One

2019/20: Relegated to League Two

2020s:

2020/21: Relegated from League Two and out of the Football League

Acknowledgements

I am indebted to my incredible mentor, Malcolm Knox from the Australian Writers Mentoring Program. Malcolm is a journalist and columnist for *The Sydney Morning Herald* and author of fiction and non-fiction books. I taught him some stuff about English football he didn't know and he taught me more about writing a sporting non-fiction book than I could have ever imagined.

Heartfelt thanks to Peter Miles and Dave Goody, United photo archive custodians, for their invaluable help in sourcing some of the images for this book. They are currently working on a historical project that will appeal to many United fans. Can't wait! My deepest appreciation goes to Chris Phillips and Michael Adkins of Newsquest/*Southend Echo* for permission to use these images. Thanks also to Jamie Cameron at Roots Hall.

I can't express my gratitude enough to Pitch Publishing for making 'Never Never Land' happen. Jane Camillin, Graham Hales, Gareth Davies, Duncan Olner, you are all heroes to me.

To my oldest friends, fellow-sufferers from the early days and purveyors of input and advice via email and WhatsApp: Jonathan Yeatts, Rob King, Keith Harris, Paul Tooley and Nigel Wilks.

To my family. My parents, Emrys and Joyce Williams, beset with United from 1964 to the end of their precious lives. To my sister, Estelle Agguini and daughter, Vickie Williams for their help and support. To my wife, Kim, who's been with me on this journey from original concept to conclusion.

And to Southend United teams, past and present, who made this book possible.

Bibliography

Bower, T., *Broken Dreams* (Pocket Books, 2007)

Dickens, C., *A Tale of Two Cities* (Originally published 1859; Octopus Books, 1986)

Editors (various), *Rothmans Football Yearbooks 1978/79 to 2002/03* (Queen Anne Press to 1991; Headline Book Publishing to 2003)

Goldblatt, D., *The Age of Football* (Macmillian, 2019)

Goody, D., & Miles, P., *Potted Shrimps* (Yore Publications, 1999)

Healey, D., *The Time of My Life* (Penguin Books, 1990)

Keane, R., *Keane* (Penguin Books, 2003)

Mason, P., *Southend United: The Official History of the Blues* (Yore Publications, 1993)

Miles, P., & Goody, D., *Images of Sport: Southend United Football Club* (Tempus Publishing Ltd, 2000)

Miles, P., & Goody, D., *Southend United Football Club: Fifty of the Finest Matches* (Tempus Publishing Ltd, 2005)

Miles, P., & Goody, D., *The Centenary History of Southend United: A Century United* (Shrimper Publishing Ltd, 2007)

Rollin, G., and Rollins, J. (editors), *Sky Sports Football Yearbook 2003/04 to 2012/13* (Headline Publishing, 2004–2013)

Rowe, K. (editor), *The Southend United Chronicles 1906–2006* (Desert Island Books, 2006)

Smith, T., *Anfield Iron* (Bantam Press, 2008)

Stevenson, R.L., *Verginibus Puerisque* (Originally published 1881)